UNEXPECTED VOICES

Theory, Practice, and Identity in the Writing Classroom

RESEARCH AND TEACHING IN RHETORIC AND COMPOSITION
Michael M. Williamson and David L. Jolliffe, series editors

New Worlds, New Words: Exploring Pathways for Writing About
and In Electronic Environments
John F. Barber and Dene Grigar (eds.)

The Rhetoric and Ideology of Genre: Strategies for Stability and Change
Richard Coe, Lorelei Lingard, and Tatiana Teslenko (eds.)

Revision Revisited
Alice S. Horning

Against the Grain: Essays in Honor of Maxine Hairston
David Jolliffe, Michael Keene, Mary Trachsel, and Ralph Voss (eds.)

Unexpected Voices
John Rouse and Ed Katz

Identities Across Text
George H. Jensen

forthcoming

Black Letters: An Ethnography of a Beginning Legal Writing Course
Randolph Cauthen

Marbles, Cotton Balls, and Quantum Wells:
Style as Invention in the Pursuit of Knowledge
Heather Graves

Basic Writing as a Political Act: Public Conversations About Writing
and Literacies
Susanmarie Harrington and Linda Adler-Kassner

Multiple Literacies for the 21st Century
Brian Huot, Beth Stroble, and Charles Bazerman (eds.)

The Future of Narrative Discourse, Literacy, and Technology
Gian S. Pagnucci and Nick Mauriello (eds.)

Tech Culture: Internet Constructions of Literacy and Identity
Gian S. Pagnucci and Nick Mauriello (eds.)

Directed Self-Placement: Principles and Practices
Dan Royer and Roger Gilles (eds.)

Who Can Afford Critical Consciousness
David Seitz

Principles and Practices: New Discourses for Advanced Writers
Margaret M. Strain and James M. Boehnlein (eds.)

UNEXPECTED VOICES

— ❖ —

Theory, Practice, and Identity in the Writing Classroom

John Rouse
St. Peter's College

Edward Katz
University of the Western Cape

HAMPTON PRESS, INC.
CRESSKILL, NEW JERSEY

Printed in the United States of America

Library of Congress Cataloging-in-Publication Data

Rouse, John, 1926-
 Unexpected voices : theory, practice, and identity in the writing classroom / Rouse John and Edward Katz.
  p. cm. -- (Research and teaching in rhetoric and composition)
 Includes bibliographical references and indexes.
 ISBN 1-57273-451-5 (alk. paper) -- ISBN 1-57273-452-3 (pbk. : alk. paper)
  1. English language--Rhetoric--study and teaching. 2. English language--Study and teaching--Foreign speakers. 3. English language--Study and teaching--South Africa. 4. English language--Study and teaching--United States. 5. Report writing--Study and teaching (Higher). 6. Second language acquisition. I. Katz, Edward, 1941- II. Title. III. Series.

PE1404.R68 2002
808'.042'071--dc21

                                                    2002068907

Hampton Press, Inc.
23 Broadway
Cresskill, NJ 07626

Contents

Preface   **vii**

1   Love and Trust and Always Trouble   **1**
The English language in a South African context; abstract
reasoning and the "bias" against soul; a structured versus
a narrative teaching approach.

2   So Much Talking, So Many Words   **23**
English as a second language; emotions in the classroom;
academic literacy; the sociolinguistics of Basil Bernstein and
that of James Gee; developing a situational classroom.

3   Everyone's Secret is the Same   **51**
Personal experience as the source of ideas; the social
construction of knowledge; individual and communal selves;
the therapeutic view of writing; writers becoming authors.

4   All the Fine Things I Might Say   **85**
Names and naming; personal expression and conceptual
thought; socialism, capitalism, and democratic individualism;
leaders who follow; the uses of despair.

5   A Self to be Confused About   **115**
Bakhtin and the free gesture; the problem of identity;
the Philosophy of This Is; from a positional to a situational
context; Bernstein's restricted and elaborated language codes;
Vygotsky's Thought and Language; Brian Street's Social
Literacies.

6   To Seek a Name and Nothing More   145
The cognitive approach in teaching writing; to have a power
name; form, content and social class; critical literacy; Vygotsky
on the social origin of language forms; Labov on nonstandard
English.

7   Of Narrative and Identity   173
Using student narratives; the "myth" of the autonomous self;
ethics and composition; postmodernism as nostalgia; the uses
of anxiety; Louis Mink on "Language as a Cognitive Instrument".

8   In Africa When the Sun Comes Up   201
From narrative to academic discourse; the socially constructed
writing classroom.

References   231
Author Index   239
Subject Index   243

Preface

He was one of those busy students we've all known—asking questions, making comments, leafing through a book, talking to someone sitting nearby. But I was glad to have him there, he wasn't simply waiting out the time. He wanted to use the minutes, he helped make the class *go*.

Then one evening as we were walking away together after a session, he said "The trouble with the way you teach is, people can be themselves."

"So what's wrong with that?"

"Well, it's risky because they just go off in different directions. Like Hector took all that time tonight telling his story and we went off on that. It was interesting, but we didn't get to whatever it was you had on your mind for the session. So there's all this anxiety because we don't know what's coming next, and there's no way to know what success would be. Maybe that's why Laverne is so unpleasant, always disagreeing with everything you say."

"As if you're always willing to agree with me! But I do like your questions, you raise issues worth talking about."

"That's because I don't know what you're really after. I'm trying to find out."

"Well, when you do find out, tell me—and then we'll both know."

We were talking about the graduate course in sociolinguistics I was giving as an adjunct professor at New York University. And long after it was over, Mr. Katz decided to renew the conversation by sending a letter to me from South Africa, where he was teaching composition at the University of the Western Cape. I was surprised to receive that letter because we had not spoken since the last day of our class. But with it he initiated a correspondence that continues to this day. He had new questions to ask, he would put me to the test again—and this book has been drawn from those letters.

One writer tells of his experiences in a South African classroom, the other comments on that account and offers stories from his teaching experience in a U.S. classroom. The contrast between the South African context and the American, as well as the surprising parallels, highlight certain issues of concern in composition studies today. In fact, the two correspondents have opposing views on a number of those issues, different answers to the questions they think important. And occasionally they do not even agree on what the question is.

These are informal but serious discussions, often moving along on a current of free association, including whatever concerns the moment suggests. The writers report to each other their experiences with young people, and the ideas suggested to them by those interactions, without pausing to condense all this into scholarly summations—they are simply writing letters. So the issues they discuss—in composition theory and practice, in sociolinguistics—have not been sorted into separate chapters but rather are commented on as they arise during their work with young people. In other words, questions that are usually discussed abstractedly in scholarly works, one topic after another, are considered here in a practical and experiential way, as theory and practice are brought together. This means that important issues—the questions or problems that come with teaching in our time—keep recurring in these pages with the interrelatedness of lived experience, and so the chapter divisions are quite arbitrary, their titles suggesting themes rather than subjects. Readers who want a definitive or summary statement of some issue, or of a chapter, must make one for themselves and in that way appropriate whatever message the book may have for them. We invite our readers to join with us in an active exploration of the concerns arising from our experiences teaching language—writing and reading—in two very different academic and social situations.

That exploration will include much close attention to interactions in the classroom. Too often in books on composition theory and practice, one may read hundreds of pages with never an illustration of the writer's own classroom practice. These two writers, however, think the essence of teaching lies in even those momentary classroom exchanges between two people when one or the other might say something new and unexpected, something worth hearing. How to make those moments happen is their concern. So they experiment, they try out one activity or another. And they improvise, following any clues they find in the lives and interests of students that suggest subjects or activities that might engage their willing participation. In short, these two find their way as they go, rather than relying on a preplanned course of study. And the book itself—with its digressions and tentative suggestions, its improvisations on whatever interest is expressed by one writer or the other—is an enactment of its major theme: the value of a narrative pedagogy. That is, a pedagogy which departs from the course of study as students find a direction or activity suggested by their own concerns and ongoing lives, so that afterward they have a story to tell of their experience together.

An experience in which they have been engaged as individuals, with thoughts of their own to express. In fact, how conceptual thought arises from individual, personal experience is important here. The reader will meet in these pages a number of young people, South African and American, who have much to think about. The Africans, by leaving their neighborhoods or villages to attend the University of the Western Cape, are moving from their local or tribal cultures into a newly forming commercial, urbanized world, and are helping to make that world as they do. The closed, intimate communities of the South African villages are being transformed by an open, large-scale market system—a transformation that brings with it the central problem in modern, urban societies: the conflict between an individualist way of life and the desire for the spiritual comfort of community. "How long will it be," Katz wonders, "before my students realize the individualist direction I am leading them in, and revolt?"

For he is teaching them a different way of using language than they' have known, and in learning it they become, by insensible degrees, a different kind of person—the self-interested individual. And the same is true of young people in any modern society who learn in schoolrooms a way of using language that sets them apart from peer group and local community. This distinction between two ways of using language was first developed by the anthropologist Malinowski, who pointed out that in premodern cultures, and in much of our own social intercourse, an utterance is typically part of a communal action rather than a representative of abstract thought:

> *phatic communion* I am tempted to call it . . .—a type of speech in which ties of union are created by a mere exchange of words. . . . Are words in Phatic Communion used primarily to convey meaning? . . . Certainly not! They fulfill a social function and that is their principal aim, but they are neither the result of intellectual reflection, nor do they arouse reflection in the listener. Once more language appears to us in this function not as an instrument of reflection but as a mode of action. (Malinowski, 1923, p. 315)

And he goes on to say that although the action-linked, community-embedded style can be found everywhere, there is another style that strives to be free of a local culture, "to control ideas and make them the common property of civilized mankind." This speech is often addressed to unseen, anonymous listeners, as, for example, his own essay. Serious cognition requires detachment from, not a return to communal involvement.

Here in Malinowski we have an early formulation of the distinction Basil Bernstein has made between the restricted and elaborated language codes. And the schools, in teaching the elaborated code of academic discourse, he suggests, are producing individuals prepared to negotiate their passage in a world of strangers—individuals who are moving on from the communal identity given by a local culture into a world of competitive individualism.

One of the forces active in making this world is evidently schooling, for it directs people to their individual improvement rather than that of the group. Another is commercialism, which draws people into urban areas where they must compete with each other for their bread and butter, leaving behind the cooperative life of the village. And a third is Christianity, which arouses a religious sense of personal responsibility for one's fate. These are forces that are active among young people in South Africa, who are responding to them often with doubt and trepidation, striving to make their adaptation to this competitive world and yet retain their communal bonds. They speak of this problem directly, and so remind us of our own unease. For we too are living with this conflict between an individualist way of life and our need for the spiritual comfort of community. And as we see this conflict developing in the South African context, we may better understand our own situation and the issues that currently engage educational writers and theorists.

For example, various assertions of postmodernist thought—the denial of an autonomous self, the belief that not individuals speak but rather language speaks through them, the suggestion that we never have objective truth but only discourse, that knowledge is socially constructed—such assertions can be seen, in the light of the South African experience, as expressing a yearning for the comfort of a communal embrace—a romantic insistence on community and culture as the necessary source of selfhood, knowledge, and the ethical life. Or otherwise we are destined to live alienated lives. And perhaps this sense that individuals must be rescued from their alienation can be seen in the growing influence of a subtle, or often not so subtle, therapeutic approach to the teaching of composition. An approach that, as we will see, sometimes involves a kind of mysticism in the search for spiritual peace.

But a peaceful mind is no great help with writing. How much better that students be agitated a little when they sit down alone with pen and paper, for we expect of them writing that expresses an individual mind coming to terms with experience in a culture undergoing rapid change. Both the African and American students are in the process of developing an individualist identity—and teachers of writing are implicated with them in that process. We will affirm young people to themselves as the individuals who have written these particular words and said these things, so they may know themselves by what they have done here with us.

Such are the concerns that have agitated these two writers. And they also bring into their letters interests from outside the classroom, one from his everyday life in South Africa and the other from his practice as a personal-vocational counselor. There are times when perhaps one might wonder just what relevance these concerns have to academic issues. Yet they do in fact relate to classroom practice, for teachers often bring to their work their concerns as private persons. The hidden motives of personal history play a decisive part in the daily encounters of those who would be helpers. This is a consideration usually omitted from scholarly, abstract discussions of teaching practice, which is after all a personal performance.

For example, in chapter 4 the writers exchange thoughts about anxiety because events in the life of one are making for some anxious moments. The reader who wonders what relevance this could have to academic concerns, may then remember a question raised in the second chapter—Are anxiety and anger emotions that are useful in the classroom?—a question returned to several times in the correspondence. For writing is an activity that draws not only on the mind but on the whole person, on the feeling intellect.

And just as we hope students will become engaged as individuals in the work we do with them, so we hope as teachers to find ourselves in the work. In fact, the kind or quality of work done in a classroom very much depends on the character of the individual teacher. And so one may well ask, "What sort of characters are these two?" We are not at all sure we want anyone to tell us.

ACKNOWLEDGMENTS

Writers and their works cited by the authors are listed in the references. However, because of the informal nature of this correspondence between two friends, information and quotations sometimes appear in the text without specific attribution; these are credited in a listing of additional sources following the references.

Those works to which we are particularly indebted include Ernest Gellner's *Language and Solitude* (which identifies the opposition between individualism and communalism as the central conflict of our time); Ronald Manheimer's *Kierkegaard as Educator* (for the concept of a "situational context" in chap. 2), and Judith Ryan's *The Vanishing Subject* (for remarks concerning empiricist psychology in chap. 7).

We would like to thank our editor, Robin B. Weisberg, for her careful and responsive reading of our text, a reading that led to many improvements.

—*John Rouse*
—*Edward Katz*

CHAPTER 1

Love and Trust
and Always Trouble

Dear John,

I suppose this letter comes to you like an uninvited guest, but I hope you will welcome it even so. Do you remember me, sitting there in your sociolinguistics class at NYU those cold winter evenings, the argumentative one? I really enjoyed our discussions about how social class affects language learning, and how we should teach writing. And we had one lively go-round about whether the self is a prisoner of language and social class, or is an independent identity possible? Hey, in that classroom at least I felt free to be myself. I've wandered some distance away these past few years—to South Africa, in fact, where arguments about language come hot and heavy. Too heavy sometimes, as if our future depends on getting the right answers. I remember talking to another passenger on a train once about what answers might work for the problems here, and he said 'There are no answers that work here.' I've not had an easy time of it, I assure you.

And why did I come to South Africa? For a woman, of course. I followed her here—a man will travel half across the world for a woman—and we married, but then after a few years we divorced and I stayed on to be near our two daughters. It's like one of those Navajo stories you tell in which the new husband goes to live among the woman's people. So now

1

I'm at the University of the Western Cape [UWC], about 23 kilometers northwest of Cape Town, and finding that teaching in South Africa is not as comfortable or quiet or predictable as teaching in the States.

And I'm wondering if the ways of working with young people that you talk about can work here. These students come from a culture that's very different from what we've known, and many of them are barely able to read and write English. In fact, there are cultural differences among the students themselves to keep in mind, tribal differences and sometimes an undercurrent of hard feeling between coloureds and Africans that can make for some uneasy moments if we touch on a volatile issue. Also, there's a history at this university of student activism—of mass meetings, demonstrations, and confrontations with the police—a history that's still in the making. So I'm in no hurry to try the sort of provocative teaching you recommend. I feel a need to be somewhat careful if I'm to keep this job.

In fact, I was lucky to get any job at all when I first came here, especially being an American and with the African National Congress [ANC] trying to maintain a boycott against foreign educators. That was part of its trade and sports boycott aimed at bringing the apartheid regime to its knees—and UWC was a centre of anti-government protest.

Also, I was arrested when I first came into the country, charged with 'Crossing the border at a point other than a border post, and being without proper documentation.' But maybe an arrest by the apartheid government was a plus for me at UWC—from jail cell to classroom, you might say. I was hitchhiking down from Kenya, and I walked through the forest around a border post so as to avoid putting up 500 rand (almost $500) for the bond required to ensure my good behavior while in the country. So here was this Brooklyn boy stumbling through that dark forest, terrified of snakes, and when I finally walked back onto the highway several kilometers farther on, a yellow police bakkie (pickup truck) came along and the border guards arrested me. I felt like a captive in Nazi Germany, and the guards sure looked the part. One of them amused himself by telling me what my face would look like if he'd turned the patrol dogs loose to bring me down. So I sat in their jail for a few days before they took me to court. The judge, a sardonic fellow, sentenced me to a long jail term, and then after enjoying my distress he reduced the sentence to time served and I was allowed to stay in the country for 3 months, which gave me enough time to get married.

But the day I appealed for a renewal of my visa I was told there was a plane leaving for the United States at 3 o'clock that afternoon and I'd better be on it. How could we get around this? My wife was already pregnant and could have stayed, being South African, but she agreed to meet me in Lesotho if I could find a decent place where we could live and have a child. Once we were out of the country the police actually called on various people with whom I had stayed and told them I'd been photographed in Swaziland with ANC cadres. A fiction, of course, although they may have considered my wife a suspect because her brother had in fact been brought up on terrorism charges and left the country while on bail. And her mother had been a staunch Marxist at one time. The Special Branch, a most feared section of the police, could lay out a web of interconnections to incriminate anyone they thought might be troublesome.

So I'm still nervous, even though the country is now in other hands. The African students are very politicized. They remember when police helicopters would come down on the campus nearly every month, and then there'd be stone throwing and tear gas. The mass meetings of the SRC (Students Representative Council) pack the Great Hall. These meetings usually begin with songs, one after another, and I tell you those voices shake the walls. And at every forceful point a speaker makes the students erupt with singing and toyi-toying. My friend Alistair points out the great gap between the way affairs get negotiated among these Africans and the way discussion takes place in the halls of learning, and I wonder if their lively engagement with great issues is going to be destroyed by all that abstract reasoning in the classroom.

I teach in the writing programme here as research assistant and lecturer, an impressive title for what is actually a temporary position. This programme was begun as a kind of experiment which aimed to prove that we can do more for language development by teaching small groups of students rather than large ones—as if that needs proving. But of course we live in a scientific age, as you would say, and all things professional must have that scientific stamp of approval, hey? Certain academic results are expected, so I'm wondering if I can bring in the sort of adventure you say ought to happen in a classroom. I've been looking at your 'Scenes from the Writing Workshop' to see how you do it, but you say things to people and do things that I'm not sure will be allowed here. It's not adventure but 'academic literacy' that's talked about, as if these students are ready for it and all we have to do is set the standard for them.

In my first tutorial they were shocked when I asked them to 'write about anything on your mind' for 10 minutes. They come here expecting to be told just what to do, as they always have in school, and in fact at UWC they go through a rigid 3-year course of study, step by step, so there's not much time for self-expression. It's a matter of following closely what lecturers say, and the students expect to be marched in the 'right' direction. And maybe my problem is I'm not sure of the direction. If you have any new thoughts about teaching I'd sure like to hear them.

Alistair is a real lifesaver. He works with me in this programme, and he seems to have a genius for taking up ideas like yours for working with young people and putting them into the South African context. And some of the readings he has found for the programme are fascinating, like *Mayombe,* a novel about the Zimbabwean war for independence, by the

Angolan writer Pepetela. It's both funny and sad, with characters named Freedom, Fearless, Struggle, and New World. I'd like to use it in my class sometime.

And I'd like to hear from you. Surely by now you have some new stories from that strange exotic land where you live, and I'm a willing listener.

Usale kakuhle (stay well)—Ed Katz

(As you see, I'm learning Xhosa from my students, but what they're learning of English from me I'm not sure.)

- - - / / / - - -

April 20

Dear Ed,

Oh yes, I remember you! You're the one in that sociolinguistics class who wanted to know, after 10 weeks of study, if any of this would be of use in your teaching. And the others were nodding in agreement, sharing your doubt. I said, "Probably not, considering that you have rejected every insight our sources have offered you"—or words to that effect. I was amused, you understand, not angry. And surprised that graduate students would find Basil Bernstein's *Class, Codes, and Control* or Jules Henry's *Culture Against Man* so threatening. Whenever I asked for a statement from either book worth commenting on, your classmates managed to find several they knew were entirely unfounded or quite false to the way people actually live and talk. So let me savor the irony of it: You now find yourself in a place where issues of language have come to the fore—where culture has been against the black man, so to speak, and issues of class, codes, and control are being lived out contentiously, even violently, every day. So now it's my turn to ask, What use is there in knowing sociolinguistics?

Certainly what you said about the gap between the way affairs are negotiated among the Africans and the way they are taken up in the academy is suggestive. In those mass meetings the young people are using language to satisfy themselves and express their communal feeling, while in the classroom they sit isolated from each other and learn the language required to satisfy professors. And no one sings in the academy. In this country hardly anyone sings, except in African-American churches or at revival meetings, now that I think about it. There's no singing in political meetings as there was during the civil rights struggle. The congregation in a white church sings hymns, of course, but they sing from hymnals since hardly anyone knows the words. The songs we once sang together as children have been forgotten, and in fact there's very little singing even in schools now. So let there be more singing, I say—particularly in schoolrooms.

Yesterday as I walked by the library, Dominick waved to me from the steps and we went on together to the cafeteria. I said, "What did you think of our poem today, Dominick?" It was "The Lonesome Dream," by Lisel Mueller.

"It was obvious," he said. "All about how our chasing after the American Dream has ruined the land and now we're dreaming about what's been lost. I liked the second verse, where death doesn't just grab your life, it's like a polite exchange."

"I don't remember hearing any of this in class. Your group was the one talking about sex, wasn't it? Did you say these things to them?"

"Oh no, they're just some ideas. Poems aren't about analyzing and ideas, they're about feelings. It's how you feel about a poem that counts."

"Yes, and your idea of the poem will influence how you feel about it. You have good ideas, so I'm wondering why you didn't tell your group these things."

"Oh you know, they'll think you're trying to show off. They'll look at you like, you know—who does he think he is?"

So I'm wondering how many there are who could sing to us but don't. How many good thoughts are lost to us because of this social pressure to remain anonymous and unremarked, so as not to be apart from the group. Here is my text, the responses spoken and unspoken among our young people to the reading and writing we do—the true text of response. And it's a text more interesting to me than the one printed in the book. If it weren't for these passing conversations outside the classroom I'd hardly know what they're thinking.

You asked me to send along any new thoughts I have about teaching, and those are my new thoughts. I'm also sending a few pages from *Provocations,* a book I'm working on that was inspired by a teacher of mine I call Mrs. M. You might find some of this interesting or perhaps even useful.

I'm still the wandering scholar, teaching part time—sometimes at Alden College, a small liberal arts school, and sometimes over at Rutgers University, in Newark. And in the evenings I counsel the bemused and the bewildered. If you're having trouble with your boss, your children, your wife or husband or lover, you come to see me. Then during the day I teach two freshman sections of basic writing. By the way, my first trouble this year came when the department head discovered that none of my students have the composition textbook. He found this very disturbing. And what if he finds out that now and then we read a short story or poem, although we're not supposed to touch literature, you understand? But I'm unwilling to give up something so useful. I'll let you know if I'm employed there next year, or if not I may have to follow you to South Africa. Will you give me a good recommendation?

I'm very pleased you thought of me after all this time. And I'd like to hear more about your experiences in South Africa and what the country is like. Now that it no longer supplies sensational headlines or video clips of street violence, we hear little of it in this country. Tell me more about the young people you work with. I'm really looking forward to hearing from you again.

Best regards—JR

- - - / / / - - -

10 June

Dear John,

You asked me to tell you what this country is like, and I'll say first that South Africa is a place where nature seems to offer a promise of peaceful days, a beautiful place. But there has been so much unrest, so much violence here, we still live with a feeling of uncertainty. The students can tell some really frightening stories. I'll take you with me on the short drive to work, about 30 minutes, so that you can see the land, and along the way you'll begin to get the feel of what living is like in this place.

We drive slowly away from my house through the tree-lined streets of Kenilworth, green and quiet with walled-in gardens and spacious driveways. Soon we're on the highway leading inland from the seashore and lovely cloud-topped Table Mountain. Those clouds cover the mountain's huge flat surface like an enormous tablecloth, hence the name. All these beautiful areas near the mountain and along the sea have been taken by whites, and stories about the removal of the mainly coloured people from here remind me that the beauty is marred by an ugly stain. In fact, the very house I now inhabit is in one of these removal areas, and often I meet people who tell me how well they know this area because they grew up here. But now I'm driving away from these green suburbs and heading east onto the broad plain of the Cape Flats, where the wind blows viciously at times—a wild southeaster that's called the Cape Doctor because it blows all the diseases away. But in our wet cold winters, with that wind blowing up from Antarctica, it may bring more disease than cure and TB is common.

Soon we can see Pinelands, another white suburb off to the left as we pass under the shadow of two enormous cooling towers belonging to the electric company. Now the road runs along the sewerage settlement lands on the right, holding pools of water for the last stage in the treatment of raw sewage (to be polite about it). We pass Langa (The Sun), an older black township, and soon we're approaching Guguletu (Our Pride), where newly built tin and cardboard shacks line the highway. A grey concrete wall, like the wall of a prison, hides many of those shacks from the view of tourists coming from the Cape Town airport. It was in there a crowd of angry Africans dragged an American college student from her car and killed her— a white woman visiting a friend. I'm sure that was reported in the U.S. And there by the road is a forbidding grey watchtower where the police are on the lookout for stone throwers who were common along here. Until recently there was no exit sign for Guguletu, another way the apartheid government erased these Africans. On a warm or humid day the smell of sewage in this area is very strong. I remember one student doing some free writing who wrote, 'Even the air in the townships is third class.'

We turn onto Modderdam Road, and on our left is part of Bontheuwel (Bont-hee-vul), a coloured township. Here are mostly old primary and secondary schools, four or five buildings, some of red brick and others covered with grey stucco, nearly every window broken. There's a vacant dusty look around these schools—large empty fields with a little grass. But energetic children play wildly in the schoolyards and buy sweets and cigarettes through the grey wire-mesh fences from wandering vendors.

And now on our right is Kalksteenfontein (Kalk-sten-fon-tain). Many place names in the Cape have the 'fontein' (fountain) ending, which suggests a spring that was the centre of some Boer farm in the old days. I always notice horse- and donkey-drawn vehicles entering this little place, and that plus the small one-room houses give it an 18th-century look. Except that the houses are made of concrete blocks, which have been painted over, many of them, sometimes very prettily in unusual colours. They were built by the apartheid government for coloured people evicted in the 1960s from District Six in Cape Town and other areas designated for whites only. For Africans nothing was built. The policy was to force them back to the Transkei and other so-called 'homelands,' or at least keep them away from Cape Town. The word *apartheid,* after all, means 'apartness'.

Oh-oh! See that dog lying there on the verge of the highway? As we go along I'm scanning the road for dead dogs and other animals, with a sort of morbid fascination to see what new victims lie along the way. There are no fences between the roads and settlements, so this sad killing goes on and on. Sometimes the bodies remain by Modderdam Road a long time, like that bulldog there that's been swelling in the sun for the past week. One day I even saw a white horse sprawled out by the road. I drive along in fear that I'll see the accident happen, and then last week a dog ran screaming into the Bishop Lavis coloured location, dragging both its back legs. A driver got out of his car and looked hopelessly after the fleeing animal. At least he looked worried, not like those drivers I imagine running down dogs to vent their frustrations.

On the right is Montana (Mon-tah-na), a cluster of well-kept homes lived in by middle-class coloureds, but very soon we come to old factory buildings, while on the left of this rubbish-lined roadway we pass a poor community of small makeshift dwellings, another resettlement. The apartheid government named this one Valhalla Park, another fancy name to gloss over the consequences of its resettlement policy. There's the acrid smell of industrial pollution all along here, and the soil looks tired, with bits of concrete, wood, plastic, and other debris from old structures littering the landscape.

Now we're passing through Bishop Lavis, a coloured slum on both sides of the road. There are few trees here, and the grass is more grey than green. There's a goat grazing near the slimy canal. Moving along with the cars and trucks we pass a horse-drawn cart loaded with all sorts of metal junk, and another pushed by three or four men. There seems to be a lot of broken glass along the side of the road. At the T-junction with the airport road a man whose fingers have been eaten away by some disease begs for money, his ragged palms outstretched.

Beyond those sand dunes on the right is the Cape Town airport. And just ahead we see what looks like a sort of ranch or homestead—an old but well-made wooden house with a galvanized tin roof. Two or three horses graze on the grey grass around the place, and there are chickens and dogs. This spread looks like something out of the old American West, so I wasn't too surprised when someone told me it's called the House on the Prairie—which bespeaks the way American popular culture and mythology have infused the South African scene. They say there's a shebeen (a speakeasy) here, and I'd like to stop sometime and check it out. The shebeens (shabeens) were first set up back when Africans were forbidden to own businesses or drink the white man's liquor, and then during apartheid they were centres of activism and social life, where all sorts of people—gangsters, teachers, musicians, nurses, agitators, everyone—met to drink and talk about everything from politics and philosophy to soccer and music. Miriam Makeba, the singer, began her career in the shebeens, and so did Hugh Masekela, the jazz trumpeter.

Spreading out beyond the House on the Prairie lies a large and growing African squatter camp known as Mandela Park—all those shacks over there of cardboard and rusty tin. Many thousands of blacks have moved from the villages and homelands to such squatter camps near the cities now that the separation laws are no longer in force. Usually, there's no electricity or plumbing, and not much law enforcement. In those camps are hordes of unemployed young men who learned to live violently during the struggle for liberation, and stories of robberies, killings, car-jackings in this area are common.

A little further on is some industrial development—construction supplies, steel piping, can manufacturing—and then open land, sand and shrubs. Over there a graveyard with wooden crosses and occasional flowers but very few tombstones, an African graveyard. We slow to a near stop where the road to Elsie's River crosses, and here beggars and work-seekers are lined along the verge on each side, 20 or more.

Now we're passing Belhar on the right, a pretty middle-class suburb inhabited mostly by coloureds. My lovely colleague Mercia Louw lives there with her husband, Lester, and their 2-year-old baby, Rachel. She tells me the place is gang-infested, and too often in the night they hear gunshots.

Hey—we're nearing the university now. A set of train tracks running up from Cape Town crosses under Modderdam Road here at Belhar Station, and goes off at an angle. In the widening space between the roadway and tracks is the Cape Flats Nature Reserve, a sandy area of 4 or 5 acres covered with green fynbos (fainbosz—fine leaves). This plant is really remarkable. One variety is a small shrub with narrow rolled leaves, and it grows all over the mountains of the Cape, blossoming with flowers in a most astonishing range of colours. And Cape reeds, which look like grasses but are tubular and more wiry. And the Protea, which can grow quite tall, about 6 feet, with rigid leaves and dense cone-shaped flower heads. There are many other varieties of fynbos—more per square metre in South Africa than any other plant in the world, I'm told.

This preserve is looked after by the UWC botany department, and by wandering skollies (hoodlums), who in fact make the area somewhat dangerous come evening time. But I wonder if there's any more danger in this country than in other crowded, overpopulated places in the world today. Do news reports of the occasional stabbing or car-jacking make us more fearful than we need be? But then, Mercia's husband was car-jacked. He wasn't harmed and the police found his bakkie later, not too badly damaged. And a taxi driver was shot dead yesterday right outside the gates of UWC, another victim in the taxi wars being fought between competing companies.

One night in Cape Town my daughter Jessica and I were walking to my car after seeing a performance of *Swan Lake*, and a young boy appeared from the darkness and asked me for money. I gave him 20 cents but he insisted that was not enough, and he pointed to large group of people huddled asleep against the wall of a building. As we walked on he inserted himself between us and I felt there was potential for violence. Police are very few, and the way these people have to live makes them desperate. The contrast between seeing *Swan Lake* and then walking into this reality in a dark street was disorienting. Finally he lagged behind and left us alone.

Well, a last rise in the road, which conceals the cops who wait for speeders here, and soon we'll be at the turnoff to the UWC campus. There's another set of train tracks over there to our left, and it was in the freight yard near the old entrance to the university that the police would gather in their yellow Casspirs, trucks, kdwelas (police bakkies), and squad cars whenever the students demonstrated against apartheid. The battle would be joined at Motterdam Road, with stones against tear gas and rubber bullets as Buffels, Hippos, and Casspirs were rolling over the campus on their huge wheels, carrying officers behind light armor.

Now we take this turnoff to the right into West Drive, and there's the university just ahead. Some say it was built way out here, 4 kilometres from any town, to make it easy for the police to isolate any agitation or political action among the students. For the hostel residents it's a boring backcountry, with no place they can go to for recreation. Tinswallo, a third-year student who is one of our tutors, says he feels like a prisoner here. The few students with a little extra cash can go over to the Belhar Station and take the train to Cape Town, but wandering skollies make that area somewhat dangerous after 4 o'clock in the afternoon when the security guards go off duty.

And that train goes through some very unsafe areas. Many of the carriages have all their windows smashed out. One day I boarded the train at Salt River Station, found a seat and sat there, trying to relax. But soon I noticed some pretty raw looking young skollies, watchful as cats while seeming to lounge with their girlfriends. Hey, this was a tough crowd and I felt sure of being knifed before we got to the next station. I ran for it into another carriage and that looked safer, with many homebound Xhosa factory workers. The atmosphere was chatty and friendly. I sat down among them and breathed the traditional sigh of relief.

But here's the checkpoint, this little building that looks so oriental with a bright red roof, where we enter university property. There's a boom on each side allowing the campus guards to stop cars, and they sometimes check your boot as you go out to see if you're driving off with yet another of the university's computers.

And now we're entering University Square, the centre of the university, surrounded by very impressive buildings of bright red and yellow brick—the Great Hall, the student centre, the library, and the new administration building. You can see it's a pretty university, really, with lawns and walks. The buildings were designed in several architectural styles to reflect a more democratic, multicultural spirit, I'm told. The Great Hall is the highest building on campus, rising four stories. On the top centre there is a huge triangle of glass, which lights the great interior spiral walkway (as in New York's Guggenheim Museum), and on the top right and left corners are large open pavilions with slanted roofs, Oriental style. Such pavilions appear also on the student centre and the new administration block. Below the steps of the Great Hall there is a decorative waterfall flowing down over a green ceramic dome, and the water is channeled towards University Square, where the police faced crowds of students singing and dancing their protest during the last food crisis.

We might say the architectural spirit here is postmodern, since there is such a mixture of styles. One side of the student centre appears as a columned Greek temple, with the words RESPICE PROSPICE (Look to the Past, Look to the Future) inscribed above, while the other side is walled with great sheets of glass. Students can sit in there eating lunch and looking out over the green lawns in front, the playing fields beyond, and in the distance the hazy Hottentot Mountains. No wonder many of them experience this place as a paradise and wish they could afford to stay on.

Nearby is a set of one-story prefabricated classrooms, with walls painted to resemble brick. These are known as the ovens, for they are very hot in summer, but in winter of course they are very cold. Beyond them the new science buildings are being built—very ultra-modern in appearance, functional, with large glass doors. If we turn here on Park Road and go along past the Great Hall, you'll see between the two arts buildings an old herb garden, somewhat overgrown, and occasionally as I walk by there to the lecture hall I can smell the dagga smoke rising, as this area is also a gathering place of Rastamans who study at the university. But the rules against this are strict and I know of one recent expulsion and a withholding forever of this fellow's degree because of selling spliff in the hostels, where the students live—those three-story, red-brick buildings over there on the right, beyond that great expanse of playing fields.

As you can see, this campus is quite extensive, and all these buildings have been built since 1960 when the government opened this place as a coloured university with about 600 students. Every year since then the enrollment has risen, and now the student population is nearly 14,000, about the same as the historically white University of Cape Town. Of course our staff numbers about half that of Cape Town's.

The student body is mixed, like the architecture. From the first days of this university the administration opposed the restrictions laid down by the apartheid regime and invited Africans and whites to come, along with the coloureds. The first rector, Jakes Gerwel, who would be classified as coloured, did not want this to be a regional university with only local students, so now the student body is almost evenly divided between the Africans and coloureds, along with a few whites. And the coloureds are far from being a homogeneous group because they include not only the mixed-bloods from African and white unions, but also Indians, both Hindu and Moslem, and Malays, descended from slaves brought over from Malaysia by the Dutch East India Company long ago. Many of these people speak Afrikaans, which developed from the Dutch and African tongues, although in urban areas the coloureds often have English as their first language. This gives them an advantage over the Africans, who speak native languages and are not as proficient in English. The Africans in this area are mainly from the Xhosa people, along with some descendants of the Khoi Khoi (once called Hottentots), who were here when the Dutch settlers came in, but our students also come from Namibia, Swaziland, and all over South Africa, so this is truly a national university. Of course there is some tension among all these groups but also they obviously have many interests in common, so the relationships among them are complex and difficult to describe.

We've had some good times together. Last week I took my class outside to watch the men at work on the new science buildings, and afterwards we wrote poems. Brenda Jaffe gave us this:

Workers

Rattle, tumble, noise all over the place
doing work with mind on own
a new house or maybe a car
Familiar to them the engine's roar
Everything happens the same everyday
Only the mind is other way.

Men in blue busy at ease
discuss what tomorrow may bring
silence is not the word so close
Construction is movement and improvement
The feeling of being of use, while
The brood is waiting at home.

We enjoyed reading these poems to each other. So as you see, we're not doing only the academic, expository kind of writing the programme requires, we're taking a hint from your 'Scenes from the Writing Workshop'. But there's so much talk here about students learning the 'language of the academy' that I'm not sure how far I can go in your direction without getting into trouble.

And I feel somewhat choked by the rectitude of the place. A friend of mine from England pointed out that she had been here for more than a month and hadn't heard one person utter a swear word. And I remember going back to New York for a visit and being shocked within an hour of my arrival by a stream of curses in the local grocery store on West End Avenue. Also, my psychedelic free-style of dancing is unusual here and people make comments. South Africa has been so strictly regulated for so long, it's almost puritanical in some ways.

But I'm adjusting, trying to keep my inner devil in check. Sometimes that's not easy, and the work here with so many students in a class is often difficult. I hope you will write soon and tell me all that you're doing.

Usale kakuhle—Ed

- - - / / / - - -

15 June

Dear John,

You probably haven't received my last letter and here I am writing another because I'd like to tell you about my work, so many questions come to me when I think about it and I'm wondering what answers you might have. It's cold down here these days—not as cold as New York in winter, but there's no central heating and these little electric heaters only warm a small area. But maybe it's the cold in my soul that's the real problem.

Alistair and I have been trying to get students to open up and write more freely by giving them exercises in creative visualization. For one of these they sat with their eyes closed while I read a passage to them about being on a small boat and coming to an island. On the island you come closer and closer to a door, take hold of the large metal handle, swing the door open and you're looking into the town. Now the students open their eyes and write down whatever they see and hear, or feel and think as they walk into the town. At the same time, we played a piece of evocative music on a tape deck to create a mood, and the students certainly got busy writing:

> The square is crowded with people. I push some of them away in able to see whose calling. And there—it was a cry! Someone is laying on a kind of altar with no fingers or toes. This man is naked and naked women are dancing and singing around him while the men play this ugly music. I felt how my heart shock of the idea that this man are going to be burn as an offer to their gods. Someone give a call and a hand take me. When I turn around I saw it . . . a huge figure of what? I don't know because it is indescribable.

That's a bit from one visualization. But sometimes I wonder where all this will take us. I mean, can we create an organized syllabus out of things like this? Alistair wants us to draw more on right–left brain research. His argument is that abstract reasoning is used too much here, and in fact that may be a problem everywhere. Too much rationality becomes a kind of cage and students hardly ever get a chance to write about their feelings.

This bias against 'soul,' you might say, is common in writing programs. And also in studies of how language is used. For example, the other day Alistair mentioned what he thought was a lack in Basil Bernstein's work on language codes, in that he leaves out the feeling individual—he's concerned mainly with how children learn the elaborated language code necessary for the abstract, intellectual kind of thinking required in school. But isn't there already too much emphasis in education on factual learning and abstract thinking? Is the expression of feeling going to be limited to activities outside of school and to the restricted code of family and neighborhood? I know you think that Bernstein's discussion of how middle-class children have the advantage of an elaborated code, whereas working-class children are handicapped by their restricted code is important, but surely Alistair has pointed to a serious limitation in Bernstein's theorizing. How much can students really learn without having some feeling for it, so to speak?

So we think it's important to spend time in a language class on experiences that draw on imagination and feeling, such as our visualization exercises. But of course we can't do only this sort of work. The syllabus requires that we teach various concepts such as tone, register, metaphor, denotation and connotation, literal and figurative, factual and emotive, and so on. There's an exam given at the end of the term, and if the students think they're not getting the exam material they complain, so we've been preparing information sheets about these concepts and then asking students to find examples of them in a short story. But at least a third of my students can barely speak English and yet they are being asked to use these sophisticated terms. Even so, maybe there's some value in presenting this structured way of examining a literary text. The need for structure here is so great, and Alistair feels strongly that the students need this approach or else they feel uneasy and uncertain. I'm more inclined to believe they need to have their individual styles emphasized and developed, but Alistair points out the communal aspect of African society and how necessary it is to build on that, with students working together on the same material. And also I fear that teaching approaches which emphasize the individual will lead to eccentricity.

In fact, this fellow Alistair makes me question your way of teaching, which has always *felt* right to me. He's very sure of himself and very persuasive. He creates these lesson plans with a certainty that I don't have, and he seems able to organize the class in such a way that students feel relaxed and trusting, willing to share their many secrets with each other. I mean, he gets them to engage somehow in an exploration of their love for one another. I'm not sure I can inspire that kind of confidence and trust in what I want to do with them. Maybe it's a lack of—oh, I don't know what. I remember you seeming to argue once that uncertainty is a sort of final state of being, that it keeps us moving and we can't hope for anything more. But I hate to think that we're destined to just always stagger along in confusion, wondering where we're going.

Perhaps the real purpose of the learning situation we're all so involved in is to create the ecstatic person. I mean, when students communicate with one another or with the teacher, don't they want most to be valued by others, commended, given warmth? Alistair pointed out that people are not as concerned with really understanding each other as they are with seeking love and respect, and developing a sense of peace. So I wonder if you've had any experiences with groups that actually succeed at creating genuinely warm spaces, that contain both provocation and love?

In fact, I'm wondering how you might work in these classes where English is a second language and many students have very little experience of it outside the classroom. This point is often thrown at me by others who believe we have to teach traditional English grammar. Diana, who worked in the program with me last year, said that students want it. She devised these exercises that showed, for example, how the police reports often used the passive voice to hide the agent, as in 'Several demonstrators were injured by birdshot in White City today', and of course it was the police who shot them. Wouldn't this be a good way to teach grammar?

Diana was certainly a lovely radical, sometimes accompanying political prisoners who were returning from Robben Island (where Nelson Mandela was imprisoned all those years). One night we were at her home in Woodstock having a party with our whole class. Later, after we left, she heard noises outside and went to the window, and suddenly her car exploded in a ball of fire right before her eyes. Then her home was broken into several times. Once she and her boyfriend locked themselves in a bedroom, terrified, while a gang vandalized the place. She believes the police were behind all this and I wouldn't doubt they saw her as another traitor to the white race. She's gone off to have a child and teach at Bops (the University of Bophutestwana).

Politics here is serious business. After all, we've been through a time when the authorities were shooting ANC supporters wherever they found them. I can't easily erase from my mind that photo of Albie Sachs crawling away from his bomb-blasted car in Mozambique. But then my ex-wife points out how the black organizations were also violent, and the leadership of the ANC is capitalist. In other words, according to her the injustices of the old system will go on despite the change in government, with perhaps a few blacks going middle class and the poor still suffering. This morning a student came by my office complaining that he was starving, so could I give him some money for food? And he's only one of many.

Well, it's getting late and I'd better send this off, although I feel there is much that is still unsaid. It helps to know there is someone outside of all this who is interested in these classroom affairs. I just hope I don't bore you with all my talk about problems. Anyway, thanks for your letter and please do write again.

Sobanna (I'll see you)—Ed

- - - / / / - - -

July 30

Dear Ed,

You took me along on your drive to UWC and that was a trip I'll remember. So perhaps I should repay the favor by inviting you to come with me through the streets of Greenwich Village to the PATH train and on to New Jersey, then the walk to school. But you already know this territory—and besides, you've got me agitated with what you say about your work with young people and I want to comment on that.

For one thing, you and Alistair seem to accept the notion of a radical division between feeling and reasoning, and you encourage young people to so divide themselves, giving them practice in creative visualization one day and information sheets to study the next. And notice that the visualization your student produced is very like something from an old penny dreadful of the Colonial period, with naked savages dancing around a human sacrifice—a stereotypical bit of fantasizing. Which must end with the "indescribable" because this student has not been given anything substantive for the mind to engage with.

I hope these comments are not too harsh, but I have no interest in right–left brain research and no patience at all with the metaphysical implications some are finding in it. Western thought is too left-brained, too analytical, we are told, whereas Eastern thought is more empathetic, more spiritual—and given the harm done to our souls by all the stress on rationality, we should strive to become more spiritual, more right-brained. But it seems to me that rationality, far from having been overemphasized or overdeveloped in our culture, is in very short supply. There is no belief so absurd that it cannot attract a following, and occult philosophies have never been more popular. Yet whatever our limitations as thinkers we are all virtuosos of feeling, convinced that whatever we feel strongly enough must be true—a belief which allows so many to substitute sincerity for critical thinking. Rather than having well-founded reasons for the beliefs they act on, these people have good intentions. The harm these good people do!

The problem is not, in fact, "too much intellect and too little soul, but too little intellect in matters of the soul." The novelist Robert Musil said that. We must go to the artists and the poets for guidance, it seems to me, because they understand the feeling intellect and give us ideas not only as they are thought but as they are felt. They understand the essential unity of the human psyche.

That poem one of your young women wrote after watching men laboring on a construction site, when she speaks of their "doing work with mind on own/a new house or maybe a car," and "Everything happens the same everyday/Only the mind is other way"—now there's a moment of singing, her heart and head engaged with it! When you took those young people back to a site they had passed every day and asked them what they could make of it, encouraging them to make old experience new, you were drawing on their essential unity and strengthening their sense of self. In fact this kind of work, as you turn the attention of your students to other lives and the world around them, tends to develop their emotional range, their ability to feel in certain directions—which is also their ability to think in certain directions, for feeling and thought are not to be separated. As you say, "How much can students learn without having some feeling for it?"

Then you go on to suggest that Bernstein's work is limited because, in Alistair's words, it "leaves out the feeling individual." It seems to make the elaborated language code used in schools simply a vehicle for abstractions, and so you wonder if the expression of feeling is "going to be limited to activities outside school and to the restricted code of family and neighborhood." This is a complete misunderstanding of Bernstein—about as far from the actuality of his work as one can get.

First, it neglects his interest in the tacit ability of ordinary speakers to express feeling and thought in language with an underlying poetic character. By his example he has encouraged other linguists to recognize that here is an aspect of language use worthy of serious study. Also, Bernstein is concerned with the social organization of emotion—with what Raymond Williams called the "structure of feeling" within a given social class or culture. He made a very important point: Our emotions are verbally mediated—and he suggested that the elaborated code allows access not only to certain ways of thinking but also of feeling. In a working-class family we may find that "The language between mother and child is public: one which contains few personal qualifications . . . [and so the] nature of language tends to limit the verbal expression of feeling. This child learns only a public language from his mother and feeling is communicated by non-verbal means" (p. 32).

However, "the further we ascend the social hierarchy, the greater the tendency to verbalize feelings, opinions and thoughts" (Bourdieu). Of course there are times when a language with few personal qualifications can express our feeling as fully as we would like, but words differentiate feeling into those more subtle and complex forms we call emotions until we come to those emotions which can only be expressed in verbal forms. If one cannot read certain works, for example, then one does not have access to the emotional experiences they offer. Learning new forms of feeling requires various social and intellectual activities that call for a generalized verbalization of experience. Bernstein describes how middle-class children tend to learn forms of feeling that are not available in a restricted language code, which far from being the sole means of emotional expression is in fact limited in the development of feeling.

So when you asked those young people to describe the construction site, to reconstruct it imaginatively, you asked them in effect to articulate new thought and feeling—for they cannot know beforehand what the result on paper will be. And the emotions suggested there, like the thought itself, cannot be separated from the words in which they are expressed. In short, such imaginative work calls on them to extend the reach of their local, neighborhood language—it tends to expand consciousness. And of course their verbal resources also develop as they read imaginative work with you and talk about it, so I wonder what poems and stories you share with them.

As for the other work you feel required to do—with tone, register, metaphor, grammar and all the rest of it—this is training in how to behave. You are being required to teach these pointless abstractions, language about language, and that passes for training in how to read or write, when the actual training is in how to sit quietly, take orders, and apply yourself to any absurdity the authorities present. This reminds me of Mina Shaughnessy. You may remember that the basic intention of her program was to acculturate all those minority students newly admitted to the City College system, and this meant teaching them discipline and respect for authority. She devised a program that gives training in the rules of grammar, in the structure of sentences, paragraphs, and essays, so that students will learn to set aside their own concerns and follow the dictates of authority, however arbitrary. My piece in *College English* pointing this out ("The Politics of Composition") upset a number of people and led one well-known scholar to publish a strenuous defense of her *Errors and Expectations,* although it seems doubtful that he had actually read the book. Once someone has gained a reputation in our profession it is no longer necessary for anyone to read the work.

Diana is moving in a better direction, it seems to me, with that exercise showing how the passive language of police reports tends to shield the police from direct complicity in the violence they wreak. She is taking up a concept of language within a real-life context and so making it meaningful to her students. But this way of teaching is highly directive, and selects material to satisfy the requirements of a curriculum which demands that concepts of language usage or grammar be taken up one after another. So to this extent Diana cooperates with an authoritarian system she otherwise opposes.

Is that too harsh a judgment? Your situation is a very difficult one and it is not for me to say how anyone there should teach. You will find your own way of living and working in that place, but it does seem important that we question what we're doing. I think if you will follow out the implications of your own thought—as when you speak of young people needing to develop their individual styles—you will find ways within your current situation to reach beyond it.

For what does it mean to have a style, except that an individual self is present in the writing? Young people are taught in most classrooms, however, to use writing simply as a utility for the impersonal transfer of information—although on occasion they may be encouraged to express their feelings on paper and be autobiographical. So they learn these two forms of prose, and there's no doubt that the expository form is the one that counts. But in fact this separation of the practical and the personal, of thought and feeling, is actually harmful to the making of good expository prose. For where do ideas come from except out of one's personal experience with the matter at hand? Let's find ways then of encouraging the individual to be present in the writing, so that it may have the conviction of style.

But you seem to fear that teaching "which emphasizes the individual can lead to eccentricity." Well, you needn't worry about that, it seems to me. "Eccentricity has always abounded when and where strength of character has abounded," and may be simply another term for originality or moral courage (J.S. Mill, *On Liberty*). "To be virtuous is to be eccentric," Mark Twain said. There's a relationship between character and liberty, so let's go ahead and encourage young people to develop their individuality, to be free.

Alistair, however, speaks of the communal aspect of African society and how you should build on that, with everyone working together on the same material. And those visualization exercises he gives are intended, I suppose, to create "genuinely warm spaces" of love and trust—a sense of community, a soothing embrace. But do they also invite those students to forget the narrow limits of their lives and dream away the time? Too bad, because the anxiety or anger they feel could be productive, they could use it in the making of something. All this talk of "warm spaces" and "peace" and "their love for one another" is too sentimental for me, not tough enough! I'm not concerned with creating warm spaces with young people— I want to get on with the doing, with the making of something. We are all there in that classroom to make something, individually most of the time and sometimes together, so we need experiences that will engage our hearts and minds with substantive issues, provoking us to respond in our various ways. So let's get on with the work!

But Alistair is worried those young people will feel uneasy and uncertain unless they're given a highly structured program. "The need for structure here is so great," you say, and so you give them structured "feeling" activities and structured learning activities. But does this radical separation of heart and mind, with all that control, all those directions, tend to serve the interests of an authoritarian system? Let us consider an alternative to the step-by-step, structured program: a course of study that develops from the lives and thoughts of young people as we go along together. For you are right to say they "need to have their individual styles emphasized and developed"—they need the freedom, so go with that thought and see where it takes you.

There's an adventure for you! Of course trouble we'll always have along the way, uncertainty or doubt, and we must learn to live with it if we're going to find out what our young people are capable of. Let it be said that when they come into your classroom they are not entering a railway carriage on the track to a known destination. In fact, you might tell them this—so they begin to understand that you must have their help to make this class go. Your uncertainty will prove in the long run to be the source of your strength, for it will keep you searching and learning. And what will come of this search there's no way of knowing in advance.

You say that perhaps the real purpose of our work with young people "is to create an ecstatic person." Well, the last time I was ecstatic I was in bed and I wasn't alone. (Sorry, but that's what talk about ecstasy does to me.) How can we know what sort of person any of those young people moving along with us will be after our time together? Perhaps we should not define the outcome so specifically.

You remind me of George Leonard and his once popular *Education and Ecstasy*, in which he speaks of "forty techniques for achieving a fuller development of human potential," and tells us that "Education, at best, is ecstatic." On the contrary, it's tiring—it's work! It leaves one with too many questions. And it depends not on a teacher with 40 techniques but on the self-movement of an individual learner. The ecstatic person? This is warmed-over Heidegger with all his talk about having an ecstatic openness to the truth of Being. One wants to say, "Oh come off it, Martin, and let's get to work!" For what else is there to our being in this world but love and work? You and Leonard, however, speak as if young people ought to have a kind of religious experience in the classroom, or a therapeutic one at least. You talk about their need to develop a sense of peace—and I hasten to tell you that a sense of peace is not productive of work. Better we agitate them a little. You talk about developing a level of trust among them so they will "share their many secrets with each other"—as if they're taking part in a group confessional, I suppose. You speak of being unable to inspire young people to have the confidence in you that will encourage them to expose themselves—but that would require not so much confidence in you as faith. Faith in a leader who knows the way, in a guru. And gurus thrive on the passiveness of their followers.

Let us resign ourselves to the fact that you and I are not destined to have followers. Nor do we want them—because we just don't know where we're going! Our satisfactions will come as we find our way along with our young people and hear now and then an unexpected voice speaking up from among them. It's not the secrets in their past that interest us but the secrets in their future—what they might make with us someday in the short time we're together. And afterward they'll think they've done it all themselves.

Well, I look forward to your letters—certainly nothing else seems to be stirring my thoughts lately. Please write soon and tell me more about the young people you work with, I'd like to be taken right into your classroom.

Best regards—JR

CHAPTER 2

— ✧ —

So Much Talking,
So Many Words

22 October

Dear John,

Your observations are always interesting, although sometimes I don't know how I should take them or if I can apply them here. Maybe there is really very little that can be taught about pedagogy, each situation being unique. I remember going into a classroom here for the first time with all those Africans sitting there, none too happy to see me, and wondering if we would get along, if I could find ways to get them interested in working with me.

This was in the old Arts Building, and the room had water streaks on the walls, black pull-down shades on the windows, a wood-tiled floor that creaked underfoot. I took over the class in midterm from a teacher who had gone on to a permanent job somewhere else. As I came in the students looked at me suspiciously, and the room was noisy with the sounds of construction going on outside, banging on steel and the whine of an engine. At that time all hell was breaking loose in the townships, with violent resistance flaring up at any provocation, while on campus there were Casspirs, police trucks and squad cars rolling in regularly, and the yellow police helicopter would come buzzing out of the sky like a huge angry wasp. Being white was not the best recommendation one could have for the job.

I started off with some free writing, thinking it would help us relax together and get acquainted, but they didn't like it. They could hardly see its relevance to the syllabus they'd been following, with its emphasis on literary concepts, or to the exam coming up, and I wasn't so sure either. My predecessor had left behind a pile of exercises in reading comprehension, with material about Nazi Germany, and I was told these students needed to learn the skills of note-taking and outlining, they were 'at risk'. So free writing was not the kind of thing they had been doing and they let me know right away they weren't happy with me. Disorganization and depression threatened.

It seemed that Mzonke Mpofana was my only hope. He sat in the half-circle in front of me, he seemed friendly, and he laughed at my enactment of a bit from Athol Fugard's play 'Sizwe Bansai is Dead'. He was willing to go along with the crazy American, he seemed to understand what I wanted us to do, maybe even saw some good in it. When he spoke it was hard not to be distracted by the large gaps where he was missing teeth, the result of a political argument he said, and he often covered his mouth in embarrassment. I couldn't help feeling let down by the authorities when he was denied admittance, despite my recommendation, to a more advanced English program after our course was over. He became a good friend.

That class was my first experience with the language problem we have here, even with students who seem to understand English. I'll be talking along, using the most ordinary words and assuming everyone is with me, only to find out later they don't really know where we're going. Even the word 'discuss' can be problematic for Xhosa speakers, because discussion among Xhosa is always carried on in a group and they don't accept the notion that one person can 'discuss' something in an essay. So if the exam tells them to 'Discuss this point', that can throw some of them.

I was trying to explain to the class what free writing is, and I was describing it as writing to explore a subject, putting down whatever comes to you about it—and some of them were listening with that sort of blank look. So I asked them what the word for 'explore' is in Xhosa, and it seems there's no exact equivalent. The only word they have for it is 'bona', which means to see or look, but it doesn't have the connotation of discovery so it's a little difficult to get across the notion of writing to explore. I wonder if Bernstein would consider this an example of moving young people from the restricted code of their neighborhood to the elaborated language of school? I suppose if you come from a culture where everyone knows what there is to know, then you don't need a word for explore.

Anyway, this means that I spend a certain amount of time in class just getting matters clear, being sure we understand each other, and maybe that's one reason I don't get into the kind of work you do, with people just going off on various projects. And also I suppose I'm not as confident as I would want to be with a self-creating class, so to speak, because I worry that emotions could run wild and the class get away from me. Alistair seems to manage the raw emotions that are brought into his classroom very well, but maybe I fear them.

In fact, I marvel at Alistair's seeming ability to rely on what I think of as a spiritual position to give him confidence. He has this notion that there is some sort of force in the universe which he hopes to tap into—through meditation, through psychic attunement—which helps us to a peaceful and spontaneous state of mind. Abstract reasoning can't give us this, it only gets in the way. And he also argued persuasively as we drove past the Athlone power plant that his students prefer to get love rather than understanding. 'What I look for when I write, and read my writing to others, is an audience who will accept me. It's a matter of love, really', he said. And perhaps this love will open the door to further understanding. So isn't it necessary to think about what emotions we're going to live with in these classrooms where we spend so much of our time?

You know, I remember a little discussion we had way back in your sociolinguistics class about anger. And I think you left us with a question as to whether anxiety and anger are emotions that are useful in the classroom. I sometimes feel quite nervous about the 'provocative' style of teaching as it can so easily arouse anger, and then how would I be able to deal with that? There's unrest and trouble enough at this university already.

Recently, there have been some vague reports of dissatisfaction in the hostels with the food. Chaka, who's in my class, claims it's 'factory-type' food, not cooked very well—like bone stew (as he called it), which is boiled cabbage with little bones in it and only a bit of meat on them. So students have been gathering in front of the administration building at lunchtime, standing there and singing. Also, the news filtered into our dull lecturers' brains that there's a problem with food credits, but who even knows what food credits are? We're so bent on leading students through the syllabus and upholding standards that little time is left for attending to the mundane problem of their sustenance. It seems that another payment of the registration and hostel fees is coming due and many of these students can't pay, so the unrest is growing.

On my way to class I saw three African students walking towards me, one of them carrying a long hard shiny cane or stick. As I passed by they gave me the look, so to speak, and I felt very white. Then behind me there was a loud whack! as that stick hit a plastic rubbish bin standing there. He meant to startle me and he did. Many of these students are quite desperate and the situation could be approaching the crisis stage, so in the classroom I'd like to keep us calm and on track.

The problem is that people here live so apart from each other, with so little understanding. I was chatting with the guitarist from the reggae group High Selassie the other night at the BASE nightclub. He was trying to explain the old South Africa, and he said 'You Americans just don't know what it's like to have your life threatened. No, that's not it—it's even worse. It's having your very thoughts controlled'. And then a certain administrator at UWC tells me about these black people, that 'Many of them need to be told, they want to conform'. Yeah, sure.

One of my students wrote about how he came to love fighting during the Soweto uprising, and he said he would go back to violence if he's kicked out of school because he can't pay the university fees. Maybe he's more ready for it than others sitting quietly in these classrooms, but there's always the possibility they'll start some really serious demonstrating, there's a history of that here. Underneath their conformance there's a spirit that waits for a call.

Here's where Alistair's spiritual outlook, his mysticism if you like, seems to give him a certain confidence. If, like Alistair Vonkeller, one holds that there is some kind of ultimately radiant state to be attained beyond ego or self, then conflicts are resolved by a softening of rigid lines and a lessening of their importance in a greater vision of things. This isn't just so much sloshing about in good feeling, there's a tough discipline involved before you reach the state of oneness and peace the mystics talk about. And isn't this sense of peace and the confidence that comes with it what we should be striving for with our students? To have the loving classroom, you might say, and move beyond anger? But I can hear you saying, 'Use it!'.

Alistair and I have been team teaching a class, and we wanted to reach some agreement with the students about what conditions in the classroom would foster learning. First we asked them to write about some bad experiences they've had as students in the past, and then some good experiences. It was shocking to find how few of them could come up with good experiences. There were stories of canings and other punishments, and many stories about instances of total embarrassment when they were required to speak English publicly. We asked them to pull from these stories some rules or guidelines that might contribute to having good experiences in a classroom, and then Alistair decided to write these up as 'Golden Agreements'. But at this point I felt he was being too prescriptive. I wonder what you think are good ways of developing discipline among students.

Oh well. Old Mike came by my house last weekend. He washes people's cars around here and sleeps in the churchyard. He plays the triangle and I get off on the guitar and vocals, mostly Bob Dylan. Music seems to open doors between people that we might usually want to keep closed, but now Mike thinks he can come sing at my place anytime. He told me he's gone into the soft drink business and I could have the four Cokes in his knapsack for only 50 rand (the bargaining starts high), so I offered him 3 rand for one bottle, which is in fact double its real price. (A rand is worth about 20 cents now.) When he asked if I had any 'hard stuff' we could drink, I lied and told him no. Instead I fixed him some health bread with peanut butter and jelly, and a cup of tea. He claims to be from Puerto Rico and that makes him definitely an Americano. He's a poet of sorts, and sometimes his remarks about ordinary things seem to imply much more. I mentioned something about mothers and he said, 'Well, women—that's another story. You've already got one newspaper and the woman is bringing you another newspaper!' He seemed agitated about this. 'I mean we already have one newspaper!' I think he was talking about women bringing babies. In the middle of a sentence he suddenly stops, and then drifts off talking to himself. Maybe he's half-mad but sweet really, and I feel bad that I don't want to spend more time with him. Maybe that's the danger of the poetic path you seem to be always pointing to, that I could easily end up on the street with Mike. After he left I opened a bottle of cane liquor and drank a shot of it, in guilt for not having offered him some.

My daughter Sarah painted a little picture of some clothes hanging on a pole, and next to it she wrote 'Daddy, I have no clothes'. I wonder if there's a special place in Hell for fathers who don't provide their daughters with enough clothes. So I keep on teaching to keep us eating, getting in a few poetic licks now and then.

Well, thank goodness it's warm here these days. Cape Town this time of year is one of the most beautiful places in the world—beaches, mountains, and forest. I can take my two daughters to Boulders, a beach only 40 minutes from my door, with huge round rocks sitting on the sand along a peaceful lagoon, and penguins walking about or lying among us as though we all belonged there together. What more could we want from Mother Nature? But in the winter it does get real chilly when we're in schools with no central heating.

Keep the pot boiling—Ed

- - - / / /- - -

November 20

Dear Ed,

You're the one keeping the pot boiling, with all that talk about love and peace and oneness, so that I'm amused and angry, impatient and resigned all at once.

Alistair tells you our students come to us hoping for love—not understanding but love. Yet why should I love them? That's not why I go into a classroom, to pass out love with the assignment. What young people need from us is not the specious suggestion that love will solve their problems, but rather they need training in the language required for mastering their life situation—and that's why they come to us, to get stronger! It's power these people want, more than love. Like Alistair himself, who tells you he writes hoping that his words will bring him love and acceptance, when in fact he writes to make his voice heard.

And that voice would like to persuade us that the schools have emphasized abstract reasoning at the expense of spiritual development, so now we need to encourage young people "to explore their love for one another" and so come into "psychic attunement" with the force of love flowing in the universe. This means teaching them to practice various exercises in visualization and meditation, I take it, so they will develop the "peaceful and spontaneous mind" that allows us to leave behind our doubts, our fears, and enter into an "ultimately radiant state" beyond ego or self. Well, the closest I've been to a radiant state recently was on the tanning table. And there while I napped my ego took a brief rest—although sometimes it seems to double itself and I meet myself in dreams, coming and going, yearning and burning. There is no going beyond self or ego until finally someone pronounces the words "Rest in peace," and then we can really sleep. There's a death wish in mysticism.

Or a failure of nerve before the disappointments and pains that life keeps bringing us, a weakness. Recently a businessman, the owner of a modeling agency, came to me for counseling because of difficulties he was having with a partner. He was very depressed. He had already been counseled by a man and wife, recent acquaintances, who had given him in effect a revival meeting and he left them feeling exhilarated, safe in the bosom of the Lord. "I slept better that night than I have in weeks," he said. It was a quick fix. But 2 days later his depression was back because of course nothing in his life had changed, he still had the same problems as before. Mr. and Mrs. Feelgood had done wonders for his mood but they could not change his life situation, which required him to take certain actions for which he had not yet found the strength. "So what are you going to *do?*" was my question. But they would teach him to shirk the business of this world on the ground that he has an important engagement elsewhere.

It may be true as you say that a tough discipline is involved in the practice of mysticism, but it requires that you submit yourself with blind faith to your master, your guru, who becomes the center of your life. You will follow exactly the regimen laid out for you, losing yourself in the contemplation of some mantra, perhaps, and learning self-hatred first of all. For that's what this talk about going beyond ego or self comes down to. And the suggestion that we have overindulged in abstract reasoning is an invitation to let someone else do the thinking for us.

And there you were the other night, sitting in a South African nightclub being told by the guitarist that as an American you don't know what it's like "having your very thoughts controlled"—and yet so many Americans are yearning for the comfort of that dispensation. That's the trouble with freedom, you have to live with your own thoughts. I see people in the gym, in the street, in the schoolyard with their earphones on, listening, unwilling to be alone with themselves ("ALONE, *adj.* In bad company." *The Devil's Dictionary*).

But if not love, you ask, then what emotions do we want to live with in the classroom? All those brought to us by young people when they speak or write of what really concerns them—the whole tortured mingle-mangle hodgepodge miscellany of uncertainty, fear, doubt, anger, ambition, even love and all that will move them to speak or act, quietly sometimes and not so quietly other times. Only as the young ones educate us in their experience, and so improve our understanding, will they allow us to work with them as they prepare themselves for the struggle. Otherwise, they're only going through the academic motions with us.

Of course that's very safe for everyone, going through the motions. Then the concerns young people bring with them into your classroom, the conflicts that could develop there, are avoided—and given the political rivalries and mix of cultures represented among the students at UWC, you could have problems. So you and Alistair worked out with them a set of guidelines or rules to be followed, a set of "Golden Agreements"—although you thought this was a little too prescriptive. Well, I'd say you're right about that because agreements, genuinely mutual agreements, arise among people in the course of their work together. We understand ourselves and others as the ongoing situation summons one response or another and so defines us, making it possible for us to give each other names. And as we learn what these others are like and what we each might do in this place, we develop ways of working together. Our doing together, whatever that turns out to be, constitutes our agreement. So let's get on with it, let's get busy and make something here! What are we going to make?—that's what I want to know.

To work in this way with young people, to live with the uncertainty of not knowing just what they'll do, risking trouble, requires a certain ironic confidence. It tells us that while we may be living in this classroom, the young ones who come to us there for instruction have their lives elsewhere. And then as they speak of themselves and begin to live with us, we become observers watching as this new drama begins to unfold, wondering how it will end. It's a story we're making here together, with the risk that our movement will suddenly slow, the gathering group fragment, disorder spread across the room. Well at least this thing has a life of its own, you or I might think—and being less impassioned than the others, intervene.

We will live with uncertainty, then, lacking as we do the safety of rules and guidelines, textbook or system. For system is the end of storymaking, and where there is no story to tell then no life is being lived. So far you've given only hints that your classroom can be a lively place, and I'd like to hear more about what you're doing with young people there, I'd like to meet some of them and see what they're making with you—hear the story of your time together.

Do you sit in a faculty lunchroom sometimes listening to the stories teachers tell of their work with young people? Perhaps we should make a collection of them, for taken together they would surely reveal the inner life of our profession as the professional journals do not. Of course you and I know better than tell our stories in lunchrooms, so perhaps there are others sitting there equally reticent. What do we talk about when we talk about teaching? (We need a Raymond Carver in the profession.)

So long for now—JR

- - -/ / /- - -

27 December

Dear John,

The agitation over food credits and fee payments simmers along, with a few hundred students marching to the administration building demanding to be registered for the next term despite outstanding unpaid loans. Yesterday one of the lecturers was telling me, 'Hey, these students want a free education. And after their meeting several of them came along, really full of themselves, and asked me for their last year's exam scripts'. It's policy here that no exam scripts are given back to students, ever— there'd be just too many complaints from these thousands of students to deal with. But another lecturer said, 'Well, eventually we're going to have to give them those scripts'.

On the way to work I picked up a student of mine from 3 years ago hitchhiking on Modderdam Road. I said, 'What do you think is going to happen with this fees crisis?' and he said 'Oh Mr. Katz, there are donors who will provide the money'. 'But will the university keep funding students who do not pay back the loans?' 'Some can pay, Mr. Katz, but many cannot. But tell me, Mr. Katz, when are you going to get a new car? This car is so rusty'. I still have the old Peugot. 'How can I afford a new car with my salary? They're so expensive and the students don't want to pay me more money'. He laughed at that.

Most of the students are still attending classes, hoping this crisis will pass and their education won't be disrupted, but if the police are called on campus that will unite them all whatever their differences and draw more of them into the demonstrations. There's a potential here for real trouble. So this issue is being lived and struggled over outside the classroom, while inside we go on with the usual academic concerns—and all of us feel this contrast, this tension. Sometimes I look at those students sitting there with me and wonder if we're just dealing in abstractions. So much talking, so many words.

Here's where Alistair has something to offer, it seems to me. Perhaps I've misrepresented him by dwelling on characteristics which are not representative of his very real creativity. When we took up 'Sizwe Banzi is Dead' (you should read it), he suggested some really good activities to go with it. We divided the play into 10 scenes, and two or three students worked on each scene, improvising from it. And elements in the play were brought out by little exercises, as when we wrote brief bits about 'Smiling, what I've experienced with it in my life'—to bring us closer to the character Styles in the play, who walks through apartheid with a 'mask of smiles'.

But Alistair's work with poetry was even better. In response to 'blues for district six', a poem by Dollar Brand about the removals from Cape Town, when the wind 'ghosted its way up hanover street/empty/forlorn', he had the students imagine they were a wind blowing 'high over the UWC campus, over Nyanga, Belhar, Guguletu—and you are blowing back into the past, back into the years before the removals . . .' and all the while a cassette was playing Dollar Brand's music 'African Herbs', a piece that was composed before District Six was classified as a white area. It had been a lively working-class neighborhood of mostly poor coloureds, with some blacks and even whites living there in defiance of the apartheid ideal— about 27,000 people. The Department of Community Development came in with bulldozers and leveled it, except for the churches and mosques, which stand there alone now and deserted. The students began free writing as they got into a mood, thinking about what had been:

> Blow along the street I saw an unsatisfied scene. People crowded in groups along the path. Children is everywhere to be seen. There on the other hand people is busying walking in a tavern. Children is crying in anger to their parents to take notice of them. But the people seems to be happy. Look they even enjoy the incideents that is happening. Some of the younger are strolling along the path in order to get their minds on the joy of the town and not to look behind that happiness of the people. Of course that is just a mask that everyone in that town is wearing. But everyone who knows will see their faces when their property is going to take it from them. [. . .]

I know you don't think much of visualization exercises, but the students seemed to enjoy this and they did write. But after activities like these I seem to find myself turning to a description of the poem or play in order to prepare the students to answer questions on the final exam, like 'How is metaphor used in this passage?' or 'Tell how the writer uses language to construct his meaning'. Why should we give an exam at all if it's going to constrain us in this way? But it's required, I have no choice. And next term I'll not be team-teaching with Alistair, so that means I'll be on my own and I wonder if I'll have the guts to try out some of your methods, or even keep on with these activities that Alistair has invented.

I've already been criticized for not being academic enough. It's not personal expression that's wanted but 'academic literacy.' At the last department meeting I was saying that personal writing helps students become competent with language, and it was explained to me that they're already 'communicatively competent'—in their social language, that is, but not in the language of the academy. So what they need now is to be initiated into the specific ideas and forms that are acceptable in a 'university culture'. The universities have evolved specific and definable genres, and these can be taught directly. One lecturer remarked that I seem to be out of touch with current theory.

So I looked into this genre stuff and the first paragraph in the first book I picked up told me all I need to know: 'A genre approach to literacy involves being explicit about the way language works to make meaning. It means engaging students in the role of apprentice with the teacher in the role of expert on language system and function. . . . It means teaching grammar again'. So that's what I'm being hammered with.

And as if that wasn't enough, later on Quinton Booi told me flat out that personal essays are a waffle, and he criticized me for being too easy with the students, not giving them the constraints and skills that Academia requires. "Students need skills in order to survive, and that's what we blacks want," he tells me. He's survived all right, he has degrees from the State University of New York and Boston U. Oh he really gave it to me yesterday. 'All this liberal stuff about creating space for the students, all this fuzzy lovey stuff—I have a visceral reaction to it', he said, like maybe it makes him want to vomit. 'I don't need some white liberal telling me in English class how I should live my life! I don't need anyone to create space for me, I'll do that for myself!' Once he got started he really let me have it. 'The only thing blacks want from that class are those skills they need to get by in this system', he said, and for him that's all there is to it.

I think he's saying that blacks want to learn just the language, the forms of English that will give them enough power at some point to get rid of European domination, which is stripping them of their culture. Vuyisile Victor, who's in my class, told me he's not giving up his culture by learning English and becoming educated. He seems to think of English as a superficial overlay he can acquire, while underneath there's a deeper cultural pattern which will remain the most powerful force in his and other Africans' lives. So there's great pressure here to teach grammar and terms and forms, which makes me doubtful about how far I can go in your direction.

But of course Vuyisile has already come a long way from his Africa just by going to university. I saw a bit of what he's leaving behind yesterday on the drive to work. I was taking a different route, along the deserted coast by the Indian Ocean, and here I come upon eight fishermen in yellow rain slickers and long black boots hauling their net out of the sea, four on each side, so I pull off the road to watch them. It's a long net, and they're drawing it slowly in to shore from the choppy waters, which are reddish on the surface with some sort of plankton. As more of it comes up from the water one fellow pulls out crabs and small fishes and tosses them back into the waves. But what catch will there be in the centre of the net? It seems strange to be watching this, men at work so directly connected to nature. I live in a world divorced from this reality, abstract, full of words and words and more words. A net of words, and what is my catch? Or am I caught? Here these people are, pulling their livelihood from the sea, and finally the centre of the net is on the beach—but there is almost nothing of consequence in it. A woman picks up a few fish and puts them in a plastic box, and offers them to me, five for two rand—perskers, she calls them. I look down at them shivering out their lives in the box. 'Are they bony?' 'Yes, too bony for me'. But later in the day at high tide, she explains, the good fish will come in. I get back into my old Peugeot and continue driving past this place, called Strandfontein, an area the apartheid government designated for blacks.

Meanwhile at the university the crowd of students demonstrating in front of the administration building at lunchtime has been growing larger, and the singing goes on longer each day. Students have been getting food credits in the form of script, about R500, for food served in the dining halls, but now the administration is refusing to give this credit unless students pay their other fees. The rector says there's no money left for food credits and the students say, 'Raise the money! We're starving!' So the SRC has called another mass meeting and 3,000 turned out for it and the situation is heating up. You have no idea how intimidating, how menacing, a mass of students can be as they come singing and dancing, toyi-toying across the campus.

Once a few years ago, several hundred students and a few lecturers, I among them, set off down Modderdam Road on foot to demonstrate at the police station in Bellville against apartheid and too much police presence. There were moments when the songs rose powerfully and we broke into a trotlike dance as African rhythms took control of our bodies and minds. Then those hundreds of feet hitting the concrete pavement in unison, the beat kept by a menacing hoot of **Huss! ! Huss Huss! ! ! Huss! Huss Huss! ! !** created a unique euphoria and sense of power—that was needed from time to time as we relaxed into a walk and could consider for a moment the possible dangers we were marching towards.

Sometimes the daily news in this country is so compelling that I often feel such things as literature are of almost no relevance—certainly not for the newly literate Africans, who must find their way among the most ominous polarities. And recent fiction by people like Oswald Mtshali, Wally Serote and Sipho Sepamla is saturated with explosive racial issues, so I have this feeling that if I brought their stories into the classroom they might put the coloureds and blacks at each other's throats. Only a fragile understanding, the fear of losing everything, keeps the country together, and there's a constant worry of absolutely horrendous possibilities arising from any episode of unrest. So just how far can I go with individual concerns when we need to keep us all together?

You can see the divide just by looking into a classroom. Africans sit with Africans, and coloureds with coloureds, although I should remark that some so-called coloureds are in fact as black as any African. It's a language divide as well, since many coloureds are more at ease with English than the Africans usually are. Once I asked for corrections to an African student's essay, and when a coloured student pointed out how one sentence could be improved there was an audible hiss from many of the Xhosa speakers. Perhaps the worst incident occurred when we were debating some points about current policies of the ANC, and one African student gave a nasty poke, saying 'You coloureds have no right to comment on these things. You were eating bread from the white man's table all those years'. Another legacy of the apartheid regime, which incited and exploited these rivalries. I had to do some serious thinking about what could and could not be discussed in that tutorial group.

It's going to be a long time before the country recovers from the suspicions and rivalries that developed under apartheid, when the people were divided by a system of racial categories. Blacks, Coloureds, Malays, Chinese, Indians, Other Asians and Whites were all considered separately. The government would give a particular privilege to one group or another to set it apart with its own interest to protect. When the Indians were given some representation in parliament, the blacks rioted against them. Coloureds were allowed to live in areas forbidden to blacks, but it was possible for an occasional black to be 'upgraded' to coloured. By the way, there was a special category for Japanese businessmen, who were called 'Honorary Whites' so they could do business here without being hampered by the rules of apartheid. And now we're still living with the ill will sewn among the people at that time to keep them from uniting against the white government.

But let's talk about something else. There are times when I need to get away from the daily hungers and struggles, which is one reason I enjoy these exchanges with you when we talk a little theory, a little philosophy. No, I don't really agree with Alistair's metaphysical ideas. And I have no trouble with the notion that 99% of this mystical stuff is just balmy and too many people go along with it. I've had students tell me they can talk in English about witchdoctors throwing lightning but they don't dare talk about it in their native language. And one said that 'When I'm back in the Transkei I believe in witches, but when I'm in Cape Town I don't'. They're living in a strange half-way place, between the new life they're learning and the old life that still has a hold on them. I hear them telling about consulting sangomas to find out who stole their property or who cast a spell to make them sick. And one student wrote a paper about how the witchdoctors tried to kidnap him when he was a child and turn him into a zombie. So there's still widespread belief in this sort of thing, and I suppose that more education is the answer.

On the other hand, science can't explain everything. There have been some events in my own life that have seemed uncanny, some exceptions to the ordinariness of everyday life that trouble my mind. In Swaziland a few years ago I had a rather uncanny experience. I was told that snakes, especially mambas, could be called by sangomas, and these snakes bring messages from the ancestors. It's permissible to kill a snake but then one is obliged to go to a sangoma to learn from her what message the snake was bringing. (A sangoma has powers, she can lift a curse or 'smell out' an evildoer.) Anyway, a friend and I took to drumming one night up there in the Swazi hills, and I played around with the thought of calling a black mamba, for in fact we knew there was one in the vicinity. Nothing happened that night, but lo and behold, the next morning I was lying on my bed when the cat set up a tremendous yowling and believe it or not a 9-foot black mamba slithered into the doorway and lifted its head! These snakes are quick to bite and their poison is deadly. I was in fact trapped there but thank God it passed me by and slithered into the child's room—Sarah's, who was a baby at the time, but she was with her mother in Johannesburg—and settled itself into a coil behind the laundry basket.

Would science say this was simply a coincidence or is there another explanation? Even in the professional journals we read that scientific laws are only 'agreements' among various persons working in that area. They do not reflect actual perceptions of reality but are a kind of compromise, the result of people cooperating, often for various and divergent reasons, in the attempt to describe reality. This seems to dovetail with Polanyi's argument that science never presents an objective picture of the universe but is twisted and bent by the human purposes which drive inquiry and theorizing. I'm wondering how far you go in thinking of science as giving us reality itself, or is it only a way of seeing the world from another point of view?

Oh well, I hope I haven't gotten carried away here. Maybe that's enough for now. Hope to hear from you soon.

Hambah kakuhl (go well)—Ed

Note: As I write this, about 300 students, almost all African, are dancing and chanting in front of the administration building, occasionally hurling abuse at the 20 or so policemen standing in front of the doorway with transparent plastic shields. This isn't just a polite, peaceful little protest, these students really mean business and they have a tradition of struggle and confrontation. They've brought registration to a halt since any student who goes in must be accompanied by a policeman in full view of the protestors. This reminds me of the really violent confrontations we've seen here in the past, and I'm hoping the issue gets resolved peacefully and soon. Will good old UWC be in session come the new semester? I wonder.

- - - / / / - - -

January 8

Dear Ed,

I'd like to hear more about people and less about miracles, to be quite direct. There is such a contrast between all that mystical speculation and events on your campus or in your classroom, as you tell about them—between the conjectural and the real. Give me the real every time! I'd like to meet those young people you work with but you haven't really taken me among them as yet.

All this talk of uncanny experiences and a black mamba summoned by drumbeat—all this tries my patience and makes me testy. Is life so drab and we so disheartened that our only escape lies in the hope of magic? Are we by some miracle to be lifted up and transformed someday, if we wait long enough, while in the meantime our affairs in this world go cursorily attended and our lives unexamined? Let's get on with the work of the world! I say, for there is no magic here except in the happiness we make for ourselves despite daily hardship. So let's get on with it!

But in the course of getting on with it there are going to be digressions, human nature being so contrary, and I've learned to go along for a time at least with whatever interest my young people what to explore, even the mystical. In fact, we spent a good part of one class period a few weeks ago talking about this matter of miracles. Jimmy was collecting information from us for a paper on what people in our community believe about the supernatural, and soon the youngsters were telling him of their marvelous experiences with fortune tellers, weeping Madonnas, premonitions, dreams coming true and the like. I listened to all this—it took an effort of will to keep silent—until finally the Imp of the Perverse tempted me to speak. I said there was something about me they did not know, something I am usually reluctant to talk about, but because they seemed sympathetic to experiences of this kind I would admit that I myself have a special power. I told them about my old grandmother, who the closer she got to the other world the more she learned about the powers that move this world, and how she taught me to put myself in tune with the higher vibrations. And if they would help me, I said, getting up from my seat among them, I would demonstrate my power.

They looked at me intrigued, wondering whether I was serious or just putting them on. If they would select some small object, I said, and conceal it on someone's person while I was out of the room, then I would come back and by means of their mental vibrations identify the person holding that object. Someone offered a key and I left the room while they concealed it, one of them watching at the door to be sure I wasn't peeking in. When they called me back, I said "Now lower your heads and think about the key, send me your thoughts, help me. I'm going to need someone as a channel for the vibrations, someone who believes, who will stand close and follow me, so Marcie will you follow me and open your mind to the vibrations and help me, hold my hand very loosely now and follow me along, and see the key, where it went, where we're going," and I walked about among them murmuring all the while about the key and vibrations. Before long I knew who had it but I delayed the discovery, asking Jimmy to stand while I walked around him with Marcie, hoping to feel the vibrations but then leaving him and trying another, until at last I said, "Oh this has been very difficult, but now I know. Gina—you have it." She reached into a pocket and drew it out. "How'd you know it was me?" she asked. "I sensed the vibrations."

Of course Marcie led me to the key. As we walked slowly along together I could feel very slight, involuntary movements of her hand as she pulled me toward it, although all the while she thought she was only following me. I'm a truthful man, I did feel the vibrations. Later I confessed and explained how the trick was done, but there are always people determined to believe despite any evidence to the contrary you give them and some youngsters insisted their thought waves must have helped me. It's easier to teach belief than skepticism.

I find it worrisome when occult movements reach into the schools, undermining a commitment to rationalism that's none too secure as it is. There's a burgeoning holistic movement in education, with supporters decrying abstract reasoning and advocating various spiritual and therapeutic concerns. Consider how many academics have taken up the postmodern notion that language cannot report an objective reality and believing otherwise is simply an outmoded habit of thought. So they prepare their students for the mysterious realm of verbal nirvana, I suppose, where language is not bound by reference or representation and we will live in spiritual comfort whatever happens in the real world. No wonder there's an outpouring of articles and books with titles like *The Spiritual Side of Writing* or *Suffering and the Remedy of Art*, while the noted scholar Jane Tompkins goes about preaching a spiritual pedagogy, giving workshops featuring meditation and visualization exercises, and asking people to draw pictures representing their deepest desires while sitar music plays in the background. An assembly (or study group) of the National Council of Teachers of English is concerned with paranormal experiences and Jungian mysticism. And then there's James Moffett, whose *Teaching the Universe of Discourse* and other works are still frequently cited in the professional literature; he outlined an instructional program in which youngsters climb the "abstraction ladder" toward a Higher Reality, which includes among other marvels telepathy, faith healing, precognition, and communication with the dead. Are these the skills we should be teaching? Well, on second thought let's hope there might be something in telepathy—that would solve my problem with the telephone company.

Examples of this mystical incursion and the therapeutic save-their-souls approach it encourages could be given endlessly, but enough already! Let us return to the mundane world in which we have our present being, and which seems quite strange enough to me. Have I told you the English department entrusted me with a class in prose fiction this term? And last week one of the full-time professors came in to observe me at work and write an evaluation. Darren was in charge that day, and we had already considered in our small groups the discussion questions he'd given us for Steinbeck's story "The Leader of the People." The entire class was now gathered in a circle (26 of us), and Darren called on each group in turn for our responses to his questions, while Professor Bowie sat there taking notes. It's interesting to me how so often in responding to a story readers will single out for objection a feature of the writing that is in fact essential to the effect—and now someone complained about all the description in this one: "It's boring, it slows down the action." The others agreed and finally I raised a hand, asking Darren for a turn to speak. "You know, descriptions can be quite revealing. Remember how Grandfather is described, how he was dressed? He comes onto the ranch wearing a black broadcloth suit, a black tie, kid leather shoes—a figure of some dignity who would be treated with respect. And of course we each dress to convey a certain impression, a certain message about ourself. Now take for example the way professors dress." I paused, and all eyes turned to Professor Bowie. He had on a suit, white shirt and tie, while I was wearing a sweater and slacks. "Now what is Professor Bowie saying about himself?"

"He expects you to know he's not just one of the crowd, he's dressed formal-like," George said. "He's even got a little handkerchief sticking out of his coat pocket." Bowie leaned over to the young woman sitting beside him and whispered something. "He says his wife made him wear it," she announced and we laughed.

"Well I'll tell you something," Bowie said. "I'm sitting in the subway and I'm wearing a nice coat and nice tie, and I notice that women are looking at me. I'm wondering if they're interested in me or my clothes. I think men don't notice a woman's clothes, they see her naked first, if you don't mind my saying so, but women look at your clothes—as if they're wondering how good a provider you might be."

"So you're dressing for the women!" Marci said. "And look at those shoes"—he was wearing a kind of loafer—"like he's saying he's not too serious, ya know."

Bowie looked a little discomfited by this scrutiny but I think he took it in good spirit. And the rest of us certainly enjoyed the moment. I'm waiting now for my copy of his evaluation report.

The next day there was an argument. Darren had finished his work with us and I was making a few closing remarks, mentioning the resentment Jody's father Carl felt toward Grandfather, who talked on and on telling yet again the old story of how he led a wagon train across the Great Plains. George said, "My old man talks about the old days all the time. Ya get tired of it."

"But there are some stories in our history we should know, aren't there?" I said. "Like the story of our revolution. I mean, how do we keep in touch with the American spirit if we don't know the old stories?

"History's boring!" Maria said quite emphatically from the far side of the room. "Who wants to hear those old stories?"

"But they tell us about the American experience, they carry with them our ideals of self-reliance, of freedom—shouldn't we know them?"

"Times change," she said. "We live in a different world now, we gotta live in the present, we gotta think about gettin jobs. Jody's father had a good point, he got tired of hearing Grandfather's old stories, they were—"

"But the hired man wanted to hear them, why not—"

"Listen!" she said. "They were Grandpa's dreams, Grandpa's values. Our whole life our parents are telling us about their values and dreams, but we want to have our own life and do something different from them, we want to make our own stories!"

This little song gave me pause. "Maria, you speak so well about this. Will you put what you're saying down on paper for us?—and I'll share it with the class. You have good ideas, so maybe you'd like to make something of them." She was willing, she had more to say, and even though no one else was asked to write about this story she did the extra work. And when I brought her paper to the class, reminding the others of our argument, they looked at me so seriously: One of their own was actually going to have the last word! And they let me know they agreed with her—but they'll remember Grandfather.

I see now that Maria and I had been acting out those characters, she taking Carl's part and I playing Grandfather. And this happens quite often when we talk about these stories, that the youngsters speak for one character or another. It seems to me this lived experience with a story is surely more important than anything I might say about form or theme or style, because it's a way of thinking. Youngsters taking the part of a character are thinking their way into the story, and often they'll talk about an issue in ways that otherwise might not have occurred to them, and perhaps sing a little. That's why I'm interested in the work you and Alistair did with "Sizwe Banzi is Dead," having the students improvise scenes from the play so they can find their own way into the experience of it. That's so much more interesting for them than just reading the play and then answering your questions about metaphor and meaning. The lived experience is what will matter to them and be remembered.

And they'll draw on it for the final exam. You worry that if you haven't given them some description or summary of the play they might not do well, but in fact they have in mind their own descriptions or summaries. And if they're asked to "tell how the writer uses language to construct his meaning," they're ready because they've been using that language, they've taken it over for themselves as they improvised and played the characters. And surely there have been discussions along the way about why those people speak as they do. If my students were asked to write about Steinbeck's use of language I'm sure they'd remember our talk about his descriptions, and how we considered the message in Grandfather's attire and Professor Bowie's. So long as the examiners don't expect polished essays from students who are doing further thinking right there with the exam, the results will likely be quite acceptable.

We do these exams to satisfy outsiders, but the really significant work has already been done. Those young people reading stories or poems with you, talking about them, will already have made some new meaning for themselves. Would Maria have found the words she did without our experience together? Of course I know we get very tired sometimes and wonder "about so much talking, so many words," as you say. But do we give up, hoping there might be some more immediate, intuitive way to understanding—to enlightenment, as the mystics would say? When you've found the True Way let me know, but in the meantime we'd better keep plodding along with our youngsters in this world, helping them make something of their experience with an essay or poem or story, encouraging them to sing now and then.

Consider the poets—who manage to transcend our everyday, sordid experience even as they make us pay close attention to it, drawing from pain some little pleasure. Frankly, such word magic is the only magic I ever expect to know in this existence. Poets are realists, after all.

And so is your friend Quinton Booi, who tells you that what blacks want are the skills they need to get by in the system, not that liberal "fuzzy lovey stuff." Well, I think we should listen to him. It's patronizing of us to imagine that we're going to lift up the spirits of those young people by giving them peace and love and space. They come to us for quite practical reasons and we should respond accordingly by helping them develop their skill with language. Of course it's naive of them to think they're going to learn English and yet remain unchanged. For example, you mentioned the misunderstandings that arise among your students when you use words like "discuss" or "explore," since the meanings those words express for you reflect a different way of life than the communal one they've known, where everyone's experience is much the same and the roles one may play are few. To learn an elaborated language code, then, simply means to learn the vocabulary and patterns of discourse necessary for playing other roles and doing new kinds of work. The question is not which code is intrinsically superior but which promotes one's viability in a changing world. Your students are moving from the communal identity and common understandings expressed by a local language code into a world of competitive individualism where they must explain themselves and what they're doing, often to strangers. They will make this move in part through the experiences they have with you in that classroom. In short, you're in the business of changing people—but let's not say so, let's just talk about the need for developing skills.

And let's keep in mind that the young Quintons sitting in our classrooms wanting practical instruction for the real world could be poets, perhaps—unlike the advanced thinkers in composition studies, many of whom seem to have drifted so far from poetry and the aesthetic experience they've lost touch with reality and live in a theoretical world. I have in mind those postmodernist epigones and the Marxists who speak of how we should "expand student agency" and "decenter classroom authority" and develop an "oppositional pedagogy," while they themselves lecture the young, "invite" them to write formal papers, and specify quite precisely what understandings they are to demonstrate. Who are, in short, authoritarians camouflaged in rhetoric. A book like Richard Wright's *Black Boy* might put them back in touch with reality but they'd rather read and talk theory.

Which reminds me that sometimes the individuals who come to me for counseling have worked out quite elaborate theories to account for their problems. They tell me these theories, intending to confine me within their understanding of a situation so as to forestall any finding that might threaten their self-image or discover them guilty. And of course I listen to all this, however long it takes, because first I must understand their situation as they do if I'm going to find a way to help them.

Recently a young woman came to see me because her son, almost 6 years old, would lose control of his bowel when he got upset or excited. Then she had to take those soiled pants off him, clean him up, tell him to be more careful, to use the bathroom, and she was tired of mucking about with him like this. But she knew why he did it, she'd read some psychology. He'd been often sick as an infant, he'd been upset when she separated from his father, and now that she had another man in the house he was being an infant again, wanting to be mothered, to keep her for himself—it was an oedipal thing. So she didn't blame him for having this problem, you understand, he couldn't help it, but he was dirtying himself two or three times a week and she was tired of waiting for him to grow out of it, so what could be done?

Well, I thought of a quite different explanation. It seemed to me more likely this boy had found a way to make his own pungent comment on the whole situation. Of course that's oversimplifying but no matter, I didn't tell this to the mother. I listened, asked questions, and then drawing on what she said we worked out some steps for her to take that might relieve the problem. First, neither she nor her companion would ever to talk about this with the boy, or say a word of criticism to him. (Her companion had been saying, "Grow up! Be a man!") When the next accident occurred, either the companion or the mother herself, whichever the boy went to, would say "Oh that's nothing, we've all done that," and then send him into the bathroom to clean himself up. Well yes, she'd been thinking of something like that and now was the time to try it. The next day the boy had another accident, and when the man of the house said, "Oh we've all done that, so just go in and get clean," the boy looked up at him for a moment, rather surprised apparently. He soon had another accident, got the same response, and that was the last time he dirtied himself.

There was no need for me to discuss theory with the mother, although she in effect invited me to—our task was to find something to do in this situation, something that would have a practical effect. So I was amused when one of your colleagues remarked that you seem out of touch with current theory, as if theory will solve our problems in the classroom. However, as one eminent authority tells us, "Theories don't prove nothing, they only give you a place to rest on, a spell, when you are tuckered out butting around and around trying to find out something there ain't no way to find out. And there's always a hole in them somewheres, sure, if you look close enough" (*Tom Sawyer Abroad*).

So let's not argue theory with these people. In fact there's no need to worry about being out of touch with the latest thought, it seems to me, as the theory mongers always have more to offer than we'll ever be able to use. Theory is like the weather—there's always plenty of it. In fact, I've added a little to the climate myself but without any effect on wind direction. So much talking, so many words, as you would say. But what are these people themselves *doing* with the students who sit with them?— that's what I'd like to know. You can read hundreds of pages of composition theory and rarely find out. The writers will tell you that "language is learned socially," for example, but of the social interactions in their own classrooms they have little or nothing to say.

And when one of them does describe an actual lesson, the others ignore it in order to talk about the theory or the good intentions back of it all. Mina Shaughnessy, for example, is much lauded for advancing our understanding of how basic writers think—for showing, among other things, that they're not stupid (cognitively deficient, I mean) but rather they just don't know the conventions of academic discourse. And how would she remedy this lack? By teaching the rules of traditional grammar, by stressing the analysis of forms. By taking up a novel like *Black Boy* and using it to demonstrate a "grammar of passages"—and doesn't the heart sink hearing that? In this way she was able to avoid its social, political, and economic implications. Talking about what's really going on in such a book could encourage the move to an elaborated language code as one explains and justifies an individual point of view, but Shaugnessy was more concerned with giving youngsters training in social discipline than in starting a conversation about real issues, for who knows where that talk would go? After all, the open admissions program she directed was in itself a daring social experiment and why put that program at risk? So her book *Errors and Expectations* turns out to be a great political achievement that satisfied her constituency, the administrators and teachers in the vast composition program at CUNY she directed. And which apparently now satisfies the composition specialists who constantly cite her rhetoric without examining her practice.

Well, I thank you again for sharing your experiences with me. Your letters do set me off sometimes, as this one did, but I like the stimulation. And they give me a reason to remember some of the young people I've worked with—to relive my experiences with them and perhaps understand what we did together. Classrooms are brightly lit but so often we work in the dark even so.

Best regards—JR

- - -/ / / - - -

16 January

Dear John,

The demonstrations on campus are getting even bigger and louder, and if the administration continues to maintain its hard line and demand payment of outstanding debts, there's a possibility the student council might call a boycott of the university. Or if this unrest continues much longer the administration might call in the police to quiet things down, and then there could be real trouble. There's a very real possibilty that I could come on campus any day now and find classrooms empty. The times are uncertain.

As for your last letter, it seems you want only the factual, the empirical, the what-can-be-demonstrated, and I have it for you but I'm not sure you're going to like it. I've been reading James Gee's *Social Linguistics and Literacies*, which seems to me to undercut, maybe even chop right down, much of what Bernstein says about language learning. And his analysis also seems quite hostile towards the approach to language teaching you favor.

For example, his attack on the idea of a 'general literacy' to be taught in a writing classroom is withering. He seems to be insisting, contrary to what you have claimed, that a subject matter is absolutely essential for language learning. Perhaps this quote (p. 173) is typical:

> There are, however, no good reasons that I can see for teaching languages or writing outside of any Discourse, since nothing but meaningless or general purpose behaviors (like banging) exist outside Discourses.

And we learn a Discourse (capital D) by learning to be a member of the group that uses it, as when we study some particular subject matter, for example. He goes on to suggest that the subject matter of a writing class ought to be 'the study of how oral and written texts of all sorts mean in their social and cultural settings' (p. 174). There's certainly no support here for the writing of personal narratives as a way to teach a 'general literacy'.

Also, I think Gee calls into question the distinction Bernstein makes between the restricted language code of working-class speakers and the elaborated code of middle-class speakers. He seems to argue that there is not this difference in elaboration at all, since these codes are equally complex and elaborate, well-suited to the social environments in which they are used. In other words, the restricted language code of the working class or local neighborhood (Gee calls this 'primary discourse') can be just as complex as what Bernstein calls the elaborated code.

But Gee's argument goes even deeper than that. It seems to me he calls into question Bernstein's notion of social controls and the supposed effects they have on language learning. Bernstein says that working-class families usually depend on positional controls with children, which define a child's lesser place in the family, and so children learn to do as they're told because that's what children must do, whereas in families that use personal controls a child is expected to give reasons for an action, to justify himself or herself individually, Where the first child might challenge the parent's authority, the second is more likely to question the reasons a parent gives for some demand. Bernstein says that

> In positional families the modes of social control depend less upon individually created and elaborated meanings and so within these families there is less need to sensitize the child towards, and promote the early development of, verbally elaborated forms of speech. (*Class, Codes and Control*, p. 156)

But Gee seems to imply that 'person-oriented' control is not so different from positional control because all discourses are constrained by the various social situations in which they are arise. He describes discourse in one of his articles ('What is Literacy?') as an 'identity kit' that 'comes complete with the appropriate costume and instructions on how to act and talk so as to take on a particular role that others will recognize'. This means that the 'autonomous subject', which supposedly develops from personal controls, is not nearly as autonomous as 'liberals' would have us believe. There are powerful social constraints and determiners acting on this 'subject' that erode the difference between positional and personal controls.

So I wonder what your response to all this will be. Have you looked into Gee's *Social Linguistics and Literacies*? I think it needs to be taken into account.

In the meantime, speaking of discourse I think it's rather curious how my students sometimes give such circuitous and formal introductions to their arguments with each other. While we were discussing 'Listen Comrades', a poem we had just read together, Zandisile said 'The word "comrade" could also just be a word meaning friend, it does not need to be political'—although in fact the poem is about African political prisoners ('comrades') being killed by their guards. Lungisa responded to him this way:

> And now good speaker, I would not wish to question your wisdom on this. But it would seem to me that we will have to follow closely the words on this page in order to fully appreciate your argument and to see that while I would not oppose your point, it seems to me that another interpretation is possible. And I would like to present that point as the writer is, or can be seen to be, political.

He went on to explain why, and that started us off on quite an interesting exchange—many lines of the poem were suitably discussed and interpreted. Also, those whose English is poor were able to hear and understand what the poem was about.

I was showing Quinton Booi some of the questions my students had written in response to this poem, and the intelligent answers they had come up with, and he said, 'But that's not the way things work in the real world, Ed. Nobody's going to give students time to just sit around and think about what they want to ask. They've got to master the discourse of the university as we give it to them. The way I get my students to write is I just tell them straight: "Write or die!" And they write, Ed.' Of course he was being a little tongue-in-cheek. I think.

Bye for now—Ed

- - - / / / - - -

February 4

Dear Ed,

You say that James Gee's *Social Linguistics and Literacies* undercuts Bernstein and is hostile toward the approach to language teaching I favor. Well, let's take a look at this. First, you point out that he attacks the notion of a "general literacy" which can be taught in a writing class because "nothing but meaningless or general purpose behaviors (like banging) exist outside Discourses." But don't the teachers of the various subjects assume their students will arrive in the classroom with a general literacy that is useful in any one of those subjects? And don't they often complain that on the contrary students are not adequately proficient in the written or even sometimes the spoken language as used in schools? Or is this school language also a Discourse that you learn by joining the group that uses it, namely the academic community? In any case, I doubt that Gee has ever taught a writing class, certainly not one with students who speak and write as ours do.

In the prose fiction class we were talking about Toni Bambara's story "My Man Bovanne," much of which is written in Black English, and Nikim said "Why they talk *country*!" He was much amused: "That's real country!" A week later he and I were sitting together looking over the first draft of his paper. "My sister read this—she's visiting me—and she said it's very good," and I explained why she thought so, pointing out the good ideas and the effective turns of phrase. Then we looked at his first paragraph, which began this way:

> Men an women go into relationship for different reasons. For a man it nothin but a game to gain female infatuation for himself, lust an sex are the only truly committed partners, an after a few minutes of pleasure has been achieve the woman will be replace by another.[. . .]

I asked him to read this aloud because students will often improve the writing as they do, but Nikim read this just as written. I put my finger on "nothin" and said, "How can you improve the spelling of this word?" He thought for moment, then said "Add g?" After a few more minutes of considering other words with him, I said "Do you notice what you've done here?" "But that the way I speak!" he said. "Yes, and there's nothing wrong with that. But do you remember how you laughed at the Black English in 'My Man Bovanne'?—you thought it was really funny. Well that's the way you talk, Nikim. But when you write you don't want your readers thinking color, that's a distraction. You want them thinking about the good ideas you have here." He considered this for a moment. "Okay I got it, I don' need ya no more." In his writing he already has the language we want, or nearly so—he has the academic rhythm, so to speak—and now he's learning the sounds that go with it.

But learning this school literacy may be experienced by some as a betrayal of one's own history and heritage:

> if I had known what I was doing I would surely not have been able to do it, I would surely not have wanted to. There was a kind of treason in it: treason toward my family, treason toward my friends. In choosing the road I chose, I was pronouncing a judgement upon them. . . .
>
> Without any conscious effort on my part, my speech had largely lost the characteristic neighborhood accent. . . . I continued to bum around with the gang . . . living the old life of the street corners, pool rooms, crap games, poker games, sports talk, sex talk. I was, to all appearances the same kid I had been before entering Columbia [University], only a little older, a little more sure of myself, a little less anxious over my status as one of "the boys." [But] I knew that the neighborhood voices were beginning to sound coarse and raucous. . . . It was the lower-classness of Brownsville to which I was responding with irritation. To wean me away from Brownsville, all Columbia had to do was give me the superior liberal education it did; in giving me such an education it was . . . ensuring that I would no longer be comfortable in the world from which I had come. (Norman Podhoretz, *Making It*, pp. 50-51)

Is this the path my friend Nikim is following away from his origins, already feeling superior to a way of speaking very like that of his own people, and I am implicated in this? So it seems. For I want him to succeed in the academic world and have any advantage it may give him later.

So how do I help him and the others learn this literacy? You tell me that Gee would consider my way unsuitable: "He seems to be insisting, contrary to what you have claimed, that a subject matter is absolutely essential for language learning." In other words, he maintains that language skills are developed in schools within the discourses of the various subjects, so a student enrolls in a business class and learns the Discourse of business, joins a literature class and learns that Discourse, and so on. Now if this means there is no such thing as the "academic essay" we can teach for general use in the various subject areas, then I would agree with him. But he goes on to say that composition should, therefore, be a Discourse with its own particular subject matter, namely "how oral and written texts of all sorts mean in their social and cultural settings." Well, he's a linguist so he would turn the writing class into a sociolinguistics class. I suggest, however, that he teach such a class himself within his own department, for we have other aims.

We have a somewhat more flexible or expansive notion of subject matter for the composition classroom. It will vary from time to time, depending on the thoughts and experiences that learner and teacher bring with them and the various searchings we undertake together—for any aspect of life and any sort of text will be open to us for investigation and report. Drawing on our respective histories, then, we will create together a social context within which there is reason to produce words—a *situational* context where you and I as helpers will live contemporaneously with our students, all of us moving along with the flow of event, uncertain of where it will end but on the lookout for possibility. There is a hope of mutuality here, as we all work together on another chapter in our ongoing histories.

Perhaps, however, this seems a little too uncertain or ambiguous, or even sentimental, for those no-nonsense types who know exactly where a class should be going, They will implement a clearly defined sequence of the understandings and skills to be practiced and acquired—they will chose to live, that is, within a *positional* context. Where a situational context has a temporal dimension in which spontaneity and process are important, a positional context is a spatial conception in which higher directs lower through the steps in a sequence of learning. Or as Bernstein would say, these teachers use positional controls, which dictate rather precisely what the students are to do. Like your friend Quinton Booi, who tells them to "Write or die!" There's an example of positional control, which relies for its authority on what "we" do in the university and defines the student's inferior position there. Like you, however, I'm more in favor of a situational context, where a personal response to events is called forth—a context in which students are expected to respond individually to a text or to a view expressed, give reasons for the position taken and so explain or justify oneself. An interactive context where, as Bernstein would say, personal controls apply.

As when your students discussed and argued about that poem "Listen Comrade." In this situation they felt a need to explain and justify their various interpretations, to give reasons for their judgments—and that sort of experience will help them acquire the language habits necessary for success in school and in the world beyond, where they must make their meanings explicit to strangers. Your natural bent as a teacher is to create these situations, which means that you and your students live with the uncertainty of personal controls, and this of course puts you at odds with standard classroom practice in the university, as your exchange with Quinton Booi suggests. However, he's not entirely wrong. Let us take what he says as a caution, a reminder to keep a balance of the situational and the positional as we strive to create a many-sided educational event.

One more point. You say that Gee calls into question the distinction Bernstein has made between positional and personal controls, that he "seems to imply that 'person-oriented' control is not so different from positional control because *all* discourses are constrained by the social situations in which they arise"—and therefore no method of control or training can develop the "autonomous subject" because our language itself not only identifies but determines us.

Consider this scene: Approaching me on the sidewalk are a mother and her young daughter, both dressed in designer clothes, the mother wearing expensive blue jeans and jacket, the daughter (about 9 or 10) in a matching jacket and dark blue sweatpants. As they pass by I overhear this exchange:

Daughter: I want blue jeans like you got.
Mother: You can't always be like me, be yourself. And
           besides, I don't have the money right now.

Certainly this is not the way I hear some mothers speaking to their children; they typically settle a contentious matter by ordering the child to accept the parent's judgment and do as they're told—they use positional controls. But this middle-class mother treats her child as an autonomous individual, and she gives the child a reason for her refusal to buy her blue jeans—she uses personal controls. Where the first child might challenge the authority of the parent, as you pointed out, the second learns to question the reasons given by the parent. Control in such a family is based on verbally elaborated meanings rather than on power, although of course power remains the real basis of authority. Bernstein has called our attention to such differences in the management of children and illustrated how the controls used in middle-class families tend to produce persons oriented more to the individual self than to the group, and with language habits that give them an advantage in school and the world beyond the neighborhood.

Now Gee can fashionably deny the autonomous subject but people are not living according to that view. Nor in fact is he—he's just repeating the current rhetoric. I'm sure he would agree that different ways of managing children will have different effects on their self-concept and on their use of language. And we need to know how the young people we work with perceive themselves, since by asking them to change their language habits or determine their own utterance we may be asking them to modify their self-conception.

It seems to me that Lungisa, in his response to Zandisile's comment on the poem "Listen Comrades," is well on his way to acquiring the self-conception that goes with an elaborated (or shall we now say academic) language. I'm referring not to the ceremonial way in which he expresses himself, but to how he sets himself apart and speaks as one individual to another, offering reasons to justify his different interpretation of the text. Accounts like this of classroom experience interest me far more than theoretical discussions because they offer a narrative that we can interpret and so perhaps begin to understand what we are doing in classrooms with young people. Theory is often at such a remove from actual classroom practice or experience! And from the lives of our students and events on campus—the demonstrations you speak of for example. But you seem determined to draw me into these theoretical discussions.

Speaking of which, I should say that *Social Linguistics and Literacies* seems to me a very interesting book, and I've commented here more on your reading of it than on the work itself. If instead of reading it to find a refutation of Bernstein, you will look for whatever confirmation it gives him, I think you will see that Gee supplies further evidence Bernstein could use. But I leave you to do that work for yourself. In fact, you've already made me do enough work for one evening and so I now take my leave of you.

Best regards—JR

CHAPTER 3

Everyone's Secret
is the Same

9 February

Dear John,

Well, the student council has called a boycott, demanding food credits for those who've been cut off for not paying all their fees, so that means mass demonstrations and tense times. They'll try to shut down the university by keeping everyone from their classes. The administration refuses to back down from its hard-line position and orders us to carry on as usual, so now the lecturer is faced with the usual dilemma: Does one obey the dictate of the administration or just not go to the classroom? It's supposed to be a peaceful boycott, without any disruption of classes, but when those protestors come singing and dancing down the corridors you better not be in the room. Yet here I am walking across the campus on my way to my first tutorial. Inside the building more than half the class, 14 or so, have gathered in the corridor. I've decided what to do. We'll go outside between the prefabs, I tell them, and discuss the situation. There's even a bench there, so when we arrive I sit down and say, 'Well, should we have class today?'

'No, Mr. Katz. If they see us in the classroom, they will beat us'.

'All right, then—let's stay here and discuss the issues, how about that? Then we can vote on whether to hold class or not'.

There are some puzzled expressions, and no one answers. 'Well, the SRC voted to boycott classes. Do you think that was a fair decision?'

'Yes, it was fair. We have no food. The university must give us food credits. How can we come to class without food? They must give us credits and then we will pay the university when we get jobs'.

'But the trouble is, students in the past have never paid such debts so now the university is owed about three million rand'.

'Yes, we are poor, we have no money to pay. The university must organize loans. How can we ever pay if we do not graduate and get jobs?'

And they have another strong argument, that subsidies are skewed in favour of the historically white universities. Back in the apartheid days the black universities, led in fact by UWC, opened registration to more students because there were so many more blacks and coloureds than whites who weren't being given an education, so now there's a long overdue adjustment in subsidies to the black universities. Then the students could register with a lesser payment of their outstanding loans.

By now groups of toyi-toying students are moving our way among the prefabs towards the new science block, so after a little more discussion I put the matter to a vote and class is canceled.

Which gives me plenty of time to answer your last letter. By the way, I was much entertained by your account some time ago of Prof. Bowie's visit to your class. My experience with someone coming for a supervisory look has always been fraught with tension, so I really enjoyed hearing about your encounter with Bowie, especially because he was the one feeling the tension. How do you do it? When an outsider comes into my classroom I'm too aware of him sitting in the back watching me, and I feel like I'm stuttering and stumbling around, but you had the whole class watching him. He must have felt more threatened than he let on, so I'm wondering what sort of evaluation he gave you.

As for this class Alistair and I have been team-teaching (mostly coloured students), I'm not sure we helped it with that attempt to get them to write up a list of 'Golden Agreements' and follow it. Getting the agreements worked out took much longer than I expected, and then sometimes we had serious confrontations about why so-and-so wasn't living up to them. I suppose the most touchy issue was attendance, since too many are absent too often, in spite of the agreement. But should the instructor have the entire responsibility for making every class so interesting that no students will ever want to be absent?

They're reading *Down Second Avenue*, by Ezekiel Mphalele, which should appeal to some. It records, in sad-making detail sometimes, the African experience in the 1940s as people moved from the rural areas to the townships and urban streets like Second Avenue: a baby's death in winter, a drunken white mistress cheating her African maid, gossiping around the tap, police raids on beer stills, superstitious fears, merciless beatings at school, the new world of American picture shows—all told by Mphalele in a wonderfully ironic style. We're having the students record their experiences with the book in reading journals, which they hand in every 2 weeks. Then I write a short response to each, but I find it almost impossible to keep my responses short and the process takes a hell of a long time, what with three groups of 20 or so students handing in journals.

I want some genuine expression from them, but sometimes what they write is very personal and I wonder if I get too personal in my responses. Nonceba (Nong-'cheh-bah, which means Mercy) wrote about the disintegration of his large family—how his brother is hooked on mandrakes, his father on drink, the violent family fights, and more. Then Ethel wrote about how she felt in class that day in her very short skirt. This kind of personal expression leaves me somewhat unnerved. Just how do I respond to it?

But maybe it does them some good to talk about what's on their minds. We also do free writing with the students as a kind of therapeutic activity, to help them relax and gain confidence. This aspect of writing is discussed by Richard Moss in *How Shall We Live*, so I'm sending a few pages of that along to you. Some of the students doing this are willing to write sincerely about themselves, like Patrick Farmer, who wrote about why he's been absent so often: got into a fight in the hostel and has been going to court. But others, like Beryl and Michelle, who attend the class every period and do all the work on time, give me writing that always seems so false. Maybe they're intimidated by Ralph, who refers to women as 'cherries'. He wrote about the Matric (matriculation) dance, which is like the American high school prom, and he said he was 'kissing my cherry like the other guys'—which upset Beryl and she told him he should keep a proper distance before marriage.

As an opposite to Ralph we have Granville de Villiers, who radiates good feeling for everyone. But his personal story was about the time he roamed the streets as a gang member, even claiming he shot two other guys. Then he got saved and he's a born-again Christian now. He's a good worker in class and I'm sure he's going to succeed at his chosen profession, which is law—he's methodical, and he's got the killer instinct required.

But Ralph is the kind that really worries me. I think he's bright, but his manner, his expression, his whole outlook is so rooted in the streets that I fear he will never succeed in academia, whereas Beryl and Michelle, with their trifling falsities, will. Even so, he brought in a fascinating interview with Rastafarian friends, and he's doing a paper on 'Is Rastafarianism for Me?'. Meanwhile, Granville is writing about spreading the Holy Word, and he complains that people don't want to listen. Ralph certainly doesn't. Sometimes I worry these two will come to blows because they actively preach their conflicting views of life at each other and they're both tough street guys. They're not making it any easier to build the loving classroom.

But then there's Sindiswa, who conquers cynicism with her talkative loving forthrightness. Answering claims that Umkhonto we Sizwe (the Spear of the Nation, the military wing of the underground ANC) had been weak and so the revolution never really got going, she talked about how 'Our boys really did try by all means to attack the South African army. They did their best but it was really tough, the might of the South African army was so intimidating!' Her speech quieted the others and made us thoughtful.

I sometimes wonder how all these people will find their way in the new South Africa, and if I can really be of any help to them. But now with the students boycotting their classes we won't be meeting for awhile, so in the meantime I stopped by Mzonke Mpofana's place on my way home from the university yesterday. He was in my very first class at UWC, as I've mentioned before, and now he's a history teacher at the high school in Guguletu. He lives in Hazeldean, which consists of a single row of about 40 small two-bedroom homes, sitting at right angles to a straight strip of tarred road along which members of the new middle class speed like mad, so it's a constant worry for parents to watch their small kids and keep them from the road. Across the way is a large field filled with rubble, grey and dusty, and beyond that miles of squatter shelters, shacks pieced together with wood, tin, and wire—some of whose inhabitants can be dangerous to those living in the new row of smart houses.

Mzonke (Um-zon-kay) lives there with his wife and two small children, and he now has teeth to fill in the gaps in his mouth that were so noticeable. He expounded on the government's new 'outcomes-driven' plan for schooling, and told me that education in South Africa must be based on the job needs of the community. My argument for a general literacy program, and for teaching South African writers like Mphalele and Fugard, did not cause him to waver. But then he asked about the play we had read in my class, 'Sizwe Banzi is Dead'. After all these years he was still enthused about it, and he talked about 'those stories we read, by Can Themba and those. Can you get a copy of the play for me?' So the stories did stay with him, and he must have learned something from our reading of them. But then he said maybe he was more of an exception, he couldn't say the others were as interested as he was, and schooling really had to be more outcomes based.

Also, he told me that the students in his high school went on strike against a teacher who was too strict and irresponsible, and after the settlement in their favor they are now demanding a part in all policymaking at the school, including hiring and firing. Mzonke is completely against this. 'The role of the student is to learn, it is our role to run the school', he said. But he was curious about my opinion, which was that student representation at faculty meetings would be useful. 'Let the students learn more about what's necessary in the running of the school, but of course they won't have equal power'. He couldn't agree with that. 'I'm more conservative now that I'm in the real world', he said.

Well, this letter has run on long enough, but one more thing before I close. Apropos of my asking in a previous letter if you think science gives us reality, Alistair was showing me a book, *Science, Order, and Creativity*, by David Bohm (a nuclear physicist who once worked with Einstein) and David Peat. They ask if the order we find in the universe is outside us in reality or is it actually in our minds? They seem to be saying there is some kind of 'generative' element in the brain that is 'implicate' in the ordering of the material world. In other words, mind contains the whole ordering of the physical world, just as each part of a hologram contains the whole figure. So in a sense all reality is part of the human spirit. What do you think of that?

Goodbye for now—Ed

News flash: More police have been called to the campus to prevent demonstrators from disrupting classes, but of course that's impossible so I'm not in my classroom, I'm in my little office typing this. Outside, the police are standing in a phalanx, with plastic masks and plastic shields, in front of the administration building facing an ever-growing crowd of students. A yellow police helicopter passes overhead like an angry wasp. When Prof. Engelbrecht, who has the unenviable task of publicly stating the position of the Rector's Committee to the students at large, appeared in one of the windows the students threw rocks at her. And we've heard they broke into the kitchens at the various hostels and stole all the equipment. One of my colleagues said, 'I remember when lecturers at Turfloop University were frog-marched out of their lecture halls. It wasn't pleasant'. But I hear a roar go up outside so something is happening, I'm closing in haste. More later.

- - - / / / - - -

February 23

Dear Ed,

Don't keep me in suspense—write soon and tell me what's happening in that unquiet place. I can only hope that all is well with you, and that you'll soon be back with your young people. In the meantime I'll report on the rather ordinary, undramatic events in my life, and perhaps comment on the issues you raise, which continue to provoke me to—well, to writing these letters at least.

What did Prof. Bowie think of my work in the prose fiction class? His report appeared in my mailbox last week and for the most part it was positive. He referred to my "innovative" methods, which drew so many students into a discussion of the story, although he did wonder if perhaps the "higher literary values" were somewhat slighted. If only he'd told me what they are!

In fact, however, you and I are more concerned with individuals than with subject matter or the higher literary values—we want to know their potential strength. Think of the classroom as a field of action where you create a situation in which all those present are involved in the making of new experience, and so are exposed along the way to the possibility of embarrassment or failure. There's a risk involved, and why should anyone there be exempt or privileged? The observer arrives expecting to look on from an aloof distance but you're not going to allow that, you're going to find some way to involve this person in the action so that he is given an opportunity to show what he is—to demonstrate self-possession or quickness of wit, responsiveness or daring. And Bowie proved himself equal to the occasion. Besides, he was getting all that attention, which is rather flattering, so afterwards it was a little difficult for him to be critical of an experience in which he had succeeded as a principal actor.

You have a number of interesting actors in your class, evidently—Ralph and Granville and others. Sometimes I've wondered why we are so interested in the difficult ones, the troubled ones like these, sinners unreformed or saved, when the continuance of our world depends on the ones we aren't paying attention to, on the Beryls and Michelles who tend quietly to their business, to work and family. Well, for one thing the delinquents are alive with a sense of issues, they're dramatic—and creative, although their creativity has gone into devising new ways of transgressing boundaries. Criminals go about their work with the same feeling as the artist, Degas tells us.

Alvin comes wearily into the classroom, eases himself down onto a seat and stretching his long legs out under the desk opens his notebook, finds a pencil in his shirt pocket and begins scrawling out another paragraph in his story. It's about his other life, at night, on a street corner in Jersey City:

> On the corner they're twenty people. The first is Razor, he's supposed to be the big man of the corner. The second is Man-G, known for stabbing someone in a second no matter who you are. Freeze is what we call the enforcer; if somebody mess up with money Freeze corrects him. Kash is what we call a runner, and he knows how to get money so that the reason he was named Kash. Prime is what we call the lieutenant. His main job is to collect money from the runners and make sure everything moves at an easy flow. Hikings was a runner but is now one of the big men of the block. He

got that name because no matter how hot it is he always wears hiking boots. Brook Money was a former big man on the block, but he got scared of the game and quit. B-Ski and P-Ski are brothers; both of them just came home from jail doing three an a half years.

Hanging on the corner is harder than what people think. First of all you have to be respected by the people on the corner or there will be fights with you every day. Then you have to watch for people who are jealous of you that might cross you by calling the cops or even stabbing you in the back. Then you have to watch out for the cops. When we see blue suit cops riding around we yell out "Yellow!" When we see the narco riding around we yell "Killer!"

The corner is like a twenty-four hour store. They're three shifts eight hours apiece, five to six people each shift. The first shift is from 8 a.m. to 4 p.m; the second shift is from 4 p.m. to 12 a.m., and the third shift is the hardest, 12 a.m. to 8 a.m. It's the best shift because they're hardly any police riding through, but you have to watch out for stick-up kids. They ride around three to four deep robbing people all night. If they catch you sleeping they will rob you of anything whether it be your money, jewelry, or even your clothes. If the stick-up kids catch you and you don't have anything for them to take they might pistol-whip you or shoot you.

Hanging on the corner there're three rules to follow and three things that can happen to you. Rule 1: never get high off your own supply. Rule 2: never mix business with pleasure. Rule 3: stash your money for a rainy day. The three things that can happen to you are: 1) you can get locked up; 2) you can get killed; 3) you can become successful at what you do.

Here we have the setting for an epic tale perhaps, the naming of heroes and the recounting of their strengths, creative in the doing and in the telling. The writer is describing, for those of us who live more innocently, the activities of young men given to risk and adventure, with a touch of self-satisfaction or even pride in his telling. But in giving us this account he gets some distance on the scene—separates himself from it, to a degree—and someday this young man might be able to write a sociological study like Elliot Liebow's *Tally's Corner*, if he can keep moving away from the corner. Surely this is one reason we encourage young people to write for us, so they may get some distance on their experience and consider what to make of it.

But what of those whose lives by contrast seem uneventful or undramatic, bound up in ordinary, everyday affairs? Or those young women who will not expose themselves before loud boastful young men? I think you're right to be concerned about the Beryls and Michelles who attend the class every period, do all the work on time, but give you writing "that always seems so false." They will learn to make one word follow another clearly enough, and one sentence follow another sensibly enough, but is that enough? We would like them to bring themselves to their work so that it has some individual character, for the world and we need their potential strength. This does not mean they must disclose the intimate details of their lives, for any writing, on whatever subject, is a personal expression so long as the writer really wants to say something. But too many of our young people are absent—holding themselves apart or keeping to a safe routine, following along step by step. In how many classrooms are rows of youngsters sitting there with only three or four actually present?

Yet does a teacher, you ask, "have the entire responsibility for making every class so interesting that no students will ever want to be absent?"— and surely that question supplies its own answer. At the end of one class, after we'd been sitting there working on our papers, a young man on his way out slouched by my desk saying "Oh, it's so boring! It's all so boring"— world-weary at 19. I said, "Well, maybe that's because you're a boring person." "Yes," he answered sadly, "I am boring." This amused me. "So what are you going to do about it?" "Oh, I'll think of something." Later he wrote a paper about going to a meeting of people interested in vampires—he was a little strange—and when he read it to us, speaking of the darker powers, one young woman was quite disturbed. She had attended a revival meeting the previous Sunday and now the spirit moved her to attempt a conversion. I wondered where all this would end.

We cannot succeed with students who are allowed to sit back saying in effect, Go ahead, get me interested! They will have to learn it's their responsibility to make this class interesting by what they bring to it of themselves. On the self-evaluation sheet I sometimes use after we've shared our papers is the question, "Was this paper the work of an interesting person? How do you know?" Of course an interesting person is one who is interested in others, or alive with an interest in something outside the self, and our young people need to learn this.

Your students have an opportunity for that with those journals in which they record their reactions to *Down Second Avenue*. Rather than reading these yourself and writing responses, why not have them read each others' and respond? Then they'll see how this story they know is looked at differently by another person and some lively exchanges might get going among them. And other subjects for further exploration might arise.

So we must help them learn to be interesting—learn that the lives and events around them, however ordinary and everyday, will supply them with all the inspiration they need. We ourselves have learned this from the poets, and now we can help these young people to that experience—send them with Mphalele walking along Second Avenue. Or with John Steinbeck to visit a family where a garrulous old grandfather starts a boy dreaming of adventures beyond the life to which his father is bound. Writers such as these suggest that something significant can be seen in every individual's experience, including one's own—if one can achieve an ironic distance from it.

After we'd gone with Nelson Algren to spend time with Augie in his working-class Chicago neighborhood, living there with his father and the second wife, remembering the mother who had given him pennies (in "a lot you got to holler"), Ekeesha told us this boy, who was stealing coins when he could, "was stealing back his mother's lost love to warm his heart, but after awhile the thieving only chilled his heart cold." She even used the word ironic. When she read her paper to us one afternoon as we sat together in a circle sharing our work, Loreny said "You know, Ekeesha—when you read to us we hear some beautiful thoughts. Like what you said about Augie paying a toll to pass through the door of his conscience. That's good! I can't do it, I can't write like that." She hesitated, glancing at me, and then in spite of our rule that we point out only the good things in what we hear, she said "But one thing's missing. We don't get to know you. That part about this other family where the father always favors the boy and the girl gets all the chores, you only mention that and it could be good! I want to hear more about how girls can have it bad too. You said the title is 'Behind Closed Doors', and it's like you're behind closed doors yourself."

The rest of us sat there listening to this and marveling. The young man next to me leaned over and whispered, "She oughta be teachin this class." I said, "Thanks a lot, fella," and then to the others: "Do you remember her opening paragraph? Read that to us again, will you Ekeesha?" It went like this:

> Many times we look at people and wonder how they became the people they are. We see them living bad lives that promise grim futures and wonder how could such a troubled person come from a wholesome family. But sometimes a law-abiding husband and wife can prove to be the pretenders of the century. You never know what really goes on behind their closed doors. The only peephole we have into their family life is through the children.

How did she do it, how did she think of those ideas? After reading about Augie and his father, and writing a paragraph of response, putting down whatever came to her about it, she wrote a brief account of another family, perhaps her own. I suggested she talk about what she'd written with someone else and look for a theme or concept she could use to open her discussion of those two stories. And when Eric heard her talking about how little we really know of other families because their doors are always closed, he said "That's a good idea, try that." But the rest of the paper is not so well done—it lacks the telling detail, the self-confident easy flow of Alvin's story of life on the corner. And yet it's more than reportage. Both writers draw on personal experience but Ekeesha has done some thinking about hers, so contrary to Loreny's impression she is very present in her writing, while Alvin seems absent from the corner and reports the scene in a detached sort of way, rather effectively putting the reader into it ("they might pistol-whip you or shoot you"). He could continue this paper by shifting from description to reflection, from we-centered experience to individuated experience as Bernstein would say. If he will think further about these stories, his own and Augie's, he may discover a theme or concept that gives him doubleness, so to speak—that puts him both within and without the lives described and so gives him ideas about them. Or I might ask him to say what beyond a street corner in Jersey City is the subject here and suggest he write a paragraph about it—about young men who are . . . what? But so far he's only done the part that comes easily to him. I'd like more thinking from Alvin, and Loreny would like more of the story from Ekeesha—and the work of both might improve if they will each try to satisfy their readers.

Now I'm not doing this with them for any therapeutic value it might have, to improve their mental health, although I'm sure it has a healthy effect. What prompts that remark is your sending me the article by Richard Moss, whose main interest in the teaching of writing, according to the introductory note, is "healing the sick." So he has young people free writing, drifting along on the flow of associations, withdrawing into themselves—and in this way he "has often created the conditions for *literally miraculous healing*" (not my emphasis). Healing, that is, which defies the laws of nature? And we lowly teachers of composition, following after this miracle worker, will rise through the practice of our art to become—healers?

Just what sort of person are we helping into being during those hours we spend in a classroom with young people? Should it be the therapeutic type, as described by Philip Rieff in his *Triumph of the Therapeutic*—people who have no loyalty to any commitment beyond their own personal "healing"? Should we go for a recovery group approach to pedagogy, as advocated and practiced by some feminist academics? Or a critical pedagogy, which would awaken the young from their dreams and open their eyes to the contradictions in society and its language so they may see the truth of life as clearly as their teacher does? Or the therapy of theory many academics now seem to practice, which supplies them with answers to questions they've forgotten and substitutes knowingness for doubt? Much of what passes for advanced thinking in composition studies has just such a strong therapeutic cast, but will any of this give South Africa the people it needs?

In short, I think this suggestion that we approach our students as healers approaching the soul-sick is in itself unhealthy.

I'd like to leave it at that but you go on to cite scientific authority, namely David Bohm, who suggests a healthy mind possesses enough spiritual energy to hold the cosmos within itself. In every generation a book such as *Science, Order, and Creativity* is written by some scientist who would minister to our spiritual ills by dropping out of science and becoming a metaphysician. So many such works have now been produced as to constitute a genre, with a predictable content updated to make the most recent scientific findings spiritually useful. Because physicists must speculate at the far edge of knowledge, where reality begins to seem very strange, they're tempted to go off the metaphysical deep end—and in the history of physics a number of eminent ones have. An interesting book could be written on this subject. Bohm, by the way, was a confirmed Marxist for much of his life but gave up Marxism for the mysticism of his "implicate order," which hardly seems like an advance to me. He was a believer in many New Age notions, including the supposed ability of Uri Geller to bend spoons by mental power alone.

You have asked if I think science gives us something like objective truth, and I'll tell you I'm tired of hearing remarks to the effect that scientific knowledge is socially constructed, that "there is no core of pure scientific truth, no detachable, medium-neutral body of facts and ideas, apart from the knowledge embedded in the social ways of scientists"—as if scientists arrive at their findings while talking over cups of tea. That quote is from a recent book on teaching academic literacy, and what an opportunity for an ironist! A little scientific literacy might be in order, it seems to me. Then the cultural critic Andrew Ross tells us that "Scientific and technical papers are saturated with the familiar narratives that literary critics have learned to deconstruct as a matter of course"—the arrogance of which is breathtaking! One hardly knows whether to be amused or distressed by the envy these people have of the scientific world and their ignorance of it. They prepare the way for mysticism, which worries me.

Incidentally, their notion that scientific theory is socially constructed—which they announce with an air of sophisticated certainty as the latest and final word, science put in its place at last—has in fact long been current among the mystically inclined. Years ago Oswald Spengler declared in his once-famous work *The Decline of the West* (1922) that the discoveries of science are simply reflections of the political and social ideas of their time. Modern scientific notions of force in the physical world, for example, derive from the Western imperialistic drive for power. Sound familiar? Atomic theory, he remarked, "is a myth, not experience"—a "socialism of the atom." And the lesson he drew from this was that we must distrust rationality, for logic as given through language betrays our deeper understanding, it denies our "instinctive, dream-sense logic," our one hope of understanding experience.

Now this sort of thinking is all too common in our profession today. A recent article in *College English* elevates imagery over language as a way of knowing—and this from a teacher of writing! I suppose we may as well spend our time in class watching films. Then too, the postmodernists tell us that we can never know an objective reality because only discourse exists (a notion deriving from the mysticism of Martin Heidegger). And they explain that rational analysis is simply inadequate for understanding the finer points of their key texts, that to draw full benefit from the obscurity of Derrida's work, for example, one must abandon the Western prejudice that favors clarity and logic—a claim mystical thinkers have always made. Meanwhile, I find it interesting that key words in the vocabulary of postmodernism ("deconstruction," "logocentrism") had their origin in the anti-science tracts written by Nazi and protofascist writers (see Anne Harrington's *Reenchanted Science*).

All of which strengthens my sense of how important it is that we help young people learn to think analytically and independently, with an eye turned to the life around them rather than fixated on their interior states and dreaming of a reenchanted world. Maybe this is a matter of mental health after all.

So let's leave these abstractions and return the classroom. Speaking of young people thinking independently reminds me that after we'd talked about Ekeesha's paper I mentioned to the group Eric's thought that Loreny could teach our class. "This disturbs me, you know, because I think he wants me to get lost, he thinks you don't need me. Thanks a lot, Eric! But if that's the popular will then I'll step aside. What do you think?" They thought it was a good idea. And Loreny was agreeable, so now I'm waiting to see what she will have us do as our next project. For a time she will be the author of the story we live together and define for us how we might act in that classroom, or indicate a direction in which we might improvise. In her own way she will encourage us to write.

Of course I'm trying to encourage the others to become not only writers but authors as well and determine a direction for themselves— which means practicing certain habits of mind. As I've said before, it's important to consider what sort of person we are helping into being when we work with young people, and that depends very much on the kind of story they learn to make for themselves while being with us. I can illustrate this point with an experience from my counseling practice.

The people I work with are healthy enough, no more neurotic than you or I, but life has put them into a situation they do not understand and cannot manage, so they feel insecure and stressed, and they come to see me. For example, a young man took a job as office boy to help pay his college expenses, but after 2 weeks the office manager, an older woman, began to ride him. She would say, "Kevin, when you answer the phone don't say 'Hello,' and don't say the name of the firm—say, 'Office boy.'" Other people there told him that's the way it goes, the first 2 weeks are a honeymoon and then she begins to ride the new office boy until he leaves and another comes in. So now she was having her fun with Kevin, she had him quite rattled. One morning he was so upset by her petty demands that he called and asked me to meet him during his lunch hour. I'd worked with him earlier on a more serious problem, so now I could be quite direct and the need was immediate. I said, "Kevin, there are two steps you can take here. I'll give you one now, and when you've done this tell me so that we can take the next step."

"Okay, I'll do whatever I have to. What is it?"

"Whenever this woman is treating you the way she should, you smile, be cheerful, do your work with a will. And whenever she mistreats you—smile, be cheerful, do your work. But just say one thing. And don't say it sarcastically, say it very nicely: 'Odette, your wish is my command.' Now you say this every time she's out of line, and only when she's out of line. Other people in the office will hear it, they'll begin to laugh, she will not be able to keep it up. But if she does keep it up, then you elaborate your routine a little, you tell her 'Odette, there's just one thing I want to say.' And you let a long pause come so that everyone is waiting to hear this one thing you're going to say. Then you say, 'Your wish is my command.'"

He thought it was worth a try. We left the restaurant, he went back to the office and as he came in she was right on him, telling him to go among the desks and pick up bits of paper from the floor. He said, "Odette, your wish is my command!"—and a woman sitting there at a desk overheard him and laughed uproariously, which was her way of giving him support.

Kevin missed his next appointment with me and I didn't see him for about 2 weeks, when he finally appeared and told me what had happened. I was quite angry, I said "Why didn't you tell me? What about Step 2?"

"There's no problem now," he said. "She's not bothering me."

"But there is a problem! You've surprised her, she's thinking about it, she's more interested in you than before! And when she's ready she'll come back at you from another angle. You have to make your move before she can do that."

"Alright," he said, looking worried again, "what's my move?"

"It's this—and you can't wait, you must do it tomorrow! When you go out for lunch you will pass a convenience store or a candy shop. Go in there and buy a little box of candy—you know, one of those little boxes with three or four chocolates in it. Wrap that up in a napkin from the place where you have lunch. Tie a piece of string around it. And when Odette is away from her desk, you leave it there with a note. And the note will read, 'From your secret admirer.'"

He shook his head doubtfully. "No, no—I don't think so. What if she asks me if it was me?"

"Then you say, 'Odette, I don't know. Because when I'm around you I get so excited I don't know what I'm doing!' Now, she will fall in love with you—or let's say she will learn that you're a loveable person—and a job will open up in that office that's better than the one you have now, and you will get it because she will give it to you. That's your goal." He got the job.

You see, when he first told me about this woman I knew exactly what she wanted from him. She wanted this young man to think about *her,* she wanted to be treated as a person, as a woman, not as another stick of office furniture. And of course when he went home each day from that office, he *was* thinking of her. But he was so wrapped up in himself and his distress that he couldn't get control of his own story, and I taught him how to do that, so to speak. That's often a good part of this work, to help people get outside themselves and the immediate moment and so acquire the power of irony.

And the same is true of our work in classrooms. If we want to change the behavior of individuals and help them become writers, then we will assist their escape from a positional context where higher directs lower and create with them a situational context in which individuals assume responsibility for their own development. A situation in which events are the outcome of decisions made by learners, who are so encouraged to begin a new chapter in the narratives they are living.

Well, thanks for listening to all this, and best regards—JR

- - - / / / - - -

20 February

Dear John,

It's night, after a day of violent happenings here. The police finally charged into the crowds of students, breaking them apart and sending them running across the campus. The rector and the Rector's Committee, meeting with the student representatives, had been prevented from leaving the administration building—held there hostage, in effect. And some students might have been moving to attack the Captain Dorego Restaurant in the student centre, so the police charged but then didn't pursue them very far. I couldn't see much of this from my office window, and when I finally walked out after the action there were rocks lying about and small piles of stones obviously placed for use—rocks against rubber bullets. And large cracks in the glass of the student centre. The rector has closed the university, and all the hostel residents have been asked to leave until calm is restored.

The university is so far in debt with unpaid fees, we worry that the threat of bankruptcy might keep lecturers' wages frozen and increasingly inadequate. So are students and lecturers in competition for the failing resources of the university? Our wages have not kept up with inflation and we've been waiting for a long overdue increase, so how willing are we to hear about more student demands? But now my sweet colleague, Mercia Louw, is organizing us to bring soup for students who are really hungry. So I guess we'll keep busy and wait for news.

Old Mike came by the house today. His hair is knotty and long, somewhat in the Rastafarian style, and hangs from his head in a kind of jumble-tumble, and his beard is a bristly mass, thick in some places but in others showing only a few threads of hair. He was wearing blue workpants, and a very old weather-beaten outer jacket over an ancient brown-checked casual jacket with huge lapels. Sometimes he sports an odour that keeps me at a distance.

On the front steps he takes off his old army knapsack and says, 'My hand's all right so I can do your car very nicely today. I got some really good polish'. His left hand is wrapped in a bandage and he tells me that 'Some guys came and pushed me where I sleep. They took all my blankets, they hurt my hand'. He went on to talk about washing cars. 'It's quite a responsible job, it's a question of trust. I take only about 10 cars. But sometimes they buy a new car and they drop me'. He speaks with a distinct American accent and claims he's from Puerto Rico, or sometimes he says Mexico, but then he says he was born in South Africa. He seems to reinvent his history as he goes along. He pulls a tin of Coke from his knapsack and holds it out to me. 'I've got enough Coke today', I tell him, 'I don't want to buy any'. I'm wondering if I'm going to get paid myself this month. 'No señor, it's a gift', he says, and hands me the tin. So after he finished washing the car I invited him in for a cheese sandwich and some coffee with a shot of Cane Spirit in it.

He's got two or three different-toned musical triangles in his pack, so I get out my guitar and we play 'Adios to the Alamo'. I drink some of the cane liquor too. The fact is that Mike is the only person I can jam away with on the guitar, middle-class folks are just too busy for these simple things. We play and I sing the old favourites from the '50s and '60s—'Earth Angel', 'House of the Rising Sun', 'Ghost Riders in the Sky', and then we get into Dylan.

After he left I sat there and had a little more cane liquor, thinking about him. Maybe he's half-mad or a poet, he speaks so strangely sometimes in disconnected but striking images. He spoke once of being 'in dismayo', which meant Pollsmor Prison. It seems the police 'pulled a great sonata' on him because of some minor transgression. One day he said, 'You know, to give a person a pair of sunglasses is to capture that person. I mean, the whole world is changed for that person'. There's a bit of singing in his words now and then, as you would say. He keeps telling me that he's going to invite me to have coffee with him at Nandos, but I have to tell him straight, 'You need to organize your act a lot differently before they'll serve you in Nandos, Mike'. I get sad thinking about him sometimes.

Another day, after a restless night:

The students are demonstrating every day for more financial support and getting more militant about it. Meanwhile, our staff association is now insisting on a 10% raise just to keep up with inflation, but the university negotiators say there's no money to pay it and their final offer is 7.5. And there's no certainty the outside funders who sponsor posts for Quinton and Mercia will come through, so can we keep them here with us? The competition for scarce resources is intense.

Having to feed my daughters and myself and find the money for our never-ending expenses is a real struggle, and I've been scraping around trying to find some way to get my hands on more cash. Part-time teaching at UWC is just not enough, so I put an ad in the local paper offering to give a 'Writing for Discovery' workshop, and I got 12 people to pay me R30 each for three 1-hour sessions. There was a high school teacher, an art student, a very athletic coloured fellow who's a runner, a teacher of retarded children, a counselor from a hospice for the dying, and a few others, mostly women, and Alistair came with two other lecturers from UWC. I rented a room for three evenings in the Waldorf School where my daughters go, a very nice old wood building converted from a home, rather rustic. I had to take down the inspirational pictures on the walls because I thought they'd be a distraction with all those saintly figures in dramatic lighting.

For the first night I borrowed an activity from you. We read Berryman's poem 'Of i826' and then wrote our own I-am poems. When these were ready I asked people to go to the far corners of the room and read to us from there so they would have to speak their lines loudly. And when I asked how we could improve our dramatic performance of the lines, one of the women suggested we should sing them. That got people going!

Imagine the counselor from the hospice, a tall thin man with a cheerful look, trying to sing this poem in his baritone voice in a slow measured sort of way, finding a bit of melody here and there:

> I am a product of the past
> I am a commodity processed and wrapped
> I am torn, sat upon, mishandled, and lost.
>
> I am stamped fragile, airmail, postage due
> I am returned to sender, address unknown
> I am planed, bussed, and carried.
>
> It is the day of delivery:
> Rejoice! The paper is unwrapped
> Remove protective covering.
> I am whole again, yet alone.

Then we paired off and people tried to interpret each other's poems, but I wasn't quite sure how we should do this. I've seen you take the most ordinary, obvious I-am poem and find a deeper meaning in it, but how do you show other people how to do that? Then someone writes a poem like this one and its meaning is so personal you wonder how personal you should get. So I don't know if anyone saw much in these poems but we had a good time talking about them.

At the next session we each wrote down the name of someone who was important in our life and wrote a cluster of words suggested by that name—which seemed to trigger a right-brain response, giving us images and ideas to work with. There is something magical in the way a seemingly miscellaneous cluster of words may come together in a meaningful, even touching poem:

> 'Suicide' the inquest concluded,
> And the coroner's report referred
> To your numbered kidneys in a bag.

Those are the last lines of a poem from one woman, writing about her brother. We got some powerful stuff.

I thought of this workshop as having a dual focus: creative writing as an art, and then as self-expression or therapy. The first evening we did things that were artistically directed, or concerned with form you might say, while the second evening we did work that was more psychological. There was something I borrowed from Ira Progoff's book *At a Journal Workshop,* in which he talks about the basic metaphor of his approach, the image of a well connecting to the underground stream:

> Each individual must go down his own well, and not the well of someone else's life. We find, however, that when, as individuals, we have gone very far down into the well of our life, we come to an underground stream that is the source of all the wells.[. . .] While the outer events of our lives take place at the surface of the well, we go inward to the underground stream to reach our deep sources. (p. 9)

Anyway, I like this idea of going down into the well so I asked the group to each go down into his or her well, take a look around and describe what they saw. Out of this came all sorts of experiences to write about, and so on the third evening we had things to share with each other, to read aloud and even perform. We had a good time.

I've also used the I-am poem in my classes at the university, but I have trouble finding an activity afterwards that will build on the experience we have with it. You've mentioned how you often find a theme in what the students write that you can go on with but that hasn't happened with me. Indeed, sometimes I worry about not having enough of these games or exercises to keep up the students' interest. Or maybe they'll begin to resist my bright ideas.

But I keep looking for activities that will really engage them. The other day I found myself remembering something you said once about each person being the hero of his or her own myth—how one's life is a kind of epic journey, and so I sat down and wrote as though I were writing my own epic story. It soon turned into a strange tale which had me becoming somehow this tiny shrunken man climbing up a gigantic woman's skirt! I was thinking of asking my students to try this, using a kind of epical language to describe some part of their own lives, but maybe not.

I wonder if when you talk about the power of myth and the individual life quest, you're admitting that we can't reject the metaphysical entirely. If mythopoetic thinking is so important in our lives, as you say, and the source of poetry, then wouldn't you agree that the ancients offer us a kind of method for developing our deeper and more profound perceptions? And so don't guys like Jung and Rudolph Steiner rate as truth-makers—or do you reject them entirely? I seem to remember you saying something one time over coffee about the desire we have for a 'higher consciousness.' Is that the secret you were referring to when you said that 'Everyone's secret is the same'?

Just wondering—Ed

- - - / / / - - -

March 6

Dear Ed,

I'm delighted that you have something new going—something both satisfying and profitable. People come to such a workshop in an evening after a long day's work hoping for a good social experience, a chance to expand their personalities among people who are unfamiliar with their ways and have no confining expectations of them. And you satisfied them, it seems, for they were all actively engaged in expressing themselves in new ways, drawing on feelings or even insights not usually expressed so openly. And doing this with strangers—who must have come to know them after this experience in a way that perhaps even their friends do not.

Then you mention your work with young people at UWC and how you have difficulty finding a way to go on with them after a writing exercise. But are you the only person in the room who can have a good idea for the work? We do an exercise with our young people now and then for some particular purpose—to introduce ourselves, to set a tone, to whet expectation, to get something going. You're right to worry that they will become resistant to your bright ideas, for they surely will. People get tired of only doing what they're told and they respond then in a perfunctory sort of way, doing the minimum required. So it's important to be less directive, to encourage those young people to become independent and self-sustaining, with some personal commitment to their work—to become authors. And when they get something going among themselves, we can retire then into the background as responsive spectators.

When Loreny took over our class she came prepared with five(!) suggestions for writing we could each chose from. These were not as demanding, as "academic" as I would like, but of course I went along with her. We were invited to write a letter to "the one person you truly hate—an old teacher or your ex-boy/girlfriend maybe." Or we could describe heaven and hell as we envision them. Or tell the story of the person we most admire. Or we might envision the whole class on a desert island and write a diary chronicling our predicament. Something serious could be done with any one of those, she said. I choose to write about a cartoon she also offered as inspiration—a drawing of three workmen laying a tile floor and captioned "Although history has long forgotten them, Lambini & Sons are generally credited with the Sistine Chapel floor." Loreny allowed us only two class periods for this project, so I had to get right to work.

Malbia and Michael had chosen to put us all on a desert island, and they were working together on this, talking and laughing about it. I wanted them to get on with the writing but they let me know that Loreny was the one in charge now, so I should go tend to my own business. After 2 days she called us together to share our work and there was considerable anticipation in the group. When my turn came, I said You know, I'm not interested in newspaper cartoons and I just glanced at this one, but then somehow I was drawn back to it. Here's what it made me think of:

History remembers Michelangelo of course, who painted the famous ceiling in the Sistine Chapel showing the hand of God reaching out to Adam and bringing him to life with a touch. This glorious art has brought inspiration to multitudes over the several centuries since it was painted. And now in this cartoon we see the forgotten Lambinis laying the tile floor under that ceiling. This sets up a contrast between work that is useful or practical, and work that is really a kind of play. Who is more important, an artist who makes pictures, which have no use except to be looked at, or a workman who makes for us something useful, something that contributes directly to the comfort or safety or movement of hundreds or even thousands of people? Is the work of a bricklayer, let us say, more important than the work of a singer or an actor or a writer of stories? The cartoon suggests that here is something for us to think about.

Notice that in this drawing the famous ceiling has not yet been painted, and so our attention is given entirely to the three men laying tile. These are the ones, people like this, who do the world's work and make the entire structure possible. They lift and carry it piece by piece [. . .]

And so on. Perhaps the fact that my father began his life's work as a carpenter influenced my choice of subject here. Then too, most of these students are from working-class families so I was assured of a sympathetic audience. I like writing along with them because then I get a turn to read aloud, and that's really the only time when I can speak to them as myself. As their teacher I have very little to tell them, so here at last was my chance to talk. When Loreny called on me and I read this paper to the group, the youngsters glanced at each other as if say, Yeah he can do it. Up to that point I suppose they thought I might be all push and no action. They think of themselves as the ones doing the real work here.

We have to take a chance now and then with these young people, and trust them to come through. That's one thing I like about the way you work, that you take chances, trying various ways of provoking them into action. Perhaps some of our colleagues may think the results are not sufficiently academic, but you and I are not giving the standard writing program, taking the youngsters through a textbook as they read one essay after another, write one response after another, and practice the various forms. We are learning how to get something started among them so they will bring themselves to the work and perhaps an unexpected voice begins to sing.

I'd like to close here but at the end of your letter you decided to provoke me, so of course I have to respond. You wonder if I admit the metaphysical or the "higher consciousness" because I've said that "Everyone has a secret, and everyone's secret is the same, and that's the secret." Well, those are not my words but rather those of a troubled young man whose dream we had just interpreted, a dream of embalmed animals and a dying dentist. He had come to me troubled by this dream, but then after we talked about it he began to understand the underlying motive for his recent actions and he felt ready then to get on with what he had to do. He said, "You know, we know the answers to all the questions, so the real question is, Which way to the inevitable?" *That's* the secret we all share, he thought—this question. Like those young people you work with who are trying to find their way, and you wonder if you can help.

Think of how many people there are who spend years in therapy as a way of delaying their answer and not doing what could be done. But David was ready now to get on with his work, having discovered why he had chosen that path. And quite happy with himself, he went on to say that if you have a motive hidden even from yourself, "a secret reason for something you do, it may be a blessing, it makes you really care about what you're doing." And he's right—for whatever the choice we make, or whatever the creative work we do, we are moved to it not only by reason but also by some deeper, underlying feeling for it. One does not reason himself into loving a woman, for example. To have only rational reasons for what you would do is not to have reason enough.

So what each youngster does with words while spending time with us will be the work of a feeling intellect drawing from the well of one's accumulated experience. And here I part company with Ira Progoff, who speaks of "the well connecting to the underground stream," which I take to be a reference to Jung's collective unconscious. So he encourages you to turn the attention of young people inward away from the world—to give them various navel-gazing exercises so they may reach down to the ancient wisdom of the race as carried by the collective unconscious. Jung himself engaged in deliberately induced visionary experiences, a practice he called "active imagination," experiences like your vision of being a "tiny shrunken man climbing up this gigantic woman's skirts." Well now!—I'm not going to touch that one. Jung's own visions were somewhat more grandiose (he once saw himself as a god), but then he held that only those of Aryan heritage would be able to follow his short-cut route the collective unconscious, so that leaves you out, along with a great many others.

I am somewhat distressed that it was in fact words of mine that led to this vision of yours—you seem determined to turn me into a Jungian. Please do not take me with you into that dark overgrown forest we know as the occult, where so many have been lost.

Our young people, if they are to make something new for themselves, cannot be sitting there endlessly exploring the wonders their psyches, contemplating their navels when there's work to be done. A little free writing or visualization is alright, but usually we write to accomplish some purpose, to make something, so let's get on with it! The Lambinis laying tile on that floor, and Michelangelo painting that ceiling above, had developed their skills by laboring long hours on earlier projects. The differences between them were a matter of ability or genius, perhaps, but when this great structure was finally completed they could all feel the satisfaction of having made an achievement and gone another distance in the life quest.

So we provoke young people to speak and write for themselves however we can—as you've done with Ralph, who talks about the Matric dance and "kissing my cherry," and Humphrey, who gives dramatic readings from *Down Second Avenue*, and Granville, who preaches his view of life, and Sindiswa defending the Spear of the Nation—and perhaps each may be moving toward the start of a new making. In any case, there's been singing in that classroom, it seems to me.

Best regards—JR

- - - / / / - - -

15 February

Dear John,

With the university shut down I have all this time, so I can write another letter. I drive over to the campus every day, not always by the same route, and yesterday on the way to Mitchell's Plain I saw a woman standing by the road hitchhiking, her clothes shabby and a doek (doo-uk, a small kerchief) on her head. It's a somewhat desolate area and she was out there alone, so I stopped to pick her up. 'Dankie, Meneer—can you take me to the Shell garage? I'm looking for work, Meneer—all day I've been looking, but nothing. Work is scarce, Meneer'.

We drive down the dusty unpaved road to Mitchell's Plain. The houses there are small but nicely painted and not so old, and one has a beautiful rock chimney rising from the patio where folks will braai (barbecue) when the weather is right. Then the road goes along a desolate strip near the shore, with dull grass growing on the sandy dunes, and we pass some goats and a flock of really fat sheep being herded by an old man. There ahead we see the Shell garage at the edge of Nyanga, an African township. This is a shantytown—small homes of tin and wood along either side of the road, some of them gaily painted, others more tumbledown, and sometimes there are chickens in the little patch of grass beside a house. The place has a comfortable, friendly vibe, more so than the quiet, spotless streets of my Kenilworth, where every home is carefully hidden from the road by walls and hedges. I'd like to walk up those narrow unpaved informal streets in Nyanga, but then I would feel so out of place. Oh, the apartheid of the mind is very deep, possibly more binding than the laws of separation once were. At the Shell garage I stop and the woman gets out, saying 'Dankie, Meneer', returning home with no good news to report.

Farther on a group of men are preparing a huge whiteish pig for roasting over a fire. It will be cut up and sold by the roadside later in the day. All sorts of things are sold along some of these roads—vegetables, baby clothes, spare parts, tires. But now the road suddenly gets even more bumpy and there is a sign: Road Closed. It used to go through to the airport road, and from there I could go on to the university, but now it has simply disappeared, unrepaired, gone. I turn left onto another dirt road, past an open-air barber shop. Some women are tending their vegetable stalls, and they have a white substance coating their faces. I don't know what that means. Another turn and I am facing a large field where little squares of grey brick, two or three feet high, are spaced at regular intervals on the flattened earth. These are probably 'site and service' places. Each square is a toilet, and a family will be invited to build their home around it. Some say this is not enough, that the program for Reconstruction and Development should do more, but others say there is no money for anything more.

Finally the road turns to the right, the car bumps around some deep ruts and I'm back on black tarmac, the airport road. Another hitchhiker is standing there. He's holding up a hand-drawn sign that says UWC so I stop to pick him up, wondering why he's going to the university when it's closed. To meet with a professor, he tells me as we start off. I ask if he's from the township. Yes, he's living there with relatives but his home is in

Port Elizabeth. I ask him if he finds the township a friendly place to live, and he tells me it is 'Mostly, but those streets you crossed back there, they are dangerous. There are people with guns there on Lansdowne Road'. I wonder if I am risking my life going through like this but he tells me 'At night mostly, it's dangerous'. 'Do you fear living here?' I ask. 'Yes, I do'. He's working for a BA, he tells me, he's going to be a teacher. "But I don't want to become a teacher, I was forced into it because of the subjects I took in high school. I really want to do business administration but now I can't change. I would have to take courses that were given in high school, like economics. It's too expensive and I have no money'.

Here is a student who is trapped, moving towards an occupation he doesn't want. How many more are there like him? I thought of Xolani Mashlowana, one of my former students who now teaches at the Harry Gwala High School, which is way at the back of Belhar, a little distance from the university. The last stretch of road into the place isn't paved, and one drives over bumps and humps to get there. Students were everywhere outside the school when I arrived one day because 'It's lunch, so they bask in the sun,' Xolani tells me. 'But many have nothing to eat for lunch, so they just stand around'. When I ask him how the work goes he says, 'How can they concentrate on what I'm trying to tell them? These kids are demoralized! So many of their parents are unemployed, so they're only thinking of how to get some money—maybe by stealing. And they get influenced by other boys to join the gangs. There is no discipline, they don't listen to anything I say. It's not like when I was in school. I'm teaching to maybe four students in the class. They hardly know English, so they cannot follow the lesson'. I mentioned that there is talk at the university about unfairness to Xhosa speakers, and he said 'When we talk Xhosa, they can understand the lessons fine'.

No wonder he doesn't want to be teaching in this school, he wants to be teaching the gospel, he tells me. But the fact is, I think he's really a poet who wants to soar and that's his interest in the gospel. When I arrived he said, 'Hey man, your hair has got some white. You're getting closer to death'. And maybe because I'm a white man, with a fat plush job at the university, he wishes I were dead. We're friends, but then there's that shadow of African poverty behind his shoulder stretching out to the horizon, and I can't bear to look at it. We stood there in the schoolyard with his disconsolate students and he said, 'I'm trying, I'm trying'.

Should I feel guilty for having all the choices that are open to me? But then my daughter Sarah, who is just out of high school, also feels trapped and complains about the capitalist system forcing people into narrow little niches. 'A few years ago', she tells me, 'you could opt out of the System, you could live off the land somewhere. You could create your own reality. But now, no chance. Everything is tied into the money economy, and land is so expensive you can't get it. You have to go work in the cities for money and you don't get much, it's just survival pay'. Her boyfriend makes jewelry, some of it quite lovely—earrings and pendants with African motifs. He has a shaved head, punk-rocker style, and sports an earring, several tattoos, and a nipple ring. Do I really understand anyone, or what's happening here?

The airport road has led into Modderdam Road, and now we're turning into the parking area at UWC. I watch the student for a moment as he walks off toward the campus and wonder if I really know anything about him even after this time we've spent together. Oh sure, he told me a few facts about himself but somehow I keep feeling there's something more these people could tell me if they only would, the secrets kept back that would reveal who they are and what they really think. You talk about how Mrs. M (in your *Provocations*) could surprise people into saying the most revealing things about themselves, but I haven't learned how to do that. I leave these encounters, and often the classroom too, thinking that we're all still strangers to each other.

It may be partly a language problem. Some of the students working with Alistair in the class we were team teaching did a study of the different expectations of English and Xhosa culture, and they pointed out the indirectness of Xhosa discourse. There's a different sensibility involved because a Xhosa tends to think as part of a whole. Their answer to even an ordinary question, for example, may be quite lengthy—indirect or roundabout as if that answer needs to be put within a social context and the person is not individually responsible for it. In fact, persons are indicated not by pronouns but by prefixes to verbs, so persons do not stand apart as individuals in that language. But then when they write in English they tend to insert pronouns unnecessarily, as in 'The woman she went to the veldt.' The students may have got on to all this because of what Vuyiswa said about her attempts to get her poetry published. She found that what she could publish in Xhosa was very different from the more direct or more individualized language that poetry in English requires. So maybe that's why I have a sense of distance between us, as if so often these students are not speaking directly to me but around me, you might say.

It was St. Valentine's Eve a few days ago and Mercia Louw sweet-talked me into paying R25 for admission to the dance her church held in the Sarepta recreation hall. This turned out to be a dark pants, dark jacket and tie affair, and I've only got my worn grey slacks and ancient brown-wool jacket, but no one minds—we're all here for a good time. Hey, this is coloured culture on the hop, a big American-style dance band on the stage and the place is jammed. And these people can dance! Quite dignified at first, a nice waltz— and there's Ikey Van De Rheede, our vice rector for academic planning, whirling by so gracefully with his pretty wife, his elbows high. A hefty young woman tells me as we dance that she once got 80% on an essay about T.S. Eliot. Then as the evening goes on the dancers whirl and prance faster, shouting as they go, getting happier and wilder with the quick step (which I've never managed), a fast fox trot, jazzing and then African group dances like the mareka (I think it's called). All this community spirit, the unspoken understanding! Sometimes I wonder what I may be missing while sitting here alone, typing the time away in the textual night.

The next day I'm back in the classroom and here are these rows of students sitting there, and what I'd like from them is some genuine personal expression. Unless they can relate our reading and writing to their personal experience and find some pleasure in the work, how can they make any sense of it? So they need to be themselves and say what's on their minds and be willing to reveal themselves. But then sometimes when they do, they reveal differences that separate us. One day Boy Boy announced that 'God does not exist, he's a creation out of our imagination,' and there was a cry of surprise, *outrage* from the other students, a kind of collective 'Haauuu . . . !' Whispers of 'Satanism!' and accusations that he didn't really believe it, he was only trying to get attention—but he did believe it and he argued with them. I was a little afraid for him having to face all those others alone. It's this raw emotion that can break out that worries me. I know you don't like the expression but we're still a long way from the loving classroom.

Too often a class gets all stirred up by some topic but then retreats when it comes time to write about it. One of our former students, Sandile Dikeni, published a story called 'Don't Be A Mugu', written in Tsotsi-taal, which is a street language often used by gangsters (tsotsis), and it's in the new course reader. Here's a bit of it:

> This is then how one shushu day a certain oubaas arrived at one Bantu community school. The ouballie wasted no time in tuning the school that he, who was Groenewald, had come to inspect them, laat die hare waai. Umhloli, an inspector that's what he said he was. And the school, three hundred of them in all, all said Umhloli! [. . .] *a white Umhloli?*

And it goes on to tell about this Afrikaans inspector who has come to this community school to examine the students in Xhosa literature. But the one selected, having forgotten the required poem, recites the Lord's prayer in Xhosa and gets full marks from the unsuspecting abelungu (white man). The point is that 'Any monolingual is, as far as I am concerned, a mugu [a fool], till proven otherwise. Jislaaik!' (Just like that, or as we would say, And that's the way it is.) One of the students gave us a reading of this piece sounding like a born news announcer for Radio 5, and the reaction was intense. I innocently needed explanations for the Xhosa and Afrikaans expressions, which added to the mirth provoked by the reading. (A 'shushu' day, they told me, is a hot day; an 'ouballie' is an old man, and 'laat die hare waai' means 'let the hair just wave'.)

As I said, the reaction to this story was intense, and the class wanted immediate discussion—no waiting to write responses to my question, 'What is this article about?', they wanted to go into it all together right then! Raaks, who is a student tutor working with us this term, came over to me with an I-told-you-so look on his face, and then with my blessing took over the meeting. His question for them was, 'Should the language in this article be the language of the new South Africa?'—which was certainly better than mine. Being an older student himself, he felt no hesitation about giving his own opinion and he challenged the common view that all the 11 languages of South Africa should be accommodated with a multilingual policy. He wrote Hindi on the board and asked how this language with its unfamiliar letters could be accommodated, but the students argued back forcefully, no silencing them! One women said that school subjects should be taught in the local tongue, and students could learn English as a second language. But another complained that the way English is taught makes people 'to be ashamed of their mother tongues'. One of the men pointed out that 'We don't just learn the language English, we also learn with it the customs of being like Europeans and we are losing our own culture'. Another said that Xhosas had to learn English to 'prove to whites that we are not dom', but someone answered that the price is too great, that African languages and cultures are being destroyed.

A discussion like this makes me think that perhaps the favored position English has enjoyed in this country is weakening. Back in 1976 when the apartheid government decreed that Afrikaans would be the required language in all schools, the students rioted and that's when the revolutionary struggle began—June 16, 1976 (it's an important date in our history). To learn English was an act of resistance. And it would allow Africans to play a part in the larger world, whereas Afrikaans would keep them isolated. But now it seems to me that African students are becoming quite insistent and chauvinistic about their own languages. One young man took me to task recently for not learning Xhosa.

But that's the first language for only about 15% of the population. Zulu has 22%, and English only 9 but growing fast. I've forgotten the percentage for Afrikaans—well under 10, although we still have five universities where it's the official language. So that leaves nearly half the population speaking the other seven languages (and some others that are not officially recognized). It's a polyglot nation we have, and how many of these people are willing to abandon their native languages in favor of English? They're beginning to feel that means giving up too much.

I think it's appropriate these local languages be used sometimes in our classes in the small group discussions, but then I often put Afrikaans speaking students and Xhosa speakers together in the same group so the only way to get work done is to use the lingua franca, which is English. With all the local languages we have in this country, it's generally agreed that English will be the 'linking language'. Without it these people will be limited, even confined to a locality. And can South Africa survive as a country without a common language?

So we had an exciting session with this question of what language or languages for the new South Africa, but will anything come of it? What sort of academic writing can it lead to? When the time comes to settle back and be alone with a sheet of blank paper, somehow the life seems to go out of so many of these students. Discussion is a communal activity for them, not something one does alone on paper. And they've already talked the subject out, so they're finished with it. Perhaps I could ask them for an individual narrative history of their experience with language learning—what would you think of that? I have the feeling so often that each one of them has something individual to say but is holding it back, not wanting to speak alone.

Well, this work certainly has its emotional ups and down, and if I keep on talking like this I'll be down, so let's change the subject. You remember those writing workshops I've been giving to supplement my income? A much needed supplement, I'll say. These have worked out very well for me, and I've been holding regular sessions, which are often much fun—although sometimes we get into serious matters. One of the men works for the hospice near here, and I wanted to know more about that so I asked him, 'From all your experience of being close to death, what can you say about it?' and he said, 'Death—is like a whisper'. I remembered that later when I was alone, at the movies.

Why does age make such a difference in the willingness to write, I wonder? I mean, these adults are so active in their writing, they have so much they want to say, but the students seem to be holding back or their minds are somewhere else, while the adults bring that somewhere else with them into the room and write about it. Oh, and these workshops even bring the promise of love, because women come to them and soon my mad soul is thinking something like this:

> *Why couldn't I be more patient.*
> *Let the apple fall on my head*
> *Rather than always climbing trees*
> *Out of season*
> *Inept*
> *Wondering if my self*
> *Knows anything at all?*
>
> *The experimental approach,*
> *That's what it is*
> *Reaching out to take your hand . . .*

But this letter has run on long enough, and I'd better end off here before you're tired of me. And I've got some 60 scripts from students to mark, writing they did before the shutdown. Giving grades seems like such a disruptive thing to do when you're trying to bring people together.

Hambah kakuhl (go well)—Ed

---///---

March 5

Dear Ed,

Reading your letters I sometimes find myself both saddened and amused. At one moment you're in the old Peugot talking with a colored woman looking for work, and then not long after you're in the arms of another who's whispering in your ear about T.S. Eliot. "In the room the women come and go / Talking of Michelangelo"—or rather of Eliot himself now, it seems, and at the colored hop of all places! I wonder about young people from villages in South Africa, or from the rural Midwest in the United States, reading someone like Eliot or perhaps Allen Ginsberg—sensibilities so foreign as to be unfathomable, I would think. Or are they voices whispering promises to them of experience more varied than what they've known? Poetry can be a powerful shaper of consciousness.

If, that is, the poem is not taken up as an *objet d'art* found on display in some anthology—or as a textual toy for poststructuralist theory to play with—but rather as experience to be lived through. So I wonder what that woman may have experienced with Eliot in the classroom. And if, by the way, she and the others read any South African poets or was only a Western sensibility to be known there?

I can understand why the young people at UWC would practice a certain reticence—how they might feel there is little in their own cultural background they can bring to the Western worldview presented with such authority by their professors. And so you wonder if you know them at all, as they seem to keep their inner selves secret from you. They will discuss an issue actively enough as a group, but then when the time comes to sit apart and commit their individual thoughts to a sheet of paper, it seems they speak reluctantly. Well, you're discovering for yourself what social scientists have told us, that people from oral cultures feel silenced by the solitary confinement of the essay form—a form that requires a high level of abstraction from immediate exchange. It implies personal and cultural values inconsistent with the patterns of thought and behavior in a tribal culture, it requires the individual who stands apart. So for those young people, learning to write an essay is not simply a matter of acquiring a few additional language skills, it requires a reshaping of consciousness—the development of an awareness that knows itself apart from the group and uses language addressed to whom it may concern.

But to be that explicit, that impersonal, is contrary to the traditional, consensual modes of resolving issues that your students have learned. We think of ourselves, when we speak directly to the point, as being open and aboveboard—sincere or genuine—but in many non-Western cultures this way of expressing oneself is felt to be confrontational, even domineering. So as I said, learning to produce the kind of writing you're asking for requires a reorientation of self, a reshaping of consciousness—you're asking people to set themselves apart, to become pushy.

And you're encouraging this development by provoking conversational exchange in the classroom, because after all writing is way of continuing the conversation. As your students begin to see this they'll be more willing to work alone. Doing so they will begin to individualize themselves, for each will write something different than the others and so discover his or her own particular secrets, which till then have been unknown to them. No wonder you feel they've not been forthcoming, that each one has "something individual to say and is holding it back"— because like the rest of us they have no individual experience, you might say, until it's been verbalized as such, and they haven't learned to do that. So they have no secrets to reveal beyond what everyone knows.

That we create such meanings for ourselves I've learned from my own experience, partly from this correspondence with you. These things I tell you in these letters are not simply meanings already in my mind, they're often discovered as I go along talking with you—and so the unexpected voice I hear is sometimes my own. When you provoke me to tell about Ekeesha and Loreny and Alvin, and what they've done, then I have to interpret their behavior and mine with them, and the insights I reach, such as they may be, are quite new to me. And of course I'm very pleased to have these new thoughts—I begin to think that maybe I know what I've done even if I don't know what I'm doing. So I mail the letter and happily share my findings with you.

Like your students, mine come from an oral culture and what they know is what they've heard. Very few of them are readers. They stroll into the classroom from noisy conversations in the cafeteria, wearing their Walkmans often, and as we sit there a beeper sounds, the owner checks it for the caller's number, feeling an urge almost as imperative as a call of nature to depart for the nearest telephone. Some actually carry a cellular phone, and only an effort of will or a steely look from me keeps them from using it right then. The difference is that my students, unlike yours from the Transkei say, are urbanized. They have no embracing communal self, having learned to be several selves and act the part required as they move from one social environment to another—as now they are learning to be academic selves. Much of the Marxist complaint about the rampant individualism of a capitalist economy is a nostalgic yearning for the communal, collective self of a tribal village, but that self is dying out everywhere and the really serious question now is, What sort of individual should we help bring into being?

Speaking of the communal self reminds me of Mrs. M's encounter with the Rainbow child. You mention how she could surprise people into saying very revealing things about themselves, and you would like to have that skill. Well, of course she knew that if people have no secrets to tell her they do have stories, and that's what she was after. Like you, she thought there is something worth knowing about every person she met, and she went out of her way to meet people. Walking through Washington Square Park one afternoon we came up alongside a young man in his late teens struggling to adjust a very large backpack, reaching behind in search of a strap. Mrs. M pulled the strap over for him, saying "Looks like you're headed for distant parts—can we go along?"

"Oh no, I just got back! I been to a Rainbow gathering in Kentucky, and it was great! Five hundred of us, and there was a thunder storm at night. And we shared our food—it was very ethical—and we walked around without any clothes on."

"That's an interesting ethic," she said as they strolled on together, but he didn't seem to hear, so enthused was he with the memory of it.

"You see, we pray for the earth—for things to grow and the earth to heal." He turned off then waving goodbye, pausing a few steps further on to look back at her for a moment and then calling out "Peace!"

For that moment she had distracted him from his plunge back into city life, back into the habitual attitude of reserve by which we keep ourselves insulated from each other in the metropolis. So he returned to a middle-class family in an urban apartment, leaving behind his self as a Rainbow child and resuming his various identities in the multifarious city. We all have this yearning for a simpler, more elemental life so to speak— your daughter is eloquent on this subject—but in fact there's no turning back now, except to say goodbye.

I read (in that capitalist rag *The Wall Street Journal*) that a favorite vacation experience for middle-aged Chinese is to return to the villages where they went as adolescents in answer to Mao's call to abandon city life for work among the peasants. So they return to drinking sour mare's milk, gnawing on boiled sheep bones, and shoveling cow dung. "This is fun!" Mr. Lu insists, shovel in hand—while his son, wearing a Chicago Bulls baseball cap and T-shirt, rolls his eyes and goes off to play video games with his friends. Later in the day Mr. Lu "belts out rowdy renditions of Communist revolutionary songs arm in arm with a group of old buddies and local herdsmen over a lunch of mutton and beer," but of course neither he nor his son wants to stay out there in the country, and after all this fun they return to life in the city and resume their various urban selves.

There is an intensification of emotional life in the city, a constant shift of stimuli, in marked contrast to the slower, more habitual, more smoothly flowing rhythm of the village and rural existence. The rhythms of the American-style dance band you heard at the community dance are the frenetic rhythms of the city, danced with abandon after a preliminary, nostalgic turn in a slower, more stately measure. And as we move about the city we present a different face to different people, so to speak—we have a variety of roles to play and who we truly are becomes problematical. But in that dance hall these separations are forgotten as the spirit of community asserts itself—all that unspoken understanding, as you say.

The next day you're back in the classroom, where rows of students sit apart and you want from each one of them some individual, personal expression, worrying all the while that getting it will make divisions among them, as when the atheist spoke up, and then something valuable may be lost with the passing of the communal spirit. But how to have our differences and yet be a community—that was the lesson when they joined so enthusiastically in a good-natured debate with Raaks over the question "Should the language of this article be the language for the new South Africa?" And the point of the article is that to be a monolingual is to be a mugu, so even here your community of students is advised of the advantage in the new South Africa of being at least a double self.

By the way, your readiness to yield control of the situation to Raaks, who conducted the discussion, shows your flexibility, your willingness to go along with the developing flow—to yield control to another so as to encourage the independence developing among those young people. Quite often, someone else in the group can do things with them we cannot because of our position or age or the expectations they have of us. We need to keep asking ourselves, What am I doing here that someone else could be doing as well or better than I? That was good teamwork with Raaks, and showed some strength on your part, it seems to me.

But then afterward you wonder what academic discourse this can lead to if the students have already talked the subject out, if the views of individuals have been expressed for them communally by one or another in the group. Of course there's much more involved here than simply a move from oral to written speech. When you ask those young people to sit alone and write, you are asking them to verbally differentiate themselves as individuals apart from the group—and this is what the new life they are entering requires of them. It requires them to relate to others in a more intellectual or matter-of-fact way than in the personally responsive way of communal life, and of course they will make this move reluctantly. But having to live now with the discontinuities and disruptions of an urban (or even campus) milieu, they must develop a more rational rather than emotional response in order to protect the inner self and their mental health (I'm paraphrasing Georg Simmel)—and their resistance to the domination of urban ways will itself make for a more self-aware and calculating individual. Furthermore, in moving from the subsistence economies of their villages to the cities, or to those great squatter camps you speak of, rural South Africans are entering a money economy, and as Simmel says, "a money economy and the domination of the intellect stand in the closest relationship to each other" (see "The Metropolis and Mental Life"). So by emphasizing with those young people the individual thought process, you're engaged with them in developing an intensification of consciousness—and one way to begin is with the individual stories they have to tell.

It's important they have opportunities for learning how to tell those stories. Their increasingly cosmopolitan experience is having the effect of individualizing them, requiring them to expand their primary language code in order to explain themselves to strangers—and so their language is changing, becoming more elaborated as Bernstein would say. Considering this, your idea of asking each of them for a narrative history of their language learning seems a good one, so why not talk with them about what such a history could be? And as they write it, some useful insight or idea about language and how it's leaned or taught may occur to them—a concept or two worth developing. Then too, out of this writing may come the next step you will take with them. In any case, you'll learn a lot.

It must be exciting for you to live in a place where a new consciousness is developing among a people, and to have a part in that development. And I can only comment on it from this great distance. There are times in these letters when you make me work very hard, and so perhaps I should thank you for these thoughts which have come to me, such as they are.

Best regards—JR

- - - / / / - - -

22 February

Dear John:

The university may have been shut down but that doesn't mean everyone goes quietly home. Modderdam Road was littered Monday with burning tires and students were demonstrating. I just heard that one of our tutors, Mjongile, was arrested with five others yesterday for an illegal poster demonstration in front of the campus, blocking traffic and holding up signs with messages like UNIVERSITY CONTINUES TO STARVE STUDENTS. He challenged me once about the topics in our course reader, like male circumcision, saying that if people discussed these things they might decide not to do them and 'this can destroy our culture.' He wanted to know why our readings question African customs but not Western culture. If I'd been quick enough I would have said something about a democratic culture being self-examining, but as it was he had me stammering for words.

Now at last, however, we've heard the university is about to reopen. Bishop Tutu (he's the chancellor of the university, mainly a ceremonial position) intervened and promised to raise money for student loans, and apparently he did just that. So tomorrow I'll be back with my students, renewing our relationship. Is the classroom going to seem a little dull after all the drama and turmoil we've experienced? Or maybe we're all tired of controversy and want to settle down to some quiet work. But I fear that perhaps the tone, the atmosphere of our sessions may change, with less openness and more suspicion. During the apartheid years there was generally a sense that students and staff were on the same side, but perhaps we're losing that now and have less trust in each other. Many of the staff definitely felt under siege themselves this time. So when I'm back in the classroom we'll need some work that will draw us closer together, but at the moment I have no idea what that should be.

Hambah kakuhl—Ed

CHAPTER 4

—✦—

All the Fine Things
I Might Say

7 September

Molo, kunjani? (Hello, how are you?)

Trying out your ideas and finding such strong currents of goodwill, even love! I took one of your little stories from *Provocations*, the one about the fellow whose father and mother tell him it's time to marry and offer to find him a bride, but he chooses for himself and then discovers the woman is a witch sent to learn his secret name. I changed the Native American names to African, so that the father, Wandering Water, became Umhambi (Traveler), and the mother, Slower-Than-You, became Nkotoza (Tongue-on-Floor-of-Mouth, or Slow Talker). I told the story one morning last week and the class was spellbound. They sat there looking at me so seriously.

I waited for them to say something without any prompting from me, but perhaps I should have waited longer for just when people finally did begin to speak up and Alberto was beginning his usual long speech, I rather took over and set them to thinking of descriptive names like those in the story to give themselves. 'Just think of a quality you need or want', I said, 'and give it to yourself in a name, give yourself a proper name you can use in time of need'. And I told them about one of my own special names, Baboon Spider. It was given to me by Benjamin, my ex-wife's son by another now-divorced husband. He called me one morning and tearfully explained that he had run away from the Afrikaner school his mother sends him to. The other boys made fun of his knapsack so he ran away. And now if he went back to that school the headmaster might very well cane him, and if he did then Benjamin swore he'd never go to that school again, ever! So I told him that running away at this time was clearly an intelligent act, one befitting a boy who's power name was obviously Leopard. And so Leopard he became, and it was amazing how quickly he calmed down. We were soon talking about his comic book hero Captain America, and then he decided to call me Baboon Spider—which is an actual spider and quite common here, about 4 inches long and hairy, with a big belly—quite beautiful, actually. It can jump some distance to avoid danger, and it's bite is very painful though not deadly. So now, thanks to Benjamin, I walk about aware of myself as a spiderman.

I told my students this story and asked them to choose power names for themselves that would help them on their way, and already many of them have. Brenda now calls herself Zama ('because it means keep trying'); Tyrone said that we are to call him Undertaker ('because I like dark places'); Buelela has become Pigeon ('because I love to travel'); and Alberto soon gave himself four or five names, like Genius, Galileo, Einstein, and such to aid him in his law studies. I suggested the name Deep Thought, hoping to give him a little control over his ever-gushing platitudes—or are they really deep thoughts? He often speaks so fast it's hard to say. But he chose to be Einstein instead.

Also, we talked about choosing a name for the class, and they decided to call themselves Students of the Third World (my other class calls itself the Dynamics). So we've been having a good time with this. It's helped draw us back together after all the demonstrations and the riot, and the college shutdown. I was worried about that, I feared there'd be some resentment brought back to the white man's classroom, but we're working together again and maybe they even feel happy to be back with me.

Your Navajo story was helpful because it doesn't reflect any of the racial or tribal tensions here, it allows the students to react simply as fellow human beings. Everyone could relate to this story, and so it made our differences incidental. And of course the element of witchcraft fascinates them. Then when they wrote about their reactions to it, some of them brought in elements from their own local cultures and so we learned something more about each other. Noma-China Klaas (a name that suggests the variety of cultures mixed in with the Xhosa people) wrote about the abductions of young girls in rural areas:

> I remember the birthday of my sister. We were living in a rural area at Transkei. It was a sunny day and everybody was excited about that. Others make a lot of noise talking to each other. My youngest sister went out looking for something [for the party]. I hear her screaming and I rush to the

scene to see what was wrong with her. When I got there I find that she was pulling by two guys. I tried to pull her at my side but they manage to take her to the car. Then they went with her.

By that time everybody was looking at us and wondering what was happening. Then I rush to the house to report that to my parents. My father comfort me and he said that I must not worry my sister will come and she will be the wife of Mahuli. I was very disappointed and we were disgrace to our friends those who were ready for the party that day. My father told them to leave the house. I was very embarassed and even now when I think of that makes me fill pain, thinking of my sister what she feel about my parents and I. I'm just thinking about me. What am I suppose to do when it come to me?

I hear papers like this and feel I'm in touch with the lives of these people. Here is Noma-China telling about ukuthwala, an arranged kidnapping, and of course Mahuli will pay the father lobola (a bride price). This is not a commercial transaction but a communal practice with complex social, legal and religious meanings. After the bride price has been paid the two families are then considered to be truly joined and the children to come will be legitimate. A payment of cattle is traditional, although in urban areas lobola is usually paid in cash, so marriage is an expensive proposition for Xhosa men. And for young women it can be a frightening experience, especially in rural areas where the old customs still have force.

When this paper was read to us some of the women began murmuring together, but Nolizwe spoke up saying that the Xhosa tradition of respect for elders requires young people to marry those chosen for them by their parents. 'My parents in Johannesburg that is far away will choose for me, and I will be happy with that choice'. One of the women tried to reason with him, saying that 'tragedy could result from this', and others joined in on both sides of the issue. Finally Nolizwe said, 'Here away from the parents you lose your respect, but when you are home in the rural areas it's not so easy to disobey them'. Everyone agreed with that.

Such practices as ukuthwala and lobola are taken by some as more evidence of backwoods ignorance, but when we hear about them as part of a story and someone's actual experience is talked about, there seems to be more respect for each other's views. People are less inclined to be dismissive of someone they meet in this way, even when that person does not share the same background or belief. There are strong intertribal rivalries and prejudices under the surface here, as when one student sneered slightly when he heard Helebha's name because 'I thought you were a Sotho.' But hearing each other's responses to the Navajo story seemed to draw us together, despite our differences. The ANC document on education calls for texts that give a knowledge of other cultures, and I think stories like this help make possible the very unity the government is after.

So we've developed a very good feeling in my two classes, and I'll say that I'm feeling good about life outside the classroom too. I've been reading A. S. Byatt's *Possession*, which seems to me a strong book. She calls it a romance, and I've taken to heart one of its suggestions and fallen totally in love. But not with a poet, as the book would have it, but with a singing teacher. We met on a mountain hike, and the surprising thing is that she seems to care for me, and seems to enjoy hearing the bits of wisdom I've gathered along life's way. She may have teacherphilia, or some such perverted but delightful passion. And I have the self-ease now that comes with doing work I really love, so it's possible for me to think about a serious relationship once more.

After seeing a movie together we took a moonlight stroll on the shore path from Muizenberg to St. James, which goes alongside False Bay, an inlet from the Indian Ocean. On the left wild crashing surf, and suddenly close by on the right the yellow carriages of the suburban train roll past, and glances are exchanged between walkers and folks looking out the windows or standing in the open doorways of the carriages. Beyond the tracks the Kalk Bay Mountains rise steeply, with green forest and fynbos at the bottom, and grey-white rocky cliffs at the top, shining in the moonlight. Now with the train gone by we hear the surf and see life in the water, cormorants, and grebes. Fishermen, usually from the coloured community, stand at certain spots fishing for octopi and other food. There are seals there sometimes too, and in December whales come into the bay. Cape Town is surely one of the most beautiful places on this planet.

So I'm going to have a picnic lunch with this ladylove of mine this very day at 12:30. I've already packed chicken sandwiches, two apples, and a few sun-dried apricots, and perhaps we'll find some sunny spot in which to rest. Oh you should know what other deviltry I've been up to! In my classes we've gone on to write our definitions of love, and we've interviewed friends, parents, and partners to find any differences in their views of this most universal and interesting of subjects. Yes, differences and discrepancies are what a writer needs—little openings and spaces in which to philosophize.

Love—Ed

- - -///- - -

8 September

Dear John,

Oh my, deceived again. The golden dream fades to reveal a bit of tarnish here, a touch of ersatz there, and a chill begins to come. So much for love. Perhaps I should have been more circumspect and not allowed my feelings quite so much expression so soon. Maybe the Africans have it right with their arranged marriages, they save themselves from a lot of anxiety and doubt, but it seems we have to prove ourselves individually, as someone worthy of being loved. Of course I have not revealed my turnaround, although I wonder if one can hide anything from a woman. I will try to overcome my doubts, my newly discovered dissatisfaction. Maybe we need to take a long hike together—romance is really more like work than a picnic, I suppose.

So let me turn to my one true love, which never fails me, my teaching. I look forward in the morning to seeing my students, but the more I know of them the more concerned I get about some of them. Loyiso, in the class that took the name Students of the Third World, shot himself in the leg and came limping into the room on crutches. He bought a pistol for self-protection, he said, and was putting it into the holster when it went off. 'I sold it now', he told me, 'it's too dangerous'. And Archie, in that same class, has been charged by the school disciplinary committee with attempted rape in the hostel, so Women Against Rape staged a march through the campus, pressuring to have him expelled. Let me tell you, there are some very rough folk in those student hostels, from very troubled communities, and I've heard that drunkenness is common on weekends.

Another student, Mabuufo (whose name, by the way, means Troubles), bursts into tears when asked about her absence on Tuesday, and tells me that she and her sister were arrested at the OK Bazaar for fraud, charged with changing price tags on certain goods. She was kept in jail from Monday to Thursday, and the Afrikaans-speaking police pretended not to understand her English and wouldn't allow her to phone out. But she professes her innocence, saying she took the items from an abandoned shopping cart. That sounds fishy, and my call to the supermarket gets the reply that the security guard saw her doing it so they won't drop the charges, and anyway they can't drop the charges, the manager claims, because 'only the police can do that', which of course is a lie. Even so, the police are still very powerful here.

And lately I've been thinking, Democracy? Yes—but what is it? And will it last? Leo Hopkins, our resident communist, was telling us over lunch the other day that even with the ANC takeover, democracy is in trouble because the economy is stumbling into chaos and needs 'management and more management, not mass demonstrations'. Incomes are shrinking fast as inflation hit 10% last month. And will capitalism do anything more for the people than exploit them? I find Marx's argument about the way surplus value is extracted from the workers a compelling point of view. And there's his account of how ideology is created, mostly to serve the interests of the ruling class, as he argues so persuasively in *The German Ideology*. Surely workers should have more control of their own work process and more representation on management boards, or do you reckon that democracy ends where the corporation begins? Without some form of socialism it seems uncertain that democracy can last in this country where there is so much poverty and desperation, and now the violence in those squatter camps and urban slums seems to be drawing closer to the white community. I read today there's a gunman who randomly shoots at cars along the cutoff to the airport, which is the road I take to the university.

Then I drive through the checkpoint and I'm in a different world, wondering if what we're doing in those classrooms is really preparing people for the reality of South Africa. Why are we still giving students a 3-hour exam in language and a 2-hour exam in literature? Having to spend my evenings preparing this already late exam certainly hasn't improved my mood. The language exam gives them a passage to read, followed by short-answer questions, and then they're asked to write an essay. And for the literature exam we give one passage from a play, and one from a short story, along with some questions. Does that sound a little ridiculous?

I constantly hear it said that literature courses in the English department cover so much material, and the exam questions require such exacting analyses of literary works, that more of our time must go to teaching all this. So we're forced to devote even the writing tutorial to instructing the students in literary terminology and the different genres, and how to write the kind of analysis required. I know you've said that a beginning course should not be tied to the literature program, that it should be concerned with general language skills and has no need of a specified curriculum. It should take the students as they are and go on with them in what I would call a 'process-oriented' way, involving them in language activities rather than teaching them language concepts or what's called a metalanguage for talking about writing. But what if you were also expected to give those same students an introduction to literary concepts and genres?

One thing I've tried is your way of having a student take over a story we're reading and bring us questions about it. Then we break into small groups to work out our responses. But it often takes too long a time for each group to report back the results, and then all sorts of disagreements arise. I get nervous when irrelevant discussions get going—like whether customers in a photography shop are customers or clients. But often these simple distinctions are so strange to these second-language learners.

Also, I was showing Quinton Booi all the intelligent questions my students had produced for one of the stories we read, and he said 'Hey Katz, the trouble with you is you imagine that people can go around asking questions, as if they can really think out and plan their own lives. Ha! Most folks here don't have any such opportunity. They've got to accommodate to the System or die'. That made me pause for thought.

Well, it's cold and rainy today and I really must go to the university to get the exam work done, so I'll send this letter off now.

—Ed

- - - / / / - - -

October 4

Dear Ed,

Two letters from you in one week—an epistolary wealth! But such an unhappy tale of love they tell. It's a hard lesson you are learning, that the real woman is always so different from the one we have been dreaming of, more definite and more demanding. Even so, I think this new affair of yours may yet prove to have some enduring quality, after you have paid the price in pain. Sadness may be an essential element of all true love affairs, for they require some comprise of the ideal along with self-surrender, and we never forget what we have given up. So even the happiest of affairs may be tinged with a touch of melancholy. In any case, continuous joy in the company of another person is simply not possible. Certainly the story of two people perpetually enjoying each other is without dramatic interest and so the attention does wander. But as the dream fades, the discovery of a real woman there offers a challenge to our powers. This can be enlivening.

As chance would have it, the day before your last letter arrived I was reading a story very much like yours. In the book *Repetition,* which Kierkegaard calls a study in experimental psychology, Constantine Constantius tells of a young man who declares his love to a young woman and finds it reciprocated, but then on the first day of his engagment falls into a deep melancholy. As the days go on he longs for the girl and yet he stays away much of the time for fear of being a burden to her, who has in fact become almost a burden to him. But she has served to awaken within him a poetic talent, and he begins to write. Already, Constantine remarks, the would-be lover has become an old man with respect to the whole relationship, which even as it continues is now simply a matter of memory and thus useful as subject matter. Eventually the young man ends the affair by taking flight—that is, by leaving town.

There's an interesting parallel here with your own story, it seems to me. For like the young man, you turned to poetry at the decisive moment, in your own way. You turned to the field of your creative endeavor, which is your classroom, and there you tried to find love, so to speak, there you introduced the subject explicitly and even asked for poems that would define it. As if love were something new that needed definition, rather than something familiar and welcome. Perhaps here was a clue that you feared your hope in the woman was misplaced, and were already preparing to make her a memory.

So in your turning to the poetry of love you enlisted the company of those young people in your classroom, who drawing now on their own memories of love, join in your concern and turn what was once a solitary move on your part into a movement. Such a need for other company in love when one already has a ladylove, suggests that perhaps she is not enough. One becomes a pieceworker at the labor of love, drawing a bit from this person, a bit from that person. And doing so for one's own consolation.

This is very different from your usual way of working with young people, which puts their interests or needs before yours. Of course we carry with us into the classroom each day our feelings, our moods, our needs— but we do not offer them as subject matter because we are only observers there. Active observers, whose task it is to find among the young, who do not know their own strength, possibilities no one knew were there. We may go to work each day with others who come riding in on their hobbyhorses, eager to enlist young people into the ranks of their particular movement, but we ourselves are only observers who come visiting without agenda or guidebook. And this requires, if I may say so yet again, the disciplined ego—the development of which is in fact our own individual and very difficult classroom project.

Let me tell a little story by Chekhov that relates to this. Reading "A Day in the Country" we follow an orphan child running through the village desperately searching for Terenty, a homeless old man. She finds him at last in the kitchen gardens and pulls him along into the forest, where her brother has his hand caught in a hole in a tree, reaching in to get a cuckoo egg for her. Terenty frees the boy, and the three of them wander on together through the afternoon, as Terenty tells them about the birds, the flowering herbs, the insects, answering their questions. The story ends with these words:

> Only towards evening our wanderers return to the village. The children go for the night to a deserted barn, where the corn of the commune used to be kept, while Terenty, leaving them, goes to the tavern. The children lie huddled together on the straw, dozing.
>
> The boy does not sleep. He gazes into the darkness, and it seems to him that he is seeing all that he has seen in the day: the storm-clouds, the bright sunshine, the birds, the fish, lanky Terenty. The number of his impressions, together with exhaustion and hunger, are too much for him; he is as hot as though he were on fire, and tosses from side to side. He longs to tell someone all that is haunting him now in the darkness and agitating his soul, but there is no one to tell. Fyokla is too little and could not understand.
>
> "I'll tell Terenty tomorrow," thinks the boy.
>
> The children fall asleep thinking of the homeless cobbler, and, in the night, Terenty comes to them, makes the sign of the cross over them, and puts bread by their heads. And no one sees his love. It is seen only by the moon which floats in the sky and peeps caressingly through the holes in the wall of the deserted barn.

That's all there is to this story, and it's enough. I take it as a model for the way we work with young people, wandering along with them, showing them something here or there by the way that draws their wonder, so they long to tell someone what they're thinking. We first learn to know the world, a poet tells us, not by our immediate initial contact with things, but rather through the signs of things—a word, a gathering phrase, a story. And now if anything in the world inspires a moment of responsive feeling, "we find that we are moved because we were previously moved by it; and we were moved because, on some day or other, it seemed to us transfigured, detached from everything else, by a word, a fable, a fancy that we connect with it." And the fancy, Pavese continues, seems to be at the time objective knowledge, reality itself, given not by invention but directly.

So we wander along with our young people, show them something here or there by the way, following the path of a story or poem, perhaps, and listen to their souls responding. And no one must see our love. For love declared always makes a claim and the young resent the presumption, while others are simply embarrassed and think you're becoming self-indulgent or even a little childish yourself.

Very good writers are able to conceal themselves in their work, so that we read it without thinking of them, caught up in the drama of ideas they present or the lives of their people. They have the concealment of style. And I think as teachers we should develop a creative style, so that our young people need not be thinking about us or our performance but rather about their ongoing work, believing they are doing it all themselves. Later they may look back and wonder, after the book is closed.

Do you remember Vitaly, in my *Provocations?* He's gruff, he's tough, he's very demanding. He wants his students to do well, and he spends much time with one or another of them, going over their work. He's the one who told his wife when they married that his students came first, then her. He went to his wedding, by the way, carrying a copy of Camus' *The Stranger* in his pocket, behavior I'm sure would interest Freud. The other day as he went out to get a hotdog from the street vendor by the campus, two young men were leaving with their orders. The vendor told him, "That boy, you know what he said? He's telling the other one you failed him but you're the only professor he'd like to have again." Vitaly's students think his interest in them concerns only the business at hand, and they feel encouraged to share that interest. He's very forceful in the classroom but keeps himself well concealed. Although you and I teach very differently than Vitaly, in this we can learn from him.

So having said these few words about your first love, I turn now to the new love in your life. This lady, so far nameless to me, will not be at all surprised by the change of heart you call your turnaround. Women are realists. We imagine that in revealing the depth of our feeling to a woman we have surprised her, overwhelmed her with our eloquence, awakened a responsiveness that draws her to us irresistibly as the monarch butterfly is drawn over great distances to a winter home in the warmth of Mexico. And all the while listening to this boyish chatter she knows exactly what she is doing. Waiting for us to grow up!

After a time the thought occurs to us that perhaps we have said too much. Carried along by enthusiasm for ourselves and desire for her we have become vulnerable to a listening ear and a watching eye. And yet we understand that despite our faults she will have us, in fact is determined to have us, and now her desire becomes a burden to us. We begin to see that she has flaws and more than her share of faults. We draw back from this powerful and determined woman who says so little, and begin to consider the options open to us, including the way out.

And yet there is something to be said for a woman who has made one enthusiastic about himself—who can hardly abide his own company and longs for someone who will listen to all the fine things he might say if only there were someone to hear them. Loneliness is the greatest misfortune. The whole problem of life, our poet remarks, is how to break out of one's loneliness, how to reach another and repossess ourselves through her. Consider also the good sense she has shown in her partiality for your company. In fact, considering the alternative, one might choose to simply wander along with her.

I send my caring regard—JR

- - - / / / - - -

October 6

Dear Ed,

In the faculty dining room we sort ourselves by rank and discipline, so that adjuncts (part timers) sit together, humanities professors together, and so on. I should sit with the other adjuncts who teach writing, of course, but occasionally I become curious about conversation among practitioners of the higher learning and find a vacant place among them. "I'm very disappointed with grades on the mid-term exam," a professor is saying as I sit down. She pauses at my intrusion, then decides to continue, bending toward her other listeners. "They can't even match authors with their works, they think Faulkner wrote 'Araby'!" The others nod as if to say they know the problem only too well. "So I put their exam papers in order, with the best one on top, and when I handed them back everyone could see who was at the top and who was at the bottom. How else do you get the attention of these people? I'm thinking of assessing each one 50 cents, and the person who writes the best paper will get the money. Money is something they understand." Most of her students are business majors taking prose fiction as a core requirement.

Before I can speak—the Imp of the Perverse urging me to go ahead, get in there, say something—"They watch television all the time and don't want to read," another professor tells us. "It's made them lazy."

"Yes, and some of those who aren't very smart think if they work hard they should get a good grade, but I don't think so. Either they understand what we read or they don't." Again the others nod. I feel an like anthropologist and resolve to write all this down immediately afterwards, for these people are not of my tribe.

Soon the others, having finished their coffee, get up from the table, leaving me there with another latecomer. "You must enjoy reading stories with those young people," I say. He looks at me dubiously. "Well," I go on, "you never know what they might say about some strange story like 'A Rose for Miss Emily'."

"But I do know! They'll say, 'Why we gotta read this stuff?'" He seems more sad about this than angry.

"When we were their age we were readers," I remark. "We wanted to read stories and talk about them."

"Yes, but then you lose interest in fiction when you get older and you've taught so much of it to so many of them." He had forgotten how to sing, perhaps, and become as matter-of-fact as the students.

All this was brought to mind by your remarks about the literature component of your writing program—the teaching of genres, of terminology, of analysis and comparison and all that good stuff. Here's another reason why literary culture is fading rapidly in our time. Surely at this beginning stage we might better participate with young people in the experience that poems and stories may give us, by which our own limited understanding of life is expanded and our minds moved to consider anew the dispensation under which we live.

And perhaps begin to question it. But when you show Quenton Booi the intelligent questions your students wrote for one of the stories they read, he tells you this is pointless: "They've got to accommodate to the System or die." But what you're doing here, it seems to me, is teaching those young people the beginning step in conceptual thinking. From their experience of the poem or story, you ask them to draw out a question, a thought, a subject to be explored—and that's the beginning of philosophy and the social sciences, you see, to comment on the poem. With the Greeks, the earliest philosophers told and retold the myth of origins, and later ones speculated on the meaning of that story, until there came a time when speculation, abstract thought, had been separated entirely from myth—that's the Greek contribution to Western thought. So if a poem or story seems to be telling us something worth knowing about human experience, then we want to contemplate that. This is the response Aristotle calls *theoria*, without which the action of the poem remains incomplete. You have an experience of the poem, as you have an experience of life, and you want to know what it means. This is one reason we ask for personal response and personal writing from our students, so they can go looking for meanings and learn the first step in conceptual thinking.

But the teaching of genre study and formal analysis to young people sets a limit to their thinking with the poem or story, and illustrates once again how "Our meddling intellect/Misshapes the beauteous form of things." For here a situational text is being taken as an object to be pulled apart, rather than as an experience to be lived through. The poets contradict the academics at every turn but they're not listening, they're expounding, and before long all other voices in the room are stilled, even the voice from the page.

When Mina Shaughnessy assigned Richard Wright's *Black Boy* to her students, she used it to give them training in "the grammar of passages." Now here is a story that would surely engage the feeling and thought of many young people with issues important to them, but Shaughnessy is not interested in their experiences with *Black Boy* but in "the perception of structure" and "the recognition of thought patterns." In this book, however, Wright tells us that it was from stories, from

> out of the emotional impact of imaginative constructions of heroic or tragic deeds that I felt touching my face a tinge of warmth from an unseen light; and in my leaving [the South] I was groping toward that invisible light, always trying to keep my face so set and turned that I would not lose the hope of its faint promise, using it as my justification for action.

Yet to many teachers of literature the poetic fiction is not a justification for action but rather material for another lesson on the grammar of form. The text itself may speak against them but they are unaware of that, deaf to the songs that poets sing.

They wish to be authorities—the expositors of an esoteric knowledge. And they teach their students to follow authority wherever it leads, however far it takes them from their own concerns or their own experience with the text at hand. All those programs which stress form—the rules of grammar, the modes of discourse, the structure of essays—have as their unstated first purpose the disciplining of the young to ensure their submission to authority. And we ask them questions to be sure they're following us!

Let us make a general rule for ourselves, that we will no longer feel impelled to demonstrate our mastery by leading young readers through a text, asking them questions as they follow us along the way. Rather, all of us will follow along with the text, meet new people and enter into their lives, experience the world as they know it and live for a time according to their values, their particular vision of life. And because our perceptions of this will differ, we will have questions to ask each other about it and soon find ourselves explaining and justifying, reaching for the language we need to describe our experience. The poetic text may yet prove have some practical value.

"Democracy, what is it?" you ask, and I'm trying to suggest an answer. It's a practice one learns by living it. My friend Warren spent last winter teaching English in a high school in Lithuania, working under a principal who had been a leader in the struggle for independence. But now as principal he used the same coercive methods as his predecessors: he spied, he gathered hearsay, he ruled by decree. Becoming democratic means learning certain habitual ways of regarding others and dealing with them, so it's important that we think about how we should live with young people in our classrooms.

I keep asking myself, "What am I doing they could do?"—and the answer is, Almost everything. They can select articles or stories for us to read together, and decide what to write about. And I invite them to make motions and vote on them: Should we have a class secretary? Should people who come late sing us a song, or give us a wise saying? Chardelle proposed that someone else be elected chairperson in my place—and the motion passed! What these young people write when they work for me doesn't really matter much to them, but they can learn to take over their class and write for themselves and then they'll care about what they're doing. Which is one reason I don't collect, edit, and grade their papers— they must learn to edit and evaluate for themselves. Those papers are not mine, after all.

Shall we call this respect for private property? I know that will seem so very retrograde among the politically advanced, but I'd like to encourage democratic individualism. You seem to be asking at one point if socialism is perhaps the best organizational system for South Africa, but under socialism there is no private property. Or perhaps you're allowed to own your house while the bureaucrats own everything else—so what scope is there for democratic individualism? We should keep in mind that the building of enterprises, the development of industry and trade, requires a high degree of individualism, and that historically there has been a relationship between capitalism and democracy. (I'm drawing here on Peter Gay's *The Enlightenment*.) Voltaire described the London Stock Exchange as a place where "the Jew, the Mohammedan, and the Christian deal with each other as if they were of the same religion, and give the name of infidel only to those who go bankrupt." The spirit of capitalism early on, as Gay reports, tended to despise tradition and question orthodoxy, to substitute reason for faith and so promote the ideals of the Enlightenment. Its celebration of industry and commerce was also a radical criticism of traditional rule by aristocrats and priests, and while valuing merchants and traders it derided military men. So capitalism has played an important part in the development of democratic individualism and of the institutions that sustain it.

Where you and I might see enterprise, however, Marx saw only selfishness. In his view, human selfishness is born of the institution of private property and bound to fade away along with it, whereas Kierkegaard on the other hand took it as an eternal trait of human nature. Which seems to you the more realistic view of the matter? Now, capitalism is selfishness put to work. And with all that power no wonder it's the only revolutionary force on the world stage today, overturning tradition everywhere it goes:

> Uninterrupted disturbance of all social conditions, everlasting uncertainty and agitation . . . all fixed, fast, frozen relations with their train of ancient and venerable prejudices and opinions are swept away. . . . All that is sold melts into air, all that is holy is profaned, and man is at last compelled to face with sober senses his real conditions of life and his relations with his kind. (Marx, Manifesto of the Communist Party)

And recent events confirm this. I've read complaints that the Eastern Europeans hurried to throw off Russian rule not so much because they wanted freedom but because they wanted VCRs and Häagen-Dazs ice cream. Well, a little acquaintance with the history of capitalism would have dispelled the utopianism back of such cynical complaints and given credit to self-interest. And now the Africans in your country are tired of being serfs and want the good things they think may come with freedom, for which they're willing to chance social and political upheaval.

But the resident Marxist tells you that democracy may have to be delayed in this difficult time for South Africa, because a faltering economy on the brink of chaos "needs management and more management, not mass demonstrations." In other words, it needs the planned management of socialism, which means not democracy—not political and civil liberties—but rather a strong hand on the steering wheel of power. Socialism, in Marxist theory, is a transitional stage on the way to communism, when life will be truly collective and bourgeois individualism stamped out entirely. Do you remember how Marx describes, in *The German Ideology*, the general all-purpose kind of somebody that communism will produce, who can "do one thing today and another tomorrow . . . hunt in the morning, fish in the afternoon, rear cattle in the evening, criticize after dinner, just as I have a mind, without ever becoming hunter, fisherman, shepherd, or critic"? So let the professors and intellectuals leave off their narrow specializations long enough to help with the harvest and learn the true communal spirit. Are you ready to go?

Or will you opt for democracy, which as Tocqueville said, "makes men forget their ancestors . . . isolates them from their contemporaries . . . and lets them imagine their whole destiny is in their hands"? As democracy develops in South Africa or elsewhere, the ideas of the lower strata in society and their ways of thought confront the accepted wisdom of the elite, who know so well how things should be done—and the elite hate it! Your resident Marxist is one of the elite and sees himself in control at Command Central. How would you like to have him as your commissar, tovarich?

So often well-intentioned people, who themselves believe in democracy and wish the best for their students, go into the classroom as autocrats—but you will stand apart there as the observer who makes a difference. I'd like to know more about those young people you work with, I'd like to see them as you do and hear them. When you tell about what happens in your classroom, how one group names itself Students of the Third World and another becomes the Dynamics, I think how exciting it must be to work with young people like those, who are trying to make a better life for themselves, and to have some part with them in the development of a new country and a new people.

Yours in the struggle—JR

- - - / / / - - -

15 October

Dear Friend,

Oh all right, so I did ride the hobbyhorse of love into the classroom, as you say, and the results were my punishment. The students avoided writing about real relationships and gave me instead episodes from TV shows, or the sort of apocryphal stories that circulate in the township. One was about a taxi driver who late one evening seduces his passenger, somewhat forcibly it's suggested, and when he telephones her the next day her mother tells him the girl died years ago. He goes to the graveyard to check out the mother's story and there he finds the jacket he lent the girl hanging on her gravestone.

Well, maybe I shouldn't feel so dissatisfied, receiving such a story, but this isn't writing that explores a personal experience or issue and gives us some individual truth to work with, like the writing generated by the names project. Asking students to write on the meanings of their names led them to reflect in writing that was both poetic and expository, and gave us a few revelations of an individual nature. (I'll copy out a couple of these to send you later.) We started with your Navajo story about the young warrior with a secret name, and unless we start with something like that to give us a direction it's too easy for students to lose themselves in the popular culture. When we wrote about love, one of them retold a story from the TV soap opera *The Bold and the Beautiful*, and when I asked her if it was true, she said yes! So what is truth? We could argue about that, I suppose—but no, this sort of summary of a TV program is just not going to lead us to something individual, something . . . moral?

The only morality that moves us now is the monetary. You talk about socialism as confining the individual but capitalism demands its own sort of conformity. And if you're not cost effective you'll be excessed— terminated, that is. The money given by the government to this university is decreasing each year, so this program I'm working in must become more cost effective, they tell us. At present we have a student–lecturer ratio of 75:1, making it the envy of other departments with their ratio of 135:1—and so, says our dean, fixing his pecuniary eye on the figures, 'If funding your program at this level means other departments will go to 145:1, then it's clear the program may have to go or the ratio must rise'. Is he preparing us for some change in our program that's already been decided—perhaps a move to the lecture hall? And what would that mean for the kind of work I like doing with students?

Speaking of which, my dear therapist, Jean Sperling, has taken me to task for not marking my students' papers. I've been procrastinating a lot, thinking of what you have said about not doing such mind-crushing work, but her position was that 'the poor students, they want and need some confirmation, some word from their teacher'. Indeed, I did mark the bloody things but I've cut down on this work by continuing on with a writing project until we have a finished piece, so I'm not reviewing the earlier drafts any more, which means I have fewer papers to grade. But suppose the dreaded dean bird finds out what I'm doing (not doing)? At the last general meeting he spent much time explaining how important it is that we all agree to give grades, etc. I could get into trouble, listening to you.

But then something rather interesting happened today. We felt the need for a little diversion, a break in the routine before starting the next project and so I asked the students to 'Write what's on your mind, just anything at all,' and the result was one of the most delightful sessions we've had. Xolisa mused, 'Can I really put what is in my mind onto paper? It's too huge, impossible! My thoughts are like snakes and scorpions'. But he did write about those snakes and scorpions, and the others laughed when he read the paper to us: 'I think I'm going crazy, I must go to a psychologist'. We all had a good time with this, and for once the conversation was not dominated by the coloured students, the Africans were as keen to participate as the others. The result was very different from what happened in my first class at UWC, remember?—when I asked them to do some free writing and they rejected that activity and me along with it. But today these students were willing to try it, and I learned something from them. When we have group projects, people get into their group identities and that's when the differences among them are so evident and worrisome to me, as if it's one group versus another. I think sometimes that real trouble could get started. But today when each person spoke simply as an individual, the others were interested and accepting, they didn't have to play identity politics. I'm not sure why this is, but it seems that encouraging individual expression helps bring us together and makes for unity.

So that was a good session. And I've been having other delightful experiences too, with the unassuming young woman I've told you about—a voice teacher, moderately well-read, and charmed by what seems to her my worldly experience. Twice last month my dear Lucy and I climbed to the top of Table Mountain, the second hike up through swirling mists and threatening wind and wet clouds. It was a bit frightening way up there, and we almost turned back. A few years ago a family of four fell to their deaths trying the climb at Second Waterfall Ravine. And Brinkwater Ravine (which used to be Stinkwater) regularly claims its victims. But somehow we managed to keep going and at the top the view was glorious, with the sun out for awhile, the Atlantic Ocean shining in the west and the Indian Ocean in the east. There was fynbos everywhere and other lovely flowers too, like the red disas blooming in the water courses. We could see down into the Valley of the Red Gods, and on the western slope was Judas Peak, one of several high outcrops that make up what are called the Twelve Apostles.

Then we went on to Tranquility Forest, a kind of underground forest, if you can believe it, that flourishes in deep crevasses, and one walks there among the yellowwood trees with a sense of being under the earth—silent, peaceful. And there we found a place to spread our picnic cloth, share our lunch and a bottle of wine. Romantic? Yes indeed.

All the best from your doubtful chela—Ed

- - - / / /- - -

October 30

Dear Ed,

The story told to you about the taxi driver and his ghostly passenger was an unexpected gift, so of course you hardly know how to receive it or how to respond at first—for it sounds a different note and calls you to follow along a new path, away from the one you have already laid out. But that's a call you might, on reflection, like to heed. Let me suggest why.

This story is one of those urban legends of the sort Jan Brunvand has collected here and published in several volumes. As such it is part of an oral culture, and you're living among people for whom word of mouth is still very important as a way of sharing cultural concerns. Passed on from person to person, the taxi-driver story seems to suggest that the modern world has not solved for us the mystery of death, or removed from our lives the influence of hidden spiritual forces. And the way these forces speak to us is through a woman. So this story expresses yet again the age-old fear men have of women, their deeply rooted suspicion that the female sex is privy to the elemental secrets of life, able to summon those darker powers that may work either good or evil—for one never knows with a woman.

I would think you might find this story particularly interesting, given your own doubtful experiences with women. But let me tell another such tale, one that puts this matter of men and women quite differently. A young woman goes with her friends to a dance, where a handsome fellow takes her by the hand and leads her onto the dance floor. There he whirls her about and she follows him, doing steps she had never learned but now with him is executing perfectly. She is entranced by the music, the motion, his smiling face—until suddenly in a quick turn he loses a shoe, and glancing down she sees not a foot but a cloven hoof. She is dancing with the devil! He immediately leaves the dance floor and disappears into the mens room, not to be seen again.

This story is commonly told in Hispanic communities, and it suggests that the young woman who gives herself too readily to a man is going to find herself in trouble. For men are devils and women are weak. It illustrates, as does the other story, how such tales express the concerns of those who tell them, concerns evidently widespread in the culture. So if your young people want to tell these stories or report on other elements of their culture, then why not go along with them? Think of the fascinating material they will bring to you! And as they consider the meanings of these stories, and the assumptions behind them, some very good thinking might be done. They could make a collection of them, with a commentary on each and perhaps an introductory essay. They'd have something of considerable interest.

Of course you know better than I what can be done in that classroom. I'm just suggesting that we should be alert to the concerns of our young people and accept their guidance when they suggest something promising. We may have our own plan of action ready for them and expect they will do serious work, but we should always be willing to follow their direction and wander along with them.

As you wander with your ladylove singing teacher, climbing mountains and rambling through the enchanted forest, finding a place at last to have your picnic lunch, with "A Jug of Wine, a Loaf of Bread—and Thou/beside me singing in the Wilderness." For the world is a wilderness through which we roam for a time, and it's good to have company as we go along in the gathering dark. You're a lucky man.

By the way, this matter of companionship has become an issue in my prose fiction class. I passed out copies of Richard Yates' story "The Best of Everything," wondering what those young people would make of it. Here is a young woman trying to decide about a young man, not sure how she feels, and her friends tell her he's no good—he says "terlet," he's only a clerk, he has no future. But then one evening when they are dancing he holds her close, sings to her in a faint whispering tenor a few words of the song, and she decides to marry him. Shortly before the wedding she waits for him one night, thinking of giving herself to him, dressing seductively, but he arrives only to say that he has come from a surprise party the boys are giving him and has to return. Very reluctantly she lets him go. In these few pages two young lives are told, more poignantly and beautifully than I can suggest here, and I wondered what thoughts they might provoke in my young people, themselves not far from marriage, some of them. We each wrote a paragraph, reacting to the story.

And the men became Ralph, trying to explain and justify his going back to the party, while the women expressed the disappointment Gracie felt. Few of them expected she would meet him the next day as planned, and none of them gave this marriage much of a chance. So then I suggested they go on to write about a couple in their own experience, "Tell us how they met, how they get along, whatever interests you about them—any couple you think of."

"This doesn't do anything for me," Rahsaan said. "I don' like this talkin bout relationships."

"You mean you're not interested in other people?"

"Oh, I'm interested but I don't want to write about it, I just live it."

"Well then, maybe you can't do this," and I sat down to begin writing. The others had already begun, and before long Rahssan decided to join us. If I were standing in front of the room giving directions and then walking around to police the work, I wouldn't have this open resistance. It would be covert and all the stronger for that, because young people need to defend their feeling of being independent.

It seems to me that much of our teaching happens in these brief and seemingly casual exchanges, so it's important we have them. There's very little I want to tell these people, but if we can get a little conversation going then I have them living in the situation along with me rather than sitting back listening, waiting for the time to pass. Of course much depends on one's improvisational skill, and on the particular character—your own or the other person's—which prompts one's words. There's no way of planning these lessons in advance of our meeting, because who knows what youngsters will say when provoked?

When they were ready, I said "Here you've each written about two couples, and there must be some idea behind this, some theme in what you've said because our minds are organized thematically—so let's find that theme. Who will work with me?" Tracey was willing, and I asked her to tell us what she had said about these two couples. Then, "You're saying Ralph is immature, he's like a boy, so Gracie has to let him go to the party—is that it? And with this other couple, the woman tells the man what to do, she acts older than he does?"

"Yes, that's the problem! Men are like children, they all need mothers!"

That remark provoked an outcry from the men, of course, and I said "Now wait a moment, you'll get your chance. Tracey, write down what you just said, you have a theme there to go with. Explain it to us, and use those stories to illustrate it."

Here Tracey begins to develop a meaning for this story in her own way. None of these young readers saw that Ralph, having spent his early life in the company of other males, trying to prove himself accepted as one of the guys, must return to his friends for a goodbye look at his past life. And that Gracie is right to let him go. She may not understand the situation in these terms, but her feeling for it is right. And when Tracey says that men all need mothers (perhaps expressing the folklore of the female community), she is saying in effect that men need women who have this intuitive understanding of them. So as I say, in her own way she makes the story meaningful, and as she writes she may see more. There's no need at this stage for me to add anything to what she says, or attempt to reshape her understanding into the literary, academic language one might use in a critical essay—I'd rather she make the story her own.

And while Rahsaan is not interested in talking about how men and women relate to each other, she is—and she offers a challenge to such men, she makes them see there is something here worth talking about. Thanks to her we have a sense that important issues are at stake. Rahsaan's paper, when he finally managed to produce it, had the title "Accept and Do Not Judge," and it began with these words:

> No matter how strange things might seem between a couple, others should not judge them. They have their own way of getting along, and the problems they have will help them understand each other better. Each one needs the other and each is strong in their own way. All that is essential is they learn to get along, and how they get along is no one elses business.

And he went on to talk about how Gracie's friends sneered at Ralph, how they looked down on him as working class—and Rahsaan questioned that presumption of superiority, almost as if he took it personally. He described Ralph as a worthy individual and one not to be controlled by a woman. So he's responding defensively, as much to Gina perhaps as to the story, but he's responding thoughtfully. And he goes beyond personal affairs to talk about the social-class implications in attitudes toward such relationships, so here Gina can learn from him. He ended the piece with the words of his title, "Accept and do not judge."

Some people might not find these classroom exchanges interesting, but to me they touch on the essence of our work—and I'd like to hear more of what the young people in your classroom are saying. But you may not have an opportunity for such exchanges if the authorities move you into the lecture hall, as you fear. At present there's always a chance that from the work people are doing together a new step will come, rather than from the dictate of the professor. There's always a chance for personal expression, when the poetic soul may speak. It would be a shame to lose that possibility. And there's no way of lecturing writing skill into people, so I'm wondering how you will manage when you find yourself standing before multitudes.

So long for now—JR

- - - / / / - - -

19 January

My Dear John,

Sorry not to have written before this, but after the cheery Holiday season (ho-ho-ho) I've been feeling so draggy about getting back to work. Am I up to arguing for poetry and the expressive voice after a shouting match with my ex-wife? These arguments totally unnerve me. I'm left feeling there has been no growth at all, no movement towards self-control, no ability to take anxiety and turn it to something constructive. And then anxiety threatens to turn slowly into despair. Kierkegaard speaks well of despair, he thinks it prepares us for making the hard choices, so maybe I should look into *Either/Or* again, I need some encouragement. 'Are you going to crack the whip', my therapist wants to know, 'and keep that family of yours within spending limits? Reality is painful!' How well I know it.

One morning I arrived at the Kenilworth train station about 20 minutes after a young man, who was described to me as only about 24 and decently dressed, was killed. He had been walking up and down the platform for some time, then he got down onto the track as though he were going to cross it (a common occurrence at these suburban stations), but as the train came on he stopped, stood in front of it and opened his arms. It was shocking to see the mutilated body there and I could hardly pull myself away, the line between life and death fascinates everyone so.

But now it's back to work ready or not. Sometimes I still feel like an outsider here—the only American in our program. In a meeting recently, one of the other lecturers remarked that I was making difficulties, and later when I asked Mercia if she thinks I'm 'difficult' she said, 'Well, you approach things from a different viewpoint than the people around here, and that can be interpreted as being difficult.' I'm just too outspoken, I suppose, and I hold to my own point of view. Which reminds me of what you said earlier about Westerners seeming to be confrontational because they speak their minds so readily, whereas people here are more concerned with fitting into the group. Ironic, isn't it? I've been trying to develop more individuality among the students and meanwhile the culture is shaping me into a more group-sensitive person. Well at least I'm trying.

And now here's our mighty dean bird, addressing the 12 of us who volunteered (some for fear of being fired otherwise) to teach a new masters course in applied linguistics, telling us how necessary that it be made rigourous and demanding. My suggestion that we let the students choose readings for the course themselves, rather than give them a required reading list, was greeted with polite surprise. It was explained to me that 'we must present students with definite information so they come away from the program with something they can use.' They will attend a day and a half of orientation at Waterkloof, and they are to leave it feeling fearful, with a sense of the great demands our coursework will make on them. No light touch here, not a trace of humor, he was deadly serious.

And he would like to start off the first evening of this orientation retreat with a 'structured entertainment', so I've been given the task of planning it, along with Alister. Some of my colleagues want us to play our guitars. Alistair can at least produce some interesting and complicated chords but I just get by with a fast strum. I was thinking of asking everyone to draw time lines showing their individual experiences with language learning, illustrated with little drawings or a few words or even a poetic phrase—nothing serious, mind you. Then we could share these, or even pin them up for all to see. Better yet, I could ask everyone to write down all the books they've read and the one with the longest list gets a master's degree on the spot. Will the dean bird go for that?

Somehow during this week-long orientation program he wants the students to have some experience with psycholinguistics, sociolinguistics, writing process theory, language teaching, stylistics, research, and aesthetics. Twelve lecturers presenting these subjects to 18 students! And as a culminating activity, he has suggested a scenario: It is some future year in the new South Africa and we are in Magistrates Court. Here is a list of persons and the offenses they are being tried for, so what linguistic issues will come up during these hearings? Not a bad idea, I thought. Well, maybe at least this orientation will help us get acquainted and perhaps even find something likeable in each other.

Later (next day, in fact):

It's 2:30 p.m. and I've just returned from visiting Alistair. He's been laid up after a hernia operation, but even when he's in much discomfort he's thinking about our work. One night he dreamt he was lying on something that caused him pain, and when he turned over to get off it he discovered it was a book with the word 'writing' on it. Freud would have no difficulty with this one, he said—a dream that reveals the discomfort work with writing instruction brings to us.

He went on to talk about how writing has the potential for putting power into the hands of students because they might use it to ask questions, and so it offers a threat—which is why writing is regularly suppressed even in the university, where its value is much touted. His example was a recent textbook introducing African literature, which asks students to write new endings to the stories but doesn't mention that they could write stories of their own. In other words, they are asked to mimic the styles of other writers but not to write in their own way, from their own knowledge of the world. He drew parallels between Freud's talking cure and discussion in the classroom, and he talked about the idea of a 'People's Education'. Oh he was on a roll! He talked of confronting the dean bird, particularly about the need for personal writing in our classrooms, because it draws on one's individual rhythm of thought and summons the student's power of language. Without this we get fake writing. He mentioned that with real writing our students have to take responsibility for what they say, and the comments of the others cause them to reflect and to revise or even transform their work and so themselves. He wants to start a small writing group with several of our colleagues, so that we're all encouraged to develop our ideas and perhaps produce something for publication. He energizes me, and after a talk like this I go back to work thinking that what we do is important for these young people.

So I go into the classroom and encourage them to write about what seems important in their lives, but then all these personal troubles appear—the lack of money to pay the fees, for example. There's one student who gave himself the name Searcher because he's always looking for accommodations he can afford, moving from place to place searching for a room, even a floor to sleep on, and squatting right now in the dorm. I wonder how he manages to get his school work done while on the move like that, but he does. Some are very determined. When we hear in class about problems like this we start talking about what can be done, and usually nothing can be done. Indeed, it's my knowing how little can be done to help these people, my pessimism, that makes me—what? Wonder, perhaps, just how much of this writing about personal experience I should encourage.

Shereen Brown, the domestic worker who washes our clothes and cleans my place top to bottom however long it takes, despite my injunction to leave at 1 p.m., all for R35 a week, whose one son became a gangster and was beaten into a week-long coma, now tells me her daughter of 16 can't get into the more selective high school because it's 'full-up' again. And so Shereen, a staunch Christian who tells me she preaches the Lord's word on the train coming here to work, who fasted for 3 days to help her son get better, now says she won't have lunch today because she's fasting again for her daughter. So I called the school and spoke with the headmaster, who said he'd think about it, but probably the girl will have to go to one of the schools that's really overcrowded.

Well, I had a week's vacation away from all this at Arniston, by the sea, with my Lucy and her two young boys. How the sea does relax one. Scraping mussels off the rocks and boiling them, with the lemon butter ready, was a pleasure too. Each night we cooked our chicken or fish on the open fire, and watched the coloured fishermen pass with octopi dangling from their hooks. Not even the sibling rivalry of the boys arguing could put me off, and I told them scary stories at night and saw their wide-open eyes shining in the firelight. Some Boer boys came by one day looking for Matthew, claiming he'd thrown stones at them. I think the Boer War continues still in various ways, yet another undercurrent in South Africa. How long can this country stay afloat?

Well, here's a toast to the world that's coming—Ed

- - -///- - -

January 29

Dear Ed,

Your last letter caused me to sit thinking for some time after I'd read it, wondering how I might respond. You speak of despair, and that word and the mood you feel reminded me of a young man who came to see me not long ago. His mother sent him one afternoon for counseling because she thought he was acting strangely, moodily, and only turned away from her when she asked what was troubling him. He was 18—just out of high school—but looked even younger, and after a time he told me this story of his school life, speaking in a hesitant, boy's voice.

"Oh, it was awful, it was terrible. It seemed like I didn't have any friends, an the teachers didn't like me, an the gym teacher called me a faggot. But it seemed like there was no one to love me, no man an no woman neither, so I decided I had to die. So I cut up twelve pieces of paper, an I wrote the name of a month on each one, an I put 'em in a bowl an I drew one. November—that's when I was gonna to do it. But I got to have a day, so I wrote down the numbers on thirty pieces of paper, an I drew one, an I got 12. November 12. So then I wrote out all the different ways I could do it, an I put those in the bowl, an I got 'cut your throat'! An I thought, Oh no—I can't do that, that's horrible. So I drew again an this time I got 'jump off the Brooklyn Bridge'. So that's what I'm thinkin a doin, in November."

He seemed rather pleased with how his story sounded, now that he had told it to someone. Despair had made him willing to tell all this to a virtual stranger and already he seemed to feel better. I thought he was unlikely to do himself in so long as there was someone willing to hear his story, and I was willing to listen until someone else came into his life who would find him interesting in the night as well as in the day. For it was evident that he despaired of ever being fully himself without someone in his life to love.

You, on the other hand, are more advanced in your despair, for unlike this young man you already have love in your life to confirm you to yourself, It's a very beautiful picture you paint of living by the sea with your woman and her boys, who need you and listen to your stories. So while my young man despairs for lack of something outside himself, you despair for lack of something within, and this thought of the missing whatever-it-is calls into question the character of your very self. So your despair is quite advanced, compared to that of my young man, and whereas he is dependent for relief on chance or some outside circumstance, your misery has given you the possibility of making a change within yourself. And also, according to Kierkegaard, you have before you the prospect of yet further advances in despair. Is that any consolation? "On beautiful terms despair is offered to you," he says, for it urges you to seek after yourself—in contrast to all those others who are lost but don't know it, and so have nothing to look for in themselves.

So you are right that Kierkegaard suggests despair may prepare us for a move, and he speaks of this in *Either/Or*. But his definitive work on the subject is *The Sickness Unto Death*—and isn't that a cheery title? However, I don't recommend that you read this complex work at this time, because you then would need to set aside your despair during a lengthy reading and so might lose the value of it. At present, despair has given you the task of looking into yourself, deciding what you will and will not accept, so as to make the self you want to have. And if one needs a name for this despair, Kierkegaard suggests, one might call it stoicism. This is the feeling expressed, I think, in remarks by the Italian poet Pavese: "It is a fine thing when a young fellow of eighteen or twenty stops to think about his own confused state of mind, clenches his fists and tries to grasp reality. But it is not so good to be doing it at thirty. And doesn't it turn you cold to think you will still be doing it at forty or later?" There must be some advantage in it.

Speaking of stoicism, I am struck by the picture you draw of Alistair lying on his bed of pain and discoursing about his work. The problem of writing instruction troubles his dreams, causing him pain both in bed and out of it. And what he says about writing being regularly suppressed in the university is often quite true, for what is usually wanted there is simply reportage, not a questioning of the way things are. And we find that what passes for training in how to write may actually be training in obedience.

Students enter a writing classroom not knowing beforehand what the *subject* will be, and then often discover that it depends on the particular penchant of an instructor or textbook writer or program director, who requires them to follow a regimen of assignments and produce a few paragraphs on whatever the topics given, and do so in correct form, so many papers of so many pages a semester, each with a thesis statement. So the students follow directions and work up a piece of writing. It takes a certain amount of stoicism on their part to give up their independence and bear with this for a semester or two, it seems to me.

But of course we want young people to take the work of writing seriously, with some sense of commitment to it. The whole age, Kierkegaard said, can be divided into those who write and those who do not write—between those who struggle to produce some meaning, I suppose, and the readers, who only consume. But he continues: "The whole age can be divided into those who write and those who do not write. Those who write represent despair, and those who read disapprove of it and believe they have a superior wisdom—and yet if they were to write, they would write the same thing." I think this suggests there is a certain pain that comes with real writing, requiring as it does serious thought about the dispensation under which one must live and strive, while readers are onlookers who feel superior to all this and wish to remain so.

Oh but see how Alistair has me going now! He and I would get along together very well. But his pain has made him angry and he talks of confronting your dean, insisting that he recognize the importance of real writing in the classroom, when students are engaged with issues important to them. I wouldn't recommend that. A confrontation is simply a contest of vanities, and whoever has the power will win the day. Your dean is not a writer but a reader, and so is satisfied that he has a superior wisdom—and he does have the power. So rather than challenge authority, let us work indirectly like secret agents, talking the accepted line while going on with our own business and achieving our conversions by degrees. It's experience that teaches, not reasons or arguments, so you and Alistair must find ways to give others experience with the kind of work you're doing with young people. Perhaps the dean bird should be invited to join the writing group Alistair would like to organize, as a visitor at least.

It seems, by the way, that your dean as a reader of people has read you quite well. He knows you can be counted on to plan a good interactive "structured entertainment" for the orientation meeting of masters students. Certainly you and Alistair should play your guitars—that's the way to start this program! And ask the others to sing with you. I once taught an in-service course for elementary school teachers called "Improvisation in the Classroom," and I arranged for us to meet in a room with a piano so every class could begin with a song. After a run through "There's a Tavern in the Town" or some other old favorite, we were ready for action. So play a tune at the retreat and ask the others to sing along with you. Teach them a song if they have none in common, and they probably haven't—but we learn a song and already we're working together. They'll be ready then to sing their way through all that heavy stuff coming, the psycholinguistics and the rest of it. By all means, let there be singing.

Yours in the struggle—JR

- - - / / / - - -

5 February

Dear John,

Today we go off to Waterkloof for the linguistics retreat, but I'm taking some time before climbing into the old Peugot to tell you about something that happened this past week. I was sitting with Alistair in the university cafeteria when a portly fellow in a yellow robe and dreadlocked hair walked by carrying in his arms a great load of newsprint. It was evident from just one look at this gentleman that we were in the presence of a comedian of the pure light indeed. He was carrying issues of his own paper, *Hei Voetsek*, which means 'Hey, Fuck Off' in Afrikaans, and I knew this had to be Rastafarian Zebulon Dread. I'd read about him in the Sunday *Argus* and also in the *Mail and Guardian*, which reported his difficulty getting anyone to print his paper because of the rude words in it. His given name is Elliott Paul, and he's a very Xhosa-looking African, but was in fact raised as a coloured in Bonteheuwel and Afrikaans was his first language. I'd been wanting to reach him, thinking I might ask him to speak to my class, or at least get a copy of his newspaper, and in fact I called a number given me by the *Mail & Guardian* with no luck. And now here he is walking by my table!

So I bought a copy of his newspaper and told him I'd been hoping to find him. He turned out to be an articulate, captivating talker, so I asked him if he would come to my tutorial that very afternoon. He played a little hard to get and wanted an honorarium if he were to address an audience, but when I told him I'd given our students the *Argus* article about him as an exam subject, he was eager for a chance to rebut it publicly. We agreed that he would come to the lecture hall that next Monday. He went on then, hopefully offering his newspaper at other tables.

Later in the afternoon I was with my Ximoko Xa Rixaka group (as they've named themselves: Shi-moko Ka Re-sha-sha, which is a Shona idiom called out in praise, meaning something like 'You're great!'), when who should appear on the road outside our prefab classroom, blabbing away to passersby and selling his newspaper? So when I told the students about him, they of course thought it would be much better to invite him in to speak with us than continue the routine work we were doing, so I went out and invited him again. Soon our classroom was ringing with his loud explanations of how he learned English by standing in front of a mirror and shouting 'I am the King! Bow down before me!' and so on. He explained that this improved his articulation, 'Especially because I listened carefully to myself and got over all my feelings of being shy with the English language. And you too have to get out of your ghetto mentality the thought that you can't learn it'. He went on to give some interesting history about ganja, explaining that the name comes from the holy Ganges River, and tracing the ban against it to the McCarthy era in the U.S., when marijuana was outlawed by politicians in order to win the white vote, he said.

He also explained that he himself does not smoke the 'holy herb' anymore, but that it can be very useful in moderation, it helps people get over their ghetto consciousness, the attachments and conditionings they've acquired in their families and tribes. He was quite wonderful. Rastafarians believe themselves to be the lost black tribe of Israel, in search of spiritual enlightenment, and his explanation that Christianity is rejected by them because it has been used to such disastrous effect against Africans, raised a clamour among the Born Agains in the class. And then when he set out to claim that Jesus, born in Nazereth and so a Nazarine, the very people from whom the Rastas get their rule not to cut their hair, was therefore a Rastaman, the questions came at him thick and fast.

On Monday he was no less effective with a much larger group. Several classes met in the lecture hall to hear him (and I did arrange to get him a R100 payment). He began with a critique of the article we had used for the last exam, 'De Bruddahs and Seestahs of Jah' (of God), demonstrating how inaccurately it presented Rastafarian beliefs and how biased it was: 'Even the title is already casting us in a poor light as being unable to speak English properly'. Next he went about the room asking students 'Who are you? And you? Who are you?'—which led to a disquisition on how 'You are not your hand or your leg or your eyes or even your brain. And if you are not that dead body of yours lying in the coffin, well then you must be something other than that body. You are universal spirit!' He went on to mention reincarnation, and he described the *Bhagavad Gita* as a step beyond the *Bible*. I liked best how he kept insisting that the students must question the beliefs they presently have:

> This is the calling of all the zombies to awakening because everyday life in this nothing new old world is driving thinking creative humans into the arms of therapists in need of therapy themselves. Here in this my message is the mother of all therapy and a dead cure from the boredom, drivel, kak and more kak that passes for life around you and me.

He said that Africans needn't be so in awe of European civilization and Sales House clothes and 'a history based on Greek civilization'—other models offered themselves, like the Shiva worshippers of India, who also wear dreadlocks. He went on, excoriating the students for dressing like 'American clones' and claiming that his yellow robe was more suitable because it was comfortable and serviceable. 'You women should go and sew your own clothes', he said. One of the students called out, 'Why are you wearing a Western wristwatch? And what about that factory-made T-shirt you're wearing?' Good old Zebulon only hesitated a moment before explaining that this was simply a stage before a more totally rural existence would be re-created: 'I won't have to wear these things when you come to visit me in the bush'. And when the students have thrown off their ghetto consciousness and made their own choice of life, they too will need to choose new names for themselves as he has done.

It was a great session and the students were energized by it, they threw a lot of questions at him. So I think you'll agree it was worth having him there. Shouldn't more ideas be brought into the classroom by outside voices like this and not everything from the teacher and the textbook? Think of all the good things they might say if they had a willing audience. Last week two Cape Flats coloured poets—James Mathews and Tyrone Appolis—read their work at the museum in Muizenberg, a strange venue for these street poets, as you might call them. One of them has been a noted drunkard, and the other has become somewhat famous for his skill with the penny whistle but now also plays guitar and thumb piano. These two have a poetic intensity in their language and they did get some of that old word magic going. At one point in the evening I heard James complain that the organizers of the new creative writing class at UWC have invited a Welsh poet to give six classes but the local poets in Cape Town are ignored. So I'm thinking that maybe I should take up the cudgels for them, but will anyone else think that maybe the locals know something the professors don't?

And now I'm off to Waterkloof—Ed

CHAPTER 5

— ✪ —

A Self
to be Confused About

17 February

My Dear Friend,

Well, the retreat was something of a delightful success, if that means getting to know each other and learning what we'll be doing together. We drove up to the place, Bloublommetzieskloof Farm, in a peaceful valley along a gravel road about an hour's drive from Cape Town on the way to Stellenbosch. (Bloublommetjes is a type of water lily that is eaten here, the flowers fried with meat, although I haven't tasted it yet.) There's a large old main house used for meetings and meals, and several smaller, Dutch-style homes painted white with thatched roofs, where we slept four to a room. A 10-minute walk through some veldt brings one to a dam holding back a small lake where we could go swimming.

To open the meeting, Alistair and I played our guitars, and then went on to provide the 'structured entertainment' called for by the dean. There were some amusing moments. When the group was told, 'Each of you walk round and tell someone else an interesting thing you've done', one of the students, Rashid, told us he was telepathic and asked if he could have a chance to demonstrate his ability. He would need only our faith and a subject who would allow his mind to be read. Sinfree Makoni, exalted head of the applied linguistics program, volunteered. He was directed to leave the room and when out of sight to assume a 'strange position'. Rashid would then receive a mental impression of this position and tell us what it was. Sinfree left the room and went into the corridor, out of sight. Rashid called to him, instructing him to communicate his position by thought waves and then to ask, 'What position am I in?' So when Sinfree called out the question, Rashid shouted back to him, 'Well, you're in the position of a fool of course!' Sinfree came back to us blushing, I'm sure, although we couldn't see it because he's quite a dark African. Surely, all this has something to do with applied linguistics.

In any case, we had a good time. Then by way of getting into the more serious matters, sociolinguistics and the rest, I asked the students to write about the best or the worst experience they'd had with language learning, and to say what idea or theory about language the teacher in question seemed to be illustrating. They told us some good stories. Lwando wrote about winning an essay contest in secondary school with a paper on how the schools could help the police do their work more efficiently, and the theory of language this experience illustrates, he said, is that the purpose of language learning is to make the work of the authorities more efficient. He is usually so evasive, so quiet and shy, but with a certain ironic look in his eye—his writing often shows an oppositional attitude. Clearly he was required to write that essay, so he gave the authorities what they wanted. In fact, the most striking aspect of these stories was how few of them reported positive experiences.

Bakhtin says that 'Only in an atmosphere of social sympathy is a free and confident gesture possible', and then every spoken or written word, 'and not one slumbering in a dictionary', expresses the hero (*Bakhtin School Papers*)—so I suppose Lwando did not feel himself a hero since his winning essay wasn't a free gesture. But with all the economic or social pressures pushing us one way or another, when is the self able to make that gesture? Where is this atmosphere of social sympathy Bakhtin speaks of? Not many of these students have found it in their classrooms, it seems.

I find him fearful reading—riveting, but fearful in his seeming claim that economic class may determine absolutely everything in an utterance. The individual person, the self, so completely disappears, leaving the mind a hollow chamber echoing and re-echoing the voices and dictates of the social forces in which we are immersed. I'm finding this thought everywhere now in the stuff they call postmodernist, and I wonder what it means for the work we do. We always talk to students as if they can really be acting subjects, making choices for themselves—so I wonder.

I'm not sure myself which way to go sometimes, towards academic discourse or individual expression. I'm having difficulty holding on to the notion that a language class should be a place where each person will express his or her particular experience of the world, including the readings we assign—that individual expression is all there is to it. And here comes the old dean bird saying 'That's just not good enough! It's banal!' When I suggested that more creative writing be done in the English department, the coordinator *hissed* at me: 'The students want practice in how to write for exams!' The writing required in that department tends toward literary criticism, which I suppose is preparation for something but no one explains what, except to say the students must get ready for the exams.

Alistair feels we must give students a strong sense that the skills they learn in this program will prepare them to fit into the university community. He's quite insistent they be taught explicitly about structure and form and the academic conventions, although in a way that doesn't rob individuals of their uniqueness. But I think you intend to promote a more distinct, even eccentric individualism—or is that too strong a way of putting it? At least you seem to have an interest in drawing out the dark, secret self in people. I'm thinking of something I heard you say once, that all the theorizing today about education lacks a sense of sin. Yes, I often feel so too, and try to get my students to feel more comfortable somehow with writing about themselves and even their transgressions. Alistair is very good at bringing up ethical issues in the classroom, and he manages to be interesting even though there's no sin anywhere is his work. He expects his students to write about various issues in expository prose and learn that skill. But then you say that narrative is the basis of all writing, and I wonder if any extended research has ever been done on this. And when you say the teaching of writing influences character or tends to produce a particular kind of person, I wonder how we're going to get evidence for that. How can we ever convince anyone else?

I was talking to my therapist about you and Alistair as sort of polar opposites in my life. The loving, sincere classroom versus the ironic, humorous and perhaps a little more dangerous classroom. She was remarking how these two persons live uncomfortably with each other in my mind, and it's difficult to find a harmony when I'm so ill at ease, wrestling with these two . . . angels . . . demons? And then the question came to me, which classroom are you really in?

I remember that in our sociolinguistics class back at NYU you said very little, so of course we wondered what you were thinking. Then whenever you did say something there was that woman who always disagreed with you, and you would go along with her. I mean, you would say 'Yes', and then go on developing her argument so that it seemed even stronger—as if you and she were working on it together. She must have got really frustrated. You played a devious game, now that I think about it— you could be on either side or both at once. You praise Bernstein but I've seen you nodding along while someone talked about his limitations. So now when I look back over our correspondence I wonder sometimes just where you do stand.

But I keep trying some of your material. When I gave our student-assistants that Navajo story about names, a very interesting discussion got going. Libra told us about a Xhosa name taboo: She's not permitted to say her father-in-law's name, ever! Nor can she use any word in which the first syllable is the same as the first syllable of his name. Her mother-in-law helped her make a list of words to use as substitutes for the prohibited words, and she had to memorize that list. So now when she speaks Xhosa, those listening to her must sort out for themselves what she's talking about. The word for this custom is *hlonipha*, which means the signs of respect a bride must show her father-in-law.

And Nobuntu Bala-Bala, commenting on how the young Navajo refused his parents' offer of a bride, mentioned the word *ukuthomba*, which refers to the prohibition against discussing love matters with one's parents until after marriage. I suppose the views of young people on the subject are not important until a marriage has been arranged. Then Dziko (Zee-koh) said that when she was born in the Transkei (one of the 'independent' homelands the apartheid government established to sequester the Africans) she was given the name Enkululeko (Freedom), but when she got older she rejected that name and chose to be Dziko (The World) instead. But now that South Africa is truly free she's willing to be called Enkululeko again. Everyone had something to say, and after a discussion like this I can't help but feel I've been with some very interesting individuals.

Yet here at the university many people act as if they've been thinking like Bakhtin or Roland Barthes all along and agree that the individual person, the subject, is a myth—so there's no need to be concerned with individual expression, they can just go on teaching the course of study, point by point. Of course there are a few dreamers here and there like me who won't surrender the self. I've just read *Sylvia*, the biography of Ashton-Warner, whom you admire, and it was a painfully entertaining book. I wonder if her story is a refutation of Bakhtin, because she was certainly a character—that is, she gave a very convincing performance as an independently acting subject. And she did some remarkably creative things with children. I'm sure I have a childish streak in me as rich as any she drew on. Not one of her books is in the university library or the public library near me. The system goes on without her, and so maybe she never really existed and Bakhtin is right.

Anyway, here's a toast to the System—Ed

- - -///- - -

March 15

Dear Ed,

Thanks for taking me along, by way of your letter, to the linguistic program's retreat, one highlight of which was certainly Rashid's demonstration of his telepathic power. I like a "structured" entertainment where the unplanned is allowed to happen and so delivers to us an unexpected message. In this case a message that might be phrased as "Those who are expecting miracles deserve to be deceived." Another stroke for rationalism, I'd say. Rashid has given a parody of those charlatans who promise to demonstrate spoon bending, faith healing, mind reading and all the rest of it—he knows how language is used to prepare the scene of revelation. Begin by offering the promise of a miracle, stress the importance of having faith, specify the steps a believer must take to help bring the miracle to pass—and if it does not happen, faith was weak or a misstep taken. Or the planets were not properly aligned—there's always an explanation. Does this have something to do with applied linguistics? Oh yes, for it concerns how language is used by miracle workers. Study that and the magic is soon gone.

Certainly this is true of literature. When a poem or story becomes an artifact for study and is no longer a lived experience, the magic goes out of it. You speak of beginning scholars at UWC writing essays "that tend toward literary criticism"—and that can be a useful training for the analytical intelligence because a situational text offers them problems of interpretation, but I hope they consider first their individual experience with the poem or story so they have both the text and themselves to examine. We already have a sufficiency of literary critics who lay out a text and dissect it happily like vivisectionists whistling while they work, or deconstructionists who find a text so riven with contradiction that one wonders how it could ever have had any life at all. And too many literary theorists who enlist the text in some ideological struggle against the patriarchy or capitalism or whatever, like a press-gang kidnapping the hapless. One doubts that these people can give themselves to a poem and have the lived experience of it. I'm reminded again of the professor who told me he's no longer interested in literature, although he continues to talk about it, explain it, analyze it—without any hope or even thought, I suppose, that one of those poems or stories might so enchant the young people who read with him as to make a subtle change in one's self.

There's a story by Chekhov that speaks of this far more persuasively than I can. "Home" is about a father who returns one evening from his work as a prosecutor to discover that his son, only 7, has been smoking his tobacco that day and the day before. "I am angry with you," he tells the boy, "and don't love you anymore." But he will not punish the child for that would only cause him to hide his vices, so he tries to reason with him: It's not right to take someone else's property, smoking is bad for you—and while he is talking the boy's attention wanders, he toys with pencil and paper. How much more easily such questions are settled in the courtroom than at home, the father thinks.

So then at bedtime he tells the child a story, making it up as he goes along, about an emperor's son who had every virtue and only one vice—smoking. The son fell ill through smoking and died, leaving his old father with no one to save him from the enemies who came and killed the old man, and destroyed the garden where they had walked together, "and now there are neither cherries, nor birds, nor little bells in that garden. That's what happened." The boy has followed this tale with rapt attention, and now "his eyes were clouded by mournfulness and something like fear; for a moment he looked pensively at the dark window, shuddered, and said, in a sinking voice, 'I am not going to smoke any more.'" The father feels guilty for having manipulated the child in this way, and wonders why morality and truth must

> never be offered in their crude form, but only with embellishments, sweetened and gilded like pills? It's not normal. . . . It's falsification . . . deception . . . tricks. . . . He thought of the jurymen to whom it was absolutely necessary to make a "speech," of the general public who absorb history only from legends and historical novels, and of how he himself had gathered an understanding of life not from sermons and laws, but from fables, novels, poems.

"Poems are spells for the soul," Plato said. And in *Laws* a poet must be at least 50 and certified by the state before he is allowed to practice his art; we must be careful, you see, about who is allowed to tell the lies that will shape youthful character. So I would think that as we read poetic fictions with youngsters we might consider what attitudes are being taught, what sort of person our work with them tends to produce.

Yet Bakhtin, you say, makes "the individual person, the subject, completely disappear," and the postmodernists have abolished the autonomous self, so you wonder what effect can we have on those young people who come to us. But consider this: If no one is an individual self, an acting subject, then who do we blame for insult and injury? There's a problem for you. No wonder so many articles and books are being produced with titles like *Postmodern Ethics, Writing and the Moral Self, Foregrounding Ethical Awareness in Composition and English Studies.* No wonder so many people are looking for leaders or gurus to tell them what to do, having lost all sense of possessing an independent volition or weary of not knowing which way to turn and feeling themselves adrift.

In fact, however, Bakhtin insists on the individual as a moral agent, on one's ethical responsibility. "There is no alibi for being," he remarks—no excuse for giving up one's moral freedom and the burden of individual responsibility. He was, after all, an admiring reader of Dostoevsky, who in the person of the Grand Inquisitor tells us that when the significance of conscious choice is denied then real agency is handed over to "miracle, mystery, and authority." So writing is not simply a matter of language exchanging words with itself, but is rather an effort to impose voice and moral will on language and give it meaningful shape. Bakhtin insisted on "answerability," on the individually answerable act (*Toward a Philosophy of the Act*). He was certainly no postmodernist, contrary to what you may have been told.

It may be true that we are all social selves—each of us a gathering of voices with no hope of ever peeling away the layers of influence to find a private, unitary, "real" self. Ibsen's Peer Gynt, late in life at the end of his adventures, sits peeling away the layers of an onion, counting off his various identities so as to reach the germ of his own true self, but of course neither he nor the onion had anything at the center. This may be a fearful thought, as you suggest, but we need not worry about it. If we have no center then it's evident that unlike Peer Gynt we must each make a choice, for good or ill, and give ourselves a center by specializing in one among our various identities, as you and I have decided to become teachers.

Of course that hasn't closed off or solved the problem of identity. A teacher, as Kierkegaard would say, is a helper who exercises his or her need to help by practicing one's own disunity among others struggling to become. Our own personal struggle limits what we can see or understand in another, but the recognition of our common striving opens the possibility of mutuality. So let us say that we have decided to become teachers of a particular kind or disposition.

No doubt in this becoming we were influenced by the social and economic forces that are part of our histories, but now as teachers we find ourselves questioning and contending with those same forces as if we have an independent self that can stand aside momentarily and judge. Our aim, as Kierkegaard would say, is to become free within the reality to which we each belong. And we might call this striving self *the hunger*. All his life Peer Gynt had said that a man ought to be himself, but finally at the end of Ibsen's poetic drama he is told, "You have never been yourself!" because he has lived aesthetically, self-indulgently, moment to moment, without the *hunger* for doing anything in particular, either good or evil. Dante would have consigned him to Limbo with the praiseless and the blameless, but finally the Button Molder comes to melt down his soul because Peer has made no use of it.

As teachers of writing we are very much concerned, it seems to me, with an individual, self-observing *hunger* making choices. We encourage young people to believe they are capable of controlling the texts they work on and becoming authors, capable of exercising their judgment and so responsible for the choices they make as acting subjects. The postmodern dismissal of the subject, however, relieves them of that responsibility and like Peer Gynt they need be no one in particular, they can live anonymously. They can wander about zombie-like, hoping to be told who they are. They can be followers. Or they may go seeking a cure, for without a center one's head becomes populated with discordant voices and that's a sickness. There are healers and mystics and gurus aplenty to take over the governance of all these people—and then they'll need your Rastafarian Zebulon Dread to wake them out of their sleep. Postmodernism encourages mysticism, it seems to me, by insisting there is no subject and all we know of reality is rhetoric. So I'll say it again: As teachers of writing, we are working to develop the acting subject, who takes very little on faith and is suspicious even of himself or herself as the case may be.

You suggest that I want to draw on the dark, secret self in people, that I'm interested in sin. How right you are! Yesterday as I was crossing Sixth Avenue a deep strong voice shouted at me: "**What you think you doin goin like that**?" and a hand reached out for me. A very large and very angry man, evidently homeless, with a battered shopping cart filled with the miscellanea of his wandering life, stood glaring at me. I had drifted out of the pedestrian crossing to pass behind him there at the curb and he didn't like that. Another troubled soul among the many now in the streets. I said, "Oh you're so right, and thank you sir!" as I turned and passed on the other side. He nodded, satisfied, having reformed a sinner. And I thought, Of course he's very concerned that everyone stay within the lines because he has such difficulty doing so himself. And this is what I mean by sin: to step outside conventional lines of thought or expression so as to explore new territory and discover new possibilities. "There is only one thing in life worth living for, and that is sin," according to Lady Francesca Wilde: "We are above respectability." To be so takes some flexibility of mind and perhaps a certain nerve.

In our work there are accepted lines of practice that teachers are supposed to follow as they shepherd their students along to the final exam, but some of us are wandering from the path. We would like our young people to produce something other than a response to the next essay in the textbook or to another assigned topic, something other than the descriptive essay, the comparative essay, the argumentative essay, each with a thesis statement. Yesterday we wrote poems—we were taking a break after 2 days of hard work—and at the end of the period, as we were leaving the room, one young woman asked me to look at hers:

> I am the woman who started it all.
> I am the sister who kept it together.
> I am the epitome of the universe.
> I am the answer to the mystery.
>
> I am an ordinary girl.
> I am the one you can talk to.
> I am my own quiet person.
> I am and always will be all this.

> It is the day my father got sick.
> Sadness is a close neighbor: pain,
>   concern, hospital, medicine, quietness,
>   life is short.
> I am the one who is thankful for tomorrow.
> (Kelly Montague)

No one outside my classroom, no one in authority that is, seems to know we do these things and never open the textbook, we don't have time for that. I went over to the department office for my mail, and the secretary there seemed abstracted, perhaps unhappy, so I sang to her: "You are my sunshine/My only sunshine/You make me happy when skies are gray/You'll never know dear/how much I love you/please don't take my sunshine away." She smiled, she thinks I'm a harmless nut.

So long for now—JR

- - - / / / - - -

22 June

Dear John,

Sorry to have delayed writing for so long. Sometimes it seems there is simply no time to write, or that writing can never keep up with living. The push to get through the work of the day makes this kind of thought a luxury and raises doubts about its power to change anyone or anything. What use or meaning will it ever have in most of the South African lives that come into these classrooms? Maybe writing is only for the rich, the poor being too busy with their starving to bother with it.

Yesterday was cold and gloomy, and the students seemed to come in reluctantly so I thought of starting us off with a song to warm us up. But Namakula said 'No, Mr. Katz—it's too cold today. We need a bowl of soup, Mr. Katz.' I only had a song for them instead of soup, but we did sing it and that drew us all together, we felt ready to go on.

Sihamba nodudu	*Let us go together*
Siyifuni sangoma	*To find the medicine,*
Sifiki sangoma	*And bring the sangoma*
Sat'um twanuyagula	*Woman to the sick child.*

Chorus:

Umtway uyagula	*The child is sick,*
Umpetwe yini na	*She is suffering.*
Umtwan uyagula	*For the sick child*
Umthaghatu sendlile.	*We must get the sorceress.*

Of course if the old dean bird walked by the door and heard this he might not understand. Like I said, I could get into real trouble listening to you. But thanks for taking the time to write your letters, I do enjoy them. Even your riff on anxiety and despair a while back lifted my spirits. But sometimes I find it odd that you are so critical of ideas that may relate to a more metaphysical way of looking at experience, since you say things yourself that seem to encourage that point of view. I've heard you talk about how everyone's philosophy is myth, how by mythmaking we feel our way to a truth that holds for us as a people and unites us against the Beast of Doubt. In fact, Alistair says that your way of thinking has more in common with mystics and esoteric thinkers than you seem to realize.

The other day he was saying that we need to identify with something larger than the self or our lives will seem meaningless. We need to live in harmony with the universe. Have you ever come across *A Way of Knowing*, edited by William I. Thompson? Maybe we can think of the world as a kind of living organism—the Gaia hypothesis. Alistair sees the human mind as part of a great living universal mind and that gives him the ability to withstand or overcome what you call the Beast of Doubt. Sometimes I think your comments about writing or the way we should work with people approach this same feeling of identity with the universe. Like that time in the sociolinguistics class when we were talking about the self as an expression of social forces, and you mentioned what you called the identity question: What is this place and this company, that I may know myself?

Doesn't that mean we know ourselves by knowing others, working with them? This year we decided to use your idea of sunshine partners in all our tutorials, so every student in the program has a partner to work with and be responsible for (as in your 'Scenes from the Writing Workshop'). That's worked very well for us, and the students like having someone to share their experience with. Isn't this how we achieve identification, by sharing ourselves, revealing ourselves to others?

This term I have three tutorial groups: One calls itself the Wake-Up Club, and the others are the Freedom Learners and the Bambanani (Hold Hands Together). First I gave them a spirited reading of your Navajo story in which the names of the characters reveal so much about them, and we talked about the meaning of the story and those names. Then they wrote about their own names, including nicknames, and what meanings they have. When they read those papers aloud I was surprised at the almost boastful pleasure they took in this reading, I thought they would be much more shy. Here's how one paper began:

My parents gave me the name Lindilizwi, a Xhosa name which means 'wait for a voice'. I grew up being called by this name. Then when I was in standard four, I started to realize that each and every name has a meaning. I used to sit by myself and wonder what my name meant. I have tried several times to think it deeply, but all in vain. I went to ask my mother to tell me exactly whose voice I must wait for. She told me that it was the Lord's voice. She added that I must always wait for a voice. I must not act behind my parent's voice or instructions. Lord, to me, does not only mean 'God,' but my parents too are my lords and I have to respect them as they too respect God. My name also means that I must not ignore other people's advice.

And this one:

Moloke is a Northern Sotho name which literally means 'You Are a Man'. I got this name after three months I spent in the initiation school [for circumcision]. Before I got this name I was known as Mpherephere which means troubles. Most people are surprised by this troublesome name. After three months I back from the Initiation School my father, mother, and my relatives had to organize a party to welcome me. It where they settled for what name should they have to give me. As a result I was recited Moloke. That is why even today proud of my name. When some one called me Mpherephere I cry because to be called by that name was no more supposed to be since I left it on the mountain.

Here's the beginning of one more, which has a certain poignancy I think:

My name is 'Mtandeni'. I was named by my father in my infancy. I was so named because I looked ugly when I was a baby. Everyone used to say, 'Hey, this child is ugly'. So my father named me 'Mtandeni' which means 'Love Him'. I like my name and it is very uncommon. I have never heard of anyone with a similar name to mine. That is why I am proud of it.

Then we went on to do a longer personal experience essay, and to get that started I gave them the phrase 'I felt oppressed when. . .', and the student could put down a note about any memory that came to mind, list the words or images it suggested, and then write about it. So Thandiwe (whose name means The Loving One) told about sitting in a schoolroom under a leaking roof while the teacher waved his switch, making the air hiss. And Paki (Witness) told us what it was like to be the linen boy in the big house bringing sheets and towels: 'My mother gave me the name Linen so the Master would be able to order his slave about easily. But I'll give my children only African names'. I wonder if this isn't just a bit ironic, everyone having such a good time writing about feeling oppressed.

But speaking of feeling oppressed, the work here drives me like a donkey and I can hardly catch my breath. Is it possible for me to live the interior life Kierkegaard speaks of in *Either/Or*, in which living well is not a matter of money? With two daughters to feed, I find the prospect scary. And somehow it begins to seem as if the 'universal' man he talks about is the most complete conformist, since 'the truly extraordinary man is the truly ordinary man'. Oh the choices K asks one to make! But there's no time here to contemplate and make either/or choices, we all just go along looking to survive day by day. There's a little poem by Han-shan on the Buddhist way of dealing with all this—maybe I should try it:

> *A thatched hut is a home for a country man,*
> *Horse or carriage seldom pass my gate:*
> *Forests so still all the birds come to roost,*
> *Broad valley streams always full of fish.*
> *I pick wild fruit in hand with my child,*
> *Till the hillside fields with my wife.*
> *And in my house what do I have?*
> *Only a bed piled high with books.*

Meanwhile, the financing for our writing program is very uncertain. It's not even in the university budget but is supported out of a special fund, so I worry about the possibility of not getting paid. Or maybe this course I teach will be absorbed into the regular English program, and then will there be a job for me at UWC next year?

How much of this uncertainty everywhere is a consequence of capitalism? It seems that knowledge itself has become a product, with more and more competition to package it for consumption, and less and less need in Academia for packagers. Then too, the so-called 'knowledge' that is required in this system becomes debased, gathered into huge catalogues of fact. Facts become the measure of intellectual wealth, and one must be processed through a giant Memorization Machine in order to have any chance at all for a job after graduation. And that may not be much of a chance since even our college graduates often can't find work. Here in South Africa the capitalist set-up makes it virtually impossible for those people with a different culture and a different language to catch up with those who got into the market first and now hold the few positions of wealth available. In spite of all the effort to keep down unrest, the country could break up into tribalism.

And then we have those horrible TV programmes from the USA, with their trivializaton of every thought and feeling. It seems that everyone is watching *The Bold and the Beautiful*. Yesterday Mikateko brought in *True Love* magazine, with a story about some fellow making love to his son's wife. The system provides people with entertainment at the most superficial level to divert their thinking from the deteriorating economic situation. Serious reading is simply not possible for most, and personal expression or independent thinking is marginalized by the mass production of trashy entertainment.

Meanwhile, outside on the streets real lives are being lived and lost. One of our bright young tutors, Jenna, was returning home from the university in a taxi, along the very taxi route I've been using, when two gunmen pulled up and shot the driver to death. She caught two bullets herself, one of which severed her spinal cord and now she's a quadriplegic. The colleague who told me about this said, 'I went to see her but she wouldn't see anyone, she's in such a deep depression. She was a dancer too, you know. It was a pirate taxi, but none of the taxis have any sort of insurance'. This episode unnerved me, and I found myself in the mind of this young girl imagining my whole life still before me while I lay there in that condition.

But I'm getting along well enough. Although I'm constantly casting about for ways to make some money. Have I mentioned my new writing workshop with senior citizens? Twelve old Jewish ladies from various parts of the world, and they have plenty to say! We meet once or twice a month and they actually pay me to sit there among them. Sometimes South Africa seems a very strange place.

Signing off for now—Ed

· - - - / / / - - -

9 July

Dear John,

Well, it seems I need to keep writing to . . . what? Make some sense of my own experience, maybe. I hope you don't mind putting up with me for a few more pages.

The Wake-up Club now has a treasurer. Vusumzi was absent from a meeting one morning and later he told me his sister had been stabbed to death. So while he was gone for the funeral, one of the students collected 30 cents from each of us for a card. Then we decided to have a permanent treasurer and we elected Bernice. Each of us gives her 5 or 10 cents a week, so we have a fund for other needs that might come up. When we were reading *Down Second Avenue* I asked the class if we should use some of the money to copy a few pages for those who couldn't afford to buy the book, but that proposal was rejected after considerable argument. It was interesting to see these students negotiating about some issue that was actually affecting us right there in the classroom.

I wasn't very enthusiastic about the reactions they wrote to passages in the book. Few of them seemed to really get into it and tell how they felt about it. (I'm enclosing a copy of the written directions I gave them.) They were only trying to do 'what Ed wants', it seemed, or they just couldn't respond freely. Most of them wrote so little of what they really felt that it was hard to find a thought or observation in any paper that the writer could go one with. I need to find some way to encourage students to expand their writing. Somewhere in *Writers Writing*, Lil Brannon suggests that students could do a second draft by writing it from a different point of view, not their own. And Peter Elbow gives a list of ideas for revision—like rewriting for a different audience, changing narrators, and so on. I was talking to Alistair about this and he said we can get better results by conferencing individually with each student, but is there time for that?

I was wondering if I've portrayed Alistair's views as accurately as possible, there may be some misunderstanding. I mean, the 'loving classroom' he talks about doesn't necessarily prescribe a particular set of practices, and he certainly does get good results from his students. I still feel it would be best if I could create the kind of classroom community wherein everyone can feel at ease with each other. We can still try to reach a consensus in spite of our disagreements about the issues we discuss, develop a class point of view and come into harmony with each other. Surely that would be a great benefit for the learning environment—this seems clear enough.

Ah, but my workshops with the old ladies keep me rolling. We meet at the Cape Seniors Club at No. 3 Bellevue Road in Seapoint, in a comfortable one-story family house that was in fact once owned by one of our ladies. Just inside the door there's a spacious lounge where the old folks watch ballet movies on Friday nights, while the writing group meets in a small room beyond, facing the street. We sit at three card tables, except for those two or three with back problems who sit close by in easy chairs. Tea and biscuits are brought in by Katy, an African domestic at the centre. And so here these sweet old ladies, who bring with them from all over the world the experience of long lives, sit with me to talk and write.

Although perhaps sweet is not quite the right word. Last week after the session one of them warned me about another: 'She's evil, I'm telling you! She told me I should maybe stop coming to our writing workshop because I'm not feeling well. Can you imagine? She tells me to give up my one enjoyment in life! She's trying to kill me, don't you see?' On the other hand, Georgette is a guardian angel. She's partly blind, can't read, has no more than a primary school education, but she writes with a sharp irony and an ear for way people talk. She doesn't write her papers, actually, but composes them in her head, fixes them in memory, and then recites them to the class when she is ready. She has a wry sense of humor, an ironic touch: 'I don't know English well. But I write in English because it is the language I know best.' After each session she invites me for a lunch of her own Mediterranean delicacies (she was raised in Syria and Egypt), and then gives me food already packaged for my daughters. She's an angel and a strict atheist—which I didn't believe was possible.

In our last workshop meeting we were trying to write short stories, and it occurred to me how difficult it is to think of plots that really work. So maybe I could help them by taking plots from the old myths, perhaps, and then we could write them up with modern-day characters. What do you think of that?

Well, it's so late I can hardly stay awake. Please do write when the urge takes you. And keep the pot boiling.

—Ed

- - - / / / - - -

August 10

Dear Ed,

So Alistair tells you that the only way to overcome one's angst and find meaning in this uncertain world is to identify with something larger than the self—but what? In answer to that call I feel perhaps the time has come for me to reveal to you the Philosophy of This Is, which offers a sustaining revelation, a secret known only to a few. And as we go along here, and if you prove yourself worthy, I may consider inducting you into the mysteries, into the Fellowship of This Is, where you will feel quite secure at last.

Alistair offers a different philosophy, one that would bring you into harmony with the universe. Perhaps, however, he and I are not living in the same universe, for the one he inhabits is a living organism that cares for its own, whereas mine is simply a field of action where we take care of ourselves. People like William Irwin Thompson, who in recent times have popularized the Gaia hypothesis, are storytellers who refurbish and pass on the old myths, and this one is very old. I rather like what Nietzche has to say about it:

> Let us beware of thinking that the world is a living being.[. . .] Let us beware of believing that the universe is a machine.[. . .] Let us beware of attributing to it heartlessness and unreason or their opposites: it is neither perfect nor beautiful, nor noble, nor does it wish to become any of these things; it does not by any means strive to imitate man. None of our aesthetic and moral judgments apply to it. Nor does it have an instinct for self-preservation or any other instinct. (*The Gay Science*, §109)

But it does offer at least a field of action where we can make something, so let's get on with it! As everyday you go into that classroom and try to make something there with your youngsters and so become yourself. What better way to live in harmony with the universe than to use it?

Yet so many feel a need to make life simpler by surrendering themselves to some higher authority. Alistair evidently shares the mystical yearnings of Heidegger, who said that "the ability to accept something greater above oneself is the true secret of greatness." In this diminishment of the individual's value or importance we have an early inspiration for postmodernism, which ridicules the very idea of self-determination. In fact, the secret of greatness seems to lie in giving up one's independent self and joining a mass movement—as Heidegger found something greater than himself in the blood and soil mysticism of National Socialism, welcoming Hitler's seizure of power as a new act in the history of Being, the dawning of a new epoch. We've seen what came of that.

But if to live and act in this world you need to be assured of a higher truth or feel yourself part of an important movement, then I have something for you. I am prepared to offer you the opportunity of a lifetime—the chance to take possession of a secret knowledge and come into harmony with the great This Is! Are you ready to enter into this fellowship and join our movement? Such a decision should not be made lightly, so think it over while I go on for now.

I'm glad to hear about your workshop for senior citizens, which sounds to me like the real thing and not too far from the Fellowship of This Is, which offers companionship if not harmony. Here you're helping these old ladies draw on their many years to make some expression of themselves, and what they tell is there on paper to give pleasure to themselves and perhaps to others. Let me make a suggestion. You mention how they've been writing short stories and finding it difficult to invent good plots, but I think the writing of a story begins not with plot but with character: We set some characters in motion and follow them around, recording what happens and that's the plot. So these women might talk about the characters they've known, and I'm sure each of them will think of someone to tell a story for her, so to speak.

It must be interesting to work with these women who are old enough to be close to the truth—and then you go on to the young people of the Wake-Up Club and the Bambanani, for whom much in life is still unknown. We are among the fortunate few, you and I, having this work we love to do and being paid for it. One's sense of worth or inner peace may not depend on the possession of wealth, as Kierkegaard suggests, but on having one's own work in the world. On the other hand, I'm sure he would agree with you that not having enough money to feed one's children is worrisome. The Buddhist poet Han-shan would invite you to console yourself with the spiritual superiority that poverty or rural isolation supposedly gives, but in the meantime your children are hungry. I seem to remember, by the way, that Jack Kerouac wove two or three of Han-shan's poems into the dialogue of *The Dharma Bums*, where the idea is to escape from the complexities of modern life into the country and its promise of inner peace. But surely this is not the time for any of us to settle into oriental resignation. All this will be further illuminated for you in my exposition of the Philosophy of This Is.

There in South Africa you're living in a dynamic society where great numbers of restless people are on the move, looking for more to eat—and what is required of them in a democratic, capitalist system is a certain individualism. You recognize this and fret that Kierkegaard, whom you admire, seems to valorize the conformist as the "universal man." In fact, Kierkegaard is very distrustful of mass man, which leads him to place great stress on the importance of the individual. When he says "The truly extraordinary man is the truly ordinary man," he is affirming the value of ordinary people and remarking on the heroism required for any of us to acquit ourselves well in a world of sorrows—a heroism that can often be observed among the most ordinary people. Surely, many of the stories or novels now being written in South Africa about the lives of individuals from the shacks and settlements, from the villages or the streets of busy towns, are in effect hero stories—like *Down Second Avenue* or Mark Mathabane's *Kaffir Boy* (which I've just read).

You are a part of this dynamism and feel so driven that you can hardly catch your breath, you say, and have "no time to contemplate and make either/or choices." Yet you contemplate the Gaia hypothesis, there seems time enough for that. Before you take it as the answer to life's conundrum, however, I would like to offer you very shortly another possibility—the choice of This Is! So be ready, be prepared!

Capitalism: You speak of how it "provides people with entertainment at the most superficial level, to divert their thinking from the deteriorating economic system." This reminds me of those deep thinkers like Herbert Marcuse who would uplift the masses by prohibiting works of fiction or other speech they regard as morally intolerable—and do so by any means at hand, by legal sanction or extralegal force if necessary. Tolerance is simply another instrument of the capitalists ("repressive tolerance," he called it). Come the new socialist state, you understand, all that is vulgar in popular culture will be swept into the dustbin of history. Along with such stories as you've mentioned reading with your students by the likes of Can Themba, I suppose, with their gangs of street children, their predatory train passengers, and the man who made his wife serve dinner every night to the suit her lover had left behind. Not uplifting enough! The masses are to spend their leisure time on worthy cultural pursuits, whether they like it or not. I myself, however, have no objection to entertainment, superficial or otherwise, and would prefer it to the mystical as a distraction from the stress of daily life. There is little difference between the cultural commissar and the guru, for neither has a sense of humor.

Why you keep going on about capitalism puzzles me. It's not capitalism but the capitalists, who will squeeze anyone for a profit, we need be concerned about. What is the difference between capitalism and communism? Capitalism is the exploitation of man by man, and communism is the opposite. (That's an old joke from Eastern Europe.) Do you feel that you have been exploited by the System? At least the System has offered you choices—but the problem with having choices to make is that we can rarely be sure of their consequences, and now there you are in South Africa! However, a person in your state of mind can hope to find salvation in the Philosophy of This Is, so take heart—I bring the answer for those ready to hear and to follow.

Now for your letter of May 9:

I enjoyed hearing about the Wake-Up Club and how they decided to elect a class treasurer. That came about because of a common concern they felt, and it seems to me that's how most of the activity in our classrooms should arise—from needs and concerns recognized by the students themselves. You are preparing them for the move from a positional context in which they receive directions to a situational context where the unexpected may happen. We get something started with them— give them *Down Second Avenue* to read, perhaps, as you did—and then wait to see what they'll make of it. But it seems the Wake-Up Club held themselves in reserve and only responded with "what Ed wants"—and no wonder, considering all the directions you gave: too many directions, a whole sheet of directions! As if to say they need only follow you along, step by step, and they'll get somewhere. No wonder they're not interested in revising their work, it's not really theirs but only something done to satisfy you. So give fewer directions, fewer steps to follow! Let choices be made and activities arise from the ongoing concerns of the students themselves, as did the decision to have a treasurer. Set those characters in motion!

In this way they learn new roles and other possibilities of being. At present, many of those young people are positional selves—they are part of a culture in which the self exists only in relation to others. Among them you are who you are because of your place in a social network of family members, clansmen, and fellow villagers. Then at UWC they enter into another positional context where they have their one role to play as followers while the teacher gives direction. But you would create with them a more fluid social environment—a situational context which offers them other roles to play. A context where, in fact, there is the possibility of inventing a role and making another self as they see opportunities for developing new activities. Moreover, in this context they will often be working together, pooling resources, while in a positional context the students sit isolated from each other as they all follow along. So it's important that we give only the minimal direction needed to get this situational process moving.

Which is one reason I agree with Alistair when he says that we needn't write comments on students' papers indicating the revisions needed, that conferencing with them is better. So let's train them to conference with each other and work as editors since we don't have time for them all. If the writer is dashing off something, getting ideas down as they come, then obviously the result is not a finished piece of work and I've often found that students want to revise it before they make their presentation to the class. I've even had to ask some students to stop working it over and read to us. The teacher should be only one more in the audience for their writing. But if they write according to a set of directions that lays out the steps, then with that last step they've finished the paper and so what more is there to do with it?

Of course there's Lil Branon's suggestion that students write a second draft from someone else's point of view, or Peter Elbow's suggestion that a paper be rewritten as for a different audience, etc., and I say to hell with that! It's so easy for teachers to sit back giving these oh so helpful suggestions while the students do this unnecessary work. We revise a piece because it will appear in some context where we want to make a particular impression, so let's help those young people build a context for the appearance of their work and they will prepare it accordingly. If one or another will not, then let that individual have the experience of appearing to others as an incomplete person. If someone doesn't mind being out of harmony with the group, then I say in effect, Go your own way. And incidentally, when after all their slow, arduous individual work these people come to know each other and feel some harmony or trust together, they will think they owe it all to themselves and not to you. Get out their way!—that's my motto.

Or do we want to be gurus in the classroom—spiritual mechanics like James Moffett, who constructed an "abstraction ladder" young people are to climb on their way to union with the Cosmic One? They can enjoy the harmony among those who are willing to be followers. Once again you speak of the great benefit for the learning environment when everyone reaches consensus in the "loving" classroom and remark that "Surely this seems clear enough." It's clear alright, and I still don't like it. We are going to feel good about each other and ourselves, in harmony with each other in that classroom, as a consequence of something we have achieved there, individually and together. So let's get right on with the work and make something!

Does it seem that I am trying to take away from you a philosophy you value? Well, I offer in its place the Philosophy of This Is. Now, since you have kept with me thus far, and have shown your altruistic dedication, your heart as big as all outdoors, your sensitivity to the finer things of life and the higher learning, well beyond the reach of crasser mortals, I feel that you are indeed a fitting candidate for the Fellowship of This Is. With us you may rest secure in the knowledge that you possess a great universal secret, one that cannot be confided to lesser souls. There will of course be a small initiation fee (10% of your yearly income), but that is really nothing at all because money is simply a reminder of the vulgar concerns from which you will be liberated in the Fellowship. Trusting that you will forward the initiation fee forthwith as a token of your selfless dedication to the Higher Truth, I am prepared at this time to reveal to you the Great Secret of the Philosophy of This Is.

Just a moment—that's strange! I'm sure it was here. How could I have possibly let it slip away? Give me a few moments, I'm certain I'll find it—if not right now, then surely in time for inclusion in my next letter. So keep the faith! Trust me! I guarantee that my next letter will provide the answer and satisfy you completely. Meanwhile, let me think about this great secret. Surely it's in the dark here somewhere.

Excuse me while I go searching—JR

- - - / / / - - -

22 September

Dear John,

Well, your talk about the Philosophy of This Is was amusing but I wonder just how useful it will turn out to be when you finally reveal it. Will it help me with my workload when I have all these midterm exams to read? I was just computing my marking time for that exam (copy enclosed), and it will take me about 41 hours to do them, which will certainly leave me bleary-eyed. Also I have the reaction-response papers to grade and the reading journals and so much more. I know you don't mark your students' papers, but how do you know enough about their work to give each of them a final grade?

I sometimes wonder if we should give this midterm exam at all, but if students need help learning how to write for other exams then I guess it makes sense. Furthermore, Alistair argues that if we have midyear and final exams then we should give students trial exams so they're really prepared. But then does this testing spread like a cancer? And I wonder if the questions we give for the reading passage practically dictate certain responses. Are they too controlling? But I must say that Alistair comes up with questions the students seem to enjoy, and they produce some really interesting responses. Which hardly seems to agree with your suggestion that we have to get out of their way to get good work from them.

Also, I've been thinking about Basil Bernstein's *Class, Codes and Control* recently, which you regard so highly, and I'm still troubled by his concept of a restricted language code. Are we to believe that all the discussions about tribal rites—lobola, circumcision, animal sacrifice, for example—are in a restricted code without continuing further elaborations? Is the academy the one place where questions and elaborations occur? Simply placing a whole language like Xhosa into the category of a local or restricted code seems problematic to me—they're a very able and creative people.

I was looking at what Bernstein says about how middle-class children learn the elaborated language code and I noticed this:

> It is possible to distinguish two modes of an elaborated code. One mode facilitates the verbal elaboration of interpersonal relations, and the second facilitates the verbal elaboration of relations between objects.

And he goes on to say that working-class students, who are likely to be oriented more toward objects than persons because of their restricted language code, will be inclined to choose fields like the applied sciences and business, where I suppose people can be treated as objects. I wonder if this weakens the argument that learning a person-centred code enables one to participate more effectively in modern power structures. Should we emphasize expository writing rather than personal expression as a way of moving students from a restricted to an elaborated code?

I find that people here resent very much the term *restricted language code*, they say it denigrates Africans, so in fact it's a little difficult to talk with them about moving students from a restricted to an elaborated code. And they refer to Brian Street's *Social Literacies*, which attacks the idea of a restricted language code—or so they say. I'm going to read the book for myself.

Anyway, when it comes to the last word on language learning, Vygotsky is all the rage. I started reading *Thought and Language*, and found it fascinating but disturbing as well. He seems to be contradicting the view of language development which puts individual expression at the centre. He says thinking is 'from the social to the individual'—that learning to generalize, to move from concrete language to more abstract language, depends very much on the 'social relationship' between teacher and student. And he talks about the importance of adult intervention. People here take Vygotsky as giving support to highly structured programs, rather than to the self-expressive and indirect approach you favor, so I'm wondering.

I was thinking about your comment that we might be giving too many directions to our students. But Alistair seems to feel they want to know where they're going and how they can get there. If learning to read a demanding text is an important part of their college work, then just asking them to react to a sentence or a passage that catches their attention, as you've suggested, lets them go off in directions that depart from the meaning there on the page. So I don't see how 'getting out of their way' is going to help. That's why we give them some fairly structured questions about a text, pointing out elements they should respond to. Then we ask them to write a 'reflection' on what they've said—to make a statement about what the text means to them—but I've noticed that most of them ignore this request. I'm not sure the directions we give them are at fault since they just haven't been asked to do anything like this before, as Alistair says.

Also, you often talk about how your way is to get the students doing something on their own, but you never mention any specific action they take once they leave the classroom. One of my first entries into the political world was as an advocate for the use of solar power back in the States. Technologies are employed by capitalism simply to make profits, in spite of the environmental destruction they cause. Indeed, I was wondering if your philosophy would ever lead you to some political action. What 'doing' have you ever got involved in besides producing more and more people who might in their turn present more and more classes where people talk about what they're going to do! And although you attack the gurus, it seems to me that you might like being one yourself.

And you talk about working with people indirectly rather than giving them direct instructions, yet when you're counseling people you seem to give them very explicit directions. In fact, I wonder about your seeming opposition to a therapeutic approach when you yourself have people coming to you for help. Of course you don't call it therapy, you call it counseling, but what's the difference? You talk as if the whole therapeutic outlook is just so much crap, but I'm not so sure. When people have to leave their communities and go it alone, that makes for a lot of maladjustment, it seems to me.

Well, I'd better end here, I've got so many more papers to read and mark, but somehow I feel better. Writing this letter has been a good break in the routine for me.

Regards—Ed

- - - / / / - - -

October 27

Dear Ed,

I am somewhat disturbed that you have expressed doubt concerning the Philosophy of This Is, suggesting that it may not offer much help with practical affairs, with your marking load for example. You will find, however, that results depend on how one completes the phrase "This is . . ." There are many completions possible, although only a few express the essence of the philosophy, capture its mystical meaning, and lend the philosopher that air of insouciance proper to one who by his grasp of Final Truth has been lifted above the petty concerns that bedevil the lives of others. I am prepared to offer you at this time a completion which satisfies these conditions, one that will also dispose of your marking load: This is **muck!**

The final examination you enclosed requires the student to spend 3 hours on a language section, which calls for reading a passage of exposition and then responding to questions about it, plus writing two papers. It requires the student to spend 3 hours on a literature section, which calls for reading passages from stories and writing reactions and explanations. Six hours in all! There has already been a 3-hour midterm examination—and you have to read and grade all this stuff! Why? Why do you people punish yourselves and those students in this way? Consider how all that time could be used for some good talk and good writing!

"Alistair argues that if we give midyear and final exams, then we have to give students trial exams so they're really prepared." And this, you say, begins to look like a cancer. How right you are! (Repeat after me: This is **muck!**)

Then you have all those journals and papers you've collected from the students to read and grade, and you wonder why I'm not doing the same. Because I'm not the audience for whom a paper is written, they write for each other. And when they read or hear the work of others they know how their own work compares with it. When the class is large and there's not time enough for every student to read a paper to us, I train them to share their work with each other in small groups, and I sit with one group, then another. Sometimes I give them a self-evaluation sheet on which they answer questions about their own work, and they put that sheet in their folders. Or they write brief commentaries for each other's papers. In short, I turn this work of evaluation, with all its attendant problems, over to the students. And by the end of the term I'm familiar enough with what each has done to assign them grades for the record—or I can refresh my memory by looking into their folders. Our students must not be waiting for us, hanging on to us every step of the way!

Which is why I object to your giving them "structured" questions about a text, pointing out elements they should respond to so they don't "depart from the meaning there on the page." Why must we treat these people as if they're simpleminded? Perhaps we have learned to do this by reading too many academic works in which directions for reading are a large part of the content. As in Brian Street's *Social Literacies,* for example, which begins with 14 pages of introduction, summary and directions for reading what is to come. Fourteen pages before you're allowed to begin the journey! Then every section and every chapter begins with yet more introduction and summary and directions, while the text itself is replete with references to "the argument discussed above" that will be "dealt with in more detail below," until finally one wants to cry out "For God's sake get on with it!" But it seems that academic readers must be led by the hand every step of the way!

So these positional texts are written for them with every morsel of information labeled and every meaning spelled out—readers need not do any thinking for themselves. Yet all those directions won't keep even the professors from finding only what they hope to find in the pages of a book and overlooking contrary evidence. You say your colleagues cite Brian Street's work as contra Bernstein, but how they read that into him I don't know. Street, like Bernstein, would have us think of a language program as a socialization process, and he believes it important that such a program take into account local experience and local literacies. He advises us to be skeptical of claims about the supposed benefits of training in "academic literacy." I recommend his book—it offers support for the kind of work you do with young people when you encourage them to use their own experience and think for themselves about what is happening around them.

For we are hoping to bring into being readers who are independent and self-reliant—who can use a text to enlarge their experience and make it meaningful. After class the other day Janine said to me, "You don't do much but I think I'm learning." Well, she's learning that I'm not going to do it for her.

However, you say that Alistair writes very good leading questions for the exams you give, and they elicit "really interesting responses" from students. This, you say, this hardly confirms my injunction that we should get out of their way. Ah-ha! So much for you, Rouse, you know-it-all! But then you wonder if those questions "practically dictate certain responses." Now here I think you're beginning to smell something that's not quite right. It's very important that aspirants to the Fellowship of This Is develop their sense of smell, for muck comes in many varieties and is often deceptively packaged.

Perhaps you wonder if those exam questions are "too controlling" because you've learned from Bernstein that using positional controls with young people tends to confine them within a restricted language code. But when children are given choices more often than directions or commands, and so must justify their choices by giving reasons for them, they tend to develop a more elaborated language. The "permissiveness" of middle-class parents is usually a dialogue—a ceaseless, intense dialogue with children, in which everything is negotiated. The permission must be won. In a working-class family, however, there tends to be less talk and more direction, so children feel less need to expand their language. They learn to rely on a restricted code in which little need be made explicit because so much is understood—the language of peer group and neighborhood, of common experience. But to make one's meanings explicit in the world beyond the neighborhood means learning the language habits and manners of the social group in which one wishes to work or have effect. Usually the middle-class child has learned those speech forms and habits of mind needed for success in school, but the lower class child may not have been socialized in the same advantageous manner.

However, in school *that child can learn an elaborated language even under positional controls.* Because the work required, the reading and writing, is predicated on it. So for me the decisive issue concerns the kind of person this schooling tends to produce. Under positional controls children are socialized to the existing order and learn to go along with things as they are—they can be followers. The elaborated code, however, has a potential for meanings that go beyond local space, time, and context—a potential that includes disorder, incoherence and a new order, a new coherence (to paraphrase Bernstein). Middle-class children, raised under personal controls at home, come to school ready to stress what "I" think as against the tribalism of what "we" think—they may be able to realize this potential for new meanings, whereas those who begin with a restricted code learned under positional controls are likely to be less interested in such potential than in simply learning to get along in the school way of using language. Positional controls do not socialize them for independence or leadership but rather for acceptance of a subordinate role.

You're troubled by talk of a "restricted" language code, however, and remark that "Simply placing a whole language like Xhosa into the category of a local or restricted code seems problematic to me—they're a very able and creative people." Bernstein would reply that each language code has its use or value, its own possibilities. So if your colleagues are put off by the negative connotations of the term *restricted,* then let's borrow Gee's term from *Social Linguistics and Literacies* and refer to the *primary code* because it comes first and is the foundation for subsequent development. An elaborated language then becomes a *secondary code.* Ah, the power of naming! In Bernstein's description a primary code has a vast potential of meanings and

> contains its own aesthetic, a simplicity and directness of expression, emotionally virile, pithy and powerful and a metaphoric range of considerable force and appropriateness. Some examples taken from the schools of this country have a beauty which many writers might well envy. It is a language in which the individual is treated as an end, not as a means to a further end.

In a technological, service economy where people are on the move, however, you cannot talk with all those you meet as if they were of your clan, for often they would in fact like to use you as a means to some further end. It's a lonely world out there beyond the village, and

> the tribal boy had to fit himself into the vast, fast-moving, frenetic life in the big city. So many habits, beliefs, customs had to be fractured overnight. So many reactions that were sincere and instinctive were laughed at in the city. A man was continually changing himself, leaping like a flea from contingency to contingency. But Abner made it, though

> most of the time he did not know who he was or whither he was going. He only knew that this feverish life had to be lived, identity becoming so large that a man sounded ridiculous boasting that he was a Mopedi or a Mosuto or a Xhosa or a Zulu—nobody seemed to care.

(That's from the story "Kwashiorkor," by Can Themba—another South African writer you have me reading.)

To make it in this feverish life as Abner did, and get ahead, means expanding one's language beyond the ways of village talk. But "Are we to believe," you ask, "that all the discourses around tribal rites are in a restricted code without continuing further elaborations?" Well, the tribal rites you refer to—lobola, circumcision, animal sacrifice—have been made problematic by Xhosa interaction with Western ideas, that's why there is all the discussion. They now feel they must justify and give reasons for their various customs, they're already moving toward an elaborated code. In the village there was no need to discuss these matters, except as gossip might be used to keep people in conformance with accepted practice. Change was slow and took place over long periods of time, furthered by occasional variations in custom. There tradition ruled. The artist was praised for his ability to recreate traditional designs, his individual creativity was not encouraged—he was not going to announce a new aesthetic. But urban life and the modern experience have opened new opportunities for the learning of new skills, and created new avenues for individual expression and creativity. To take advantage of these opportunities, however, means learning the vocabularies and patterns of discourse used in schooling, in commerce, in technical research, and in a great many metalinguistic activities. In other words, one needs to learn an elaborated language and the individualist identity that goes with it, moving on from the communal "we" of a primary code, in which so little need be explained because so much is understood.

Here is where we start with many young people. The so-called basic writers in the city colleges of New York, as described by Mina Shaughnessy in *Errors and Expectations*, match in every Bernsteinian particular the users of a primary language code: they put down opinions without giving evidence or reasons; the connections between their statements are usually implicit because they assume a reader understands what is in the writer's mind; they often fail to name the object or person they write about, or state explicitly their main idea, making vague references instead to "it" and "they" and "thing"; the pleasures of peer and neighborhood talk have a strong hold on them. In short, their writing shows that after twelve years of schooling many "have never successfully reconciled the worlds of home and school." Now if these students are going to move beyond their origins, they will need to develop an elaborated language and become the individuated self.

However, Bernstein himself remarks that this division between restricted and elaborated codes is too simple, and as you point out he goes on to describe two uses of an elaborated code, one oriented to persons and the other to objects. Working-class students, he suggests, are more likely to move toward the object mode rather than the person mode of the elaborated code:

> In concrete terms, we might expect working-class children to move towards the applied sciences than towards the verbal arts. This shift from authority to rationality for working-class children may involve a less traumatic change in their role relations, systems of meaning and control, than a shift from authority to identity [to the uncertainties of interpersonal relations]. Authority and rationality are both positional in the sense that the individual works within a framework, within a system or structure, without the critical problem of ambiguity of ends.

Perhaps this is why almost all the working-class students I teach go on to major in such subjects as biology or accounting. The exceptions are usually women, whose experiences in the working-class family helping with the care of younger siblings have made them more person-oriented than their brothers. As for the middle-class students, the careers they choose seem somewhat more varied, although in fact many of them become business majors—they're going where the money is.

You wonder if this argues against the person-centered language activities we encourage, in favor of a more structured and object-oriented approach. And it's true that the young people we work with will sometimes demand lessons in grammar and language forms—they're comfortable in structured, rationalized programs with clearly defined objects of study. So should we emphasize the object-directed form of the elaborated code with these students—which would mean, I suppose, less narrative and more book research and reporting of facts?

Well, we're going to have both. Remember that any writing is personal so long as the writer is truly engaged with the matter at hand rather than simply working through an academic exercise. What one says or writes should have a certain force, and that comes only with the writer's self-investment. I've read that success in many careers goes to those who can make a convincing presentation of self—who can express themselves well in public settings, as in a meeting. So whether our students are person- or object-oriented they need practice in presenting themselves and their work to others.

And this means for many of them a move from the communal self to the individuated self. Consider the middle class mother I spoke of who told her child to "Be yourself!" Of course that raises for the child a very difficult question: "Who am I?"—and she will spend a lifetime working on it. Bernstein suggests that children in these person-centered families "may well develop acute identity problems concerned with authenticity." And as working-class students expand their primary language codes to develop an elaborated language, they will move from the certainty of who "we" are to the uncertainty of who am "I"? In short, they too may develop a self to be confused about.

So that's what we're implicated with in the teaching of writing— adding to the confusion. Our classroom will not be a place where young people are defined in advance, where they come to get their orders and all follow along in the same direction, but where they are let loose to make their own meanings and define themselves. They are moving away from the tribalism of their neighborhoods toward the lonely individualism that is the modern experience.

You seem to feel this experience, with its attendant alienation and disquiet, calls for a therapeutic approach in education, but rather than be a healer to the young, I would be the one responsible for showing them alternatives and opening the range of possibility. You ask if perhaps I feel the "whole therapeutic outlook is just so much crap." Well, those are your words, not mine, but let me say that I feel you're beginning show an aptitude for the Philosophy of This Is, which calls for the practice of skepticism and critical thinking—along with the ability to find the right names for things.

I must say that you go on to show a healthy skepticism when you ask me "What 'doing' have you ever got involved in besides producing more and more people who might in their turn present more and more classes where people talk about what they're going to do!" Socko! Pow! But why stop there? "Although you attack the gurus, sometimes it seems to me that you might like being one yourself." Well, if someone wants me to play that role, then I'm happy to oblige. But I told you earlier in this correspondence that you and I are not destined to have followers, and now it's evident that I must march on alone for the only person who's been listening to me has fallen away. But at least I have my students, and so I'll follow along with them for company—although I know they're going to abandon me before long.

Some years ago, during a flight to Madrid, I met a young man who was on his way to join the Marharishi Mahesh Yogi for a winter retreat on Majorca. He invited me to come along and share the experience, and because he claimed to have some influence I agreed to go if he would arrange for me to interview the Maharishi. So 2 days later I found myself surrounded by transcendental meditators in an old wood-framed hotel on Majorca, about to meet the Maharishi. For the occasion his devotees, several hundred in number, gathered in a large, low-ceilinged, dimly lit meeting room where they sat on the floor, while I was allowed to sit on the lower step of a dais from which above us the Maharishi, seated on cushions, addressed the assemblage in his high sing-song voice. He answered each of my questions without a moment's hesitation and at considerable length. He assured me that Transcendental Meditation has an important role to play in education. Later I was asked by one of his lieutenants if I would like to become a teacher of the doctrine, and I must say this suggestion—that I too might someday sit before a multitude of upturned young faces smilingly aglow in nodding readiness to hear my words—this had a certain appeal. However, I decided against becoming a guru in the classroom as some others yearn to be, like Jane Tompkins or James Moffett for example, and perhaps your friend Alistair Vonkeller. To become a spiritual leader of the young, loved and loving, is not my ambition. I only want to help them find ways to say a few good things while we're together, that's enough for me.

And writing this letter I've done enough for one evening. Do keep in mind the Philosophy of This Is, of which I am the Archon, Guiding Light, and Big Cheese! Among its virtues you will find it useful as a guide through the textual maze of postmodern theory, in which a great many have been lost. It disposes of so much and perhaps we may find something useful in the residue. Meanwhile I hope you will write again before long since no one else is agitating my thoughts these days.

Yours in fellowship, JR

CHAPTER 6

— ✿ —

To Seek a Name
and Nothing More

5 April

Dear John,

   Last night, Diana surprised me with a call from way up at the University of Bophutetswana [Bops], near Sun City. Do you remember my mentioning her, our lovely radical who would bring political prisoners back from Robben Island? Since then she's 'mellowed out', she told me. 'Too bad', I said. Then she told me about the baby she found on a rubbish heap, a Tswana baby about 3 months old. The police investigated but never turned up a mother, so Diana and her husband adopted it as a brother for their own child, Ben. And she named the child Goitseone, which is Tswana for 'God only knows'—who he came from, I suppose. Diana can operate at the extreme even when mellowed out.

   She told me about her work at Bops and it was shocking to hear that she lectures alone to two groups of 250 students each, and there are no small tutorial groups such as we have at UWC. But enrollments are rising here too and there's no money for hiring additional staff, so that's going to mean larger classes. In fact, I've heard that our programme may soon be moving into the lecture hall, as at Bops. Does that mean we'll be giving lectures on the forms of academic discourse and no more of the expressive writing we've been doing? There are some on our staff who look forward to that. They say it's not enough simply to write, the students must learn a

145

metalanguage for talking about it, terms from rhetoric and grammar or linguistics—like thesis, assumption, literal/figurative, tenor, field and mode—so they really know what they're doing.

There's a definite trend in this programme away from expressive writing. And perhaps I feel a little guilty when I hear their talk about how a student-centered process approach only delays the development of rigorous thinking. Maybe I've been remiss in not asking my students more cutting questions, like those used by the cognitivists, as they call themselves—as in the assignments of William Coles in *The Plural I*:

> Here is a statement: "A professional, whether paid or unpaid, is the man that counts. An amateur is a clumsy bastard." Where do you stand on this issue?

So the student has to explain the meaning of 'professional' and 'amateur' and go on from there. What do you think of this assignment? Sometimes I feel I'm just blundering along like a clumsy bastard amateur myself, and others times I actually feel rather professional, so I could write about this issue but I'm not sure my students would enjoy working with it. Where's the humour in it for them? That's one thing that keeps us going I think— the chance for a bit of humour now and then.

We had a good time with the names project, there were some laughs with that, but did the writing go as far as it should, was it reflective enough? I don't remember anyone musing deeply about, let's say, the use of names and labels in society, or the power of naming in general. Maybe we should have done something a little more demanding with it.

Oh well. On the first day of class this term I asked my students to draw a gravestone for themselves on their writing paper and then write an epitaph, noting down when they died and what they wanted to be remembered for. I borrowed this exercise from something I'd read, thinking we could get to know each other this way and maybe something else would come of it. They'd be writing about things close to them, important to them, and maybe some topic would come up that we could all go on with. In a small class I can take this kind of chance, but if the dean increases class size to 30 or more, or moves us into the lecture hall, it will be impossible to identify a genuine concern we share and move freely with it.

On the other hand, I wonder sometimes if we can really do that even in a small class. You talk about going along with the students, with what they want to do, but just how seriously do you take the notion of allowing them to negotiate the curriculum? I mean, sorcerers are adept at bringing people around to their way of seeing things, and you're devious enough for that, you work indirectly. So where is the direction really coming from? I insist that each student chair a week's class, but then I'm the first and usually the only one who puts up a hand, so I give the assignment for the day. My democratic pretensions are so often undermined by my commanding voice and offhand jokes. You're smoother than that, somehow, and you don't talk very much. I wonder what your secret power name is—Beelzebub?

The fact is, I fear the class being taken over by some long-winded and boring speaker, as when Morné wanted to talk about street law and then lectured us for half an hour about what our legal rights are in the street. But maybe he wasn't so boring, now that I think about it. It seems I'm not sure when to give directions and when to let them go their own way. What if they wander off and I lose them?

Also, there are certain things they need to learn, that require some directed attention, like how to examine a piece of writing and say what makes it effective or not. But instead of commenting on the writing they just talk about whatever it happens to make them think of. So to help them keep on track I listed three different things to look for in a piece of writing and demonstrated the kinds of comments they could make. Then Constantia read her paper to us. We had written lines beginning 'Once I was . . . Now I am . . .', and extended them to make a longer, fuller statement. Here's her paper:

> Once I was cruel and heartless towards my younger sister, I would beat her and even ask my friends to take her away. My mother tried to explain to me that I would be lonely without her. 'Who would play games with you? And she helps you with all the work around the house'. She even took me to church, but I did not know good from evil at that time.
>
> I was too close to my mother, sleeping in the same bed. So I didn't want my sister to share that love.
>
> But one day my mother took me to church and the preacher was reading the Ten Commandments and it was so beautiful, and he read one that said you must love one another as you do yourselves, and I change immediately. I understood the words and now I am loving to everyone but especially to small children.

Does that sound convincing? This 'Once I was lost, now I am saved' theme comes up too often, it's common property. Everyone in the room has a story like this. But who knows what secrets or even wise thoughts Constantia might tell us if she could only be persuaded to speak truly of herself? I know these students have interesting histories to draw on but many of them resist becoming autobiographical.

After Constantia read her paper to us I asked the others to write for 3 minutes about the writing itself, to comment on what they noticed in the piece and what they liked. The first three who read their comments to us said they were glad Constantia had seen the light of the Ten Commandments—which provoked from me a too long talk to the effect that approving of Constantia's moral gain is not the same as commenting on her writing. They listened, and then a student said, 'What I want to know is, did Constantia repent?' Well, I can understand how some people might think that's funny but at the time I didn't see the humour of it: How do you get students to comment on the *writing*, to be reflective?

Speaking of humour, I was thinking the other day how so much of American literature is humourous, an ironic kind of humour you might say—Woody Allen, Updike, Kurt Vonnegut—but South African stories are often so literal, so overdetermined, with meanings spelled out for the reader. Oh yes, there's humour in Ezekiel Mphalele and some of the older ones, but now with Gordimor and Ndebele, for example, the literature being written is very serious, very political. Of course there are touches of humor in them, and the Coetzee of *Dusklands* is a grim comedian of sorts, but they don't leave you laughing. The situation here is so divided culturally that I suppose people feel this is not a time for laughter. And also there's the problem that what amuses one group may anger another, so humour is kept close to home. But I think finding something in common to laugh about could be a way of bringing people together. And we surely need a few laughs now, when the situation in South Africa just keeps getting murkier.

Butshabethu, one of my students, said 'Even talking to you and being a friend is difficult. My political friends see me as a sell-out. They want to know, "How can you take a ride to Cape Town with a white man?" I explain that we are in a transitional period now that we have taken political power, we no longer need be so limited in our thinking. I can think what I like, talk and be friends with anyone. But they don't see it that way. They feel the political struggle is still hot'.

And when Shereen came to clean the house today I asked her if life is easier now than when she was young. 'No, Mr. Katz, life was much easier then. We lived on a farm, and we had some land where we could grow vegetables. And every month the farmer would give us a sheep or goat to eat, and one to raise for ourselves. My father was rich, he had so many goats. Yes, life was good until the government came to take our land. They came with a very big truck and just threw everything from the house on the truck and forced us to go to this other place. But it was no good, it was sandy. And there was rain only sometimes in the spring. We could grow nothing there. They were cruel'. She doubts there will peace in South Africa. 'These blacks, they don't like the Afrikaners, and if they don't know who you are, they will kill you. And these gangs, they make so much crime now'.

She's right about that. Two nights ago Rashied Staggie, one of the leaders of the Hard Living Boys, was shot in the head and set afire on a street in Salt River by vigilantes. These gangs virtually control the streets in many areas and they dominate the squatter camps, Then there's the wonder, and sadness, of their names—the Sexy Boys, the Young American

Gigolos, the Mongrels, the Dixie Boys, the Cape Town Scorpions, and the JFKs (Junky Funky Kids). I said something like 'They're trying to be somebody', and Quinton Booi shot back, 'There's nothing romantic about these gangs'. Even so, many of our students admire and emulate them, in dress at least. A vigilante group calling itself PAGAD (People Against Gangsters and Drugs) has been trying to take back the streets, and at Staggie's funeral 2,000 gang members turned out for him, promising revenge. A picture of the bloody corpse was on the front page of the newspaper, lying in the street wearing a bright white baseball jacket. I woke up in the night feeling again of the horror of it.

In my class, Moses Kula wrote about 'A bad thing happened to my younger sister' one night when she was attacked in the street by 'gang boys' and stabbed. I remind myself that these things are happening among the most alienated and poverty-stricken people, but I cannot allow myself to think too much on the horror that must rule in these circumstances. So I wonder how to respond to this paper Moses has written about the violence that shadows so many of these young lives.

Well, those are my concerns at the moment. By the way, I hear that the science faculty is objecting to all the personal writing we do in this program, so maybe I've been making a mistake by advertising that feature of the course and our emphasis on the expressive voice. Anyway, our propaganda envoy to the Academic Development Committee has changed the description of our program, eliminating 'personal experience writing' and substituting 'orienting students to the academic environment'. Ah, the power of a good slogan!

Tot Siens (all the best)—Ed

- - - / / / - - -

April 25

Dear Ed,

I must say that reading your letters can be quite a unique experience. They sometimes start a train of thoughts or associations that otherwise might never have occurred to me, and I get to musing about the oddest things. And sometimes laughing too. Now this last one, for example: Here you talk about the need for a few laughs now and then while we work, and how you wish for more humor in South African writers, while in your classroom the young people are drawing tombstones and writing their epitaphs! Well alright, I suppose humor and death can go together. There's a three-part canon by John Hilton (1599-1657), written as an epitaph, that goes like this:

Here lies a woman.
Who can deny it?
She died in peace,
Though lived unquiet.
Her husband prays,
If o'er her grave you walk,
You would tread soft.
For if she wakes,
She'll talk.

I sang this for a young friend of mine and he said, quite seriously, "Oh that's bad, what he says about her. I wonder how they got along." And this from a loquacious fellow who expects that a woman will be silent and listen to *him*. I said, "You're funnier than the song." He looked puzzled, for he certainly hadn't intended to be humorous. Such people approach themselves with a certain solemnity.

But humor can help lighten our burdens, particularly the heavy weight of self. I think of the epitaph Dorothy Parker wrote in one of her bibulous moments: "Excuse my dust." And one by John Gay:

Life is a jest, and all things show it,
I thought so once, and now I know it.

So it's important that we not take ourselves too seriously or we lose the ability to go as the moment requires. We must be willing to contradict ourselves. You have this flexibility, it seems to me, because you have a sense of humor—although you worry that a penchant for offhand jokes undermines your "democratic pretensions." By always giving you the last word I suppose. But then, you recognize at some point when the joke is on you—when you have made yourself comical by violating your own principles. As when having insisted that a student lead the class for a week, you then sit among the others and deliver your instructions from there. If we can't laugh at ourselves we never can do any good, for who would feel safe with us? To see the humor in this is already to have made a move beyond it—but in what direction? You want these young people to be self-moving and yet you're afraid that without your guidance they will not be productive. So you've been thinking about this and now you wonder if we really can just go along with them, find some concern we all share and see what comes of it. You suggest that perhaps I somehow manage to bring them around to my way of thinking while making them believe they have found their own direction. You speak of this as a kind of sorcery or deception and speculate that perhaps I have taken Beelzebub as my power name. You *are* a funny man!

Well, there's a truth of sorts in this, I must admit. Nietzsche remarks that an educator is a dissembler who pretends to one position or another according the learner's need: He is beyond good and evil, but no one must know it. And so I go along with the interests or concerns of my young people in order to direct their energies to some useful outcome. Of course I could lay out an entire course of study for them, one project after another, but then they would only be going through the prescribed motions with little investment of themselves. They would be riding in my vehicle, following my itinerary, and I become responsible for making it all interesting somehow. Do I want to work that hard, against their covert resistance or at best with only their polite conformance? I would rather get some commotion started among them and then go along helping them find the forms by which to learn what they are feeling and thinking on their way to a destination they anticipate without knowing just what it is.

So the moment when you should intervene becomes crucial. That Morné felt free to get up and go on lecturing about one's legal rights in the street for 30 minutes says something about the way you work with young people. At some point one might ask him a question about the *unwritten* rules of street behavior. There's a subject that would interest those young people, for street life is obviously of some concern to them. And if they were to write about those informal rules, then what you would have from them is not simply personal experience but also thoughtful consideration of it written at a distance, and you could stand with the writer at that distance, so to speak, and comment on those thoughts and how they're expressed. The result might be pages like those we read in Elijah Anderson's *Streetwise*. So why not discuss the possibility with them, and perhaps ask Morné to organize the work with those who want to take this path? Others might decide to consider the unwritten rules that govern behavior in the family, in the hostels, in the university—or even in your classroom, and wouldn't that be interesting? Along the way they might make some interesting discoveries about the circumstances of their lives, and perhaps in the process do some good writing.

Of course I'm not sure that any of us want to submit ourselves to this kind of scrutiny, but some interesting insights might eventuate if we did. Let's consider for example the unspoken rule in your classroom that the highest valuation goes to writing which reveals the self—which is in fact confessional. For you seek a genuine expression of the self rather than writing that is done as a duty, perfunctorily, without real commitment. But even so, despite your caring interest, these young people resist opening themselves to you or the others, and keep their secrets safe as Constantia did, by providing a formulaic confession.

And yet what an interesting example of the form she has given you! By confessing error—"Once I was cruel and heartless towards my younger sister"—she intends to demonstrate the wholeness, the integrity of her present self. She has been converted from sinful ways to the way of Christianity and found herself. So this story is another in a long series of confessions that begins with Augustine, and like those others it carries the eloctionary force of a demand for exculpation, so that free of guilt one becomes one's true self, whole and self-directing.

To answer this demand for exculpation a listener, a reader, is needed to confirm the success with which the troubled soul has found its salvation, and so by this confirmation the new identity is made secure. You have difficulty being that listener for you suspect the story may be a contrivance, not a true revelation of self. And besides, as a teacher you want to talk about this confession as a text, as a piece of writing to be improved, and you urge the others to join you. But they are trying to be the readers this text demands and so are faithful to the moment. They offer the writer confirmation by saying they're glad she has seen the light. And ignoring your demand that they comment on the writing itself, they ask the writer "Did you repent?"—and so prompt Constantia to perfect the form, as she claims to have perfected herself. In their own way they're doing what you ask of them.

As churchgoers they have had certain social experiences which have made them responsive to this form. With other kinds of writing, however, they are not responsive to the form but rather to its content, they "talk about whatever it happens to make them think of," as you say—their response is more emotive than intellectual. They have not had the social experiences in the home or community that could make them sensitive to form or structure in general. Consider the following:

> When the children were invited to tell a story about some doll-like figures (a little boy, a little girl, a sailor and a dog) the working-class children's stories were freer, longer and more imaginative than the stories of the middle-class children. The latter children's stories were tighter, constrained within a strong narrative frame. It was as if these children were dominated by what they took to be the *form* of a narrative and the content was secondary. (Bernstein, p. 180)

And what is true for narrative is true for the other modes of discourse: middle-class children want to get them *right*, and that means in correct form. They're ready for the demands of a formal education. This suggests a twofold question: What social experiences can we provide in the classroom that will develop a sensitivity to form in those who need it, and develop in others a concern with producing imaginative and interesting content?

Here's where your use of literature can be important. Suppose, for example, you read a fable with your students, encourage them to tell the fables they know and then to write one themselves. This work would tend to make them sensitive to forms that move toward a definite conclusion, as the fable illustrates a moral point, so that later when they're doing other writing you can ask them, "What's the point of this, what thought are you going to leave us with?" Shirley Brice Heath describes how middle-class children who have been read bedtime stories and talked about them with a parent learn to build book knowledge into their experience of the world—they come to school prepared to write, having internalized cultural assumptions and patterns of discourse operative in classrooms. And now as our students read poems, stories and essays with us, and share their individual responses to them, they sharpen their awareness of various discourse patterns. And with their classmates as an audience, they will be stimulated in this public setting to produce writing with an interesting, imaginative content.

I'm not suggesting that narrative be the only kind of writing we do, but rather just illustrating one sort of social interaction that may develop a sensitivity to form. Of course we cannot replicate in our classroom the family experience of middle-class children—I don't want to become the father of all those young people—but what Bernstein and others tell us about how language is learned in those families whose children are successful in school, certainly has implications for our work helping students develop their writing ability. It suggests that personal expression in the classroom should be encouraged; that individuals be called on to explain and justify what they say; that they develop with us a classroom procedure and patterns of interaction so they will become alert to the cues that signal the need for another step in an orderly sequence of activity or discussion, and respond accordingly—all so they develop a sensitivity to form as well as content.

And we teachers have a learning task as well: to develop our sensitivity to the responses of the young people we work with, to the content of what they say. Perhaps here I should make a confession myself. There are times when I realize I've not really been listening to the students, I have so many good ideas for them and know so well just what the next step should be. One day last week Magda came over to me with her paper, not sure it was going right. She had written about a security guard at a Toughman Contest (described by the journalist Bob Greene), who was lured into a restroom and beaten by several men; then she had gone on to tell about seeing a fight in a bar, when a bully who had been beaten down by several men rose up and shot a bystander. What interested her in all this was the part that fate or chance had played in the lives of those two injured men. But I pointed out that what had happened to that guard and that bystander were only incidental events within larger narratives about male combat, and so could she find a theme more central to those narratives? We settled on the ready anger in men who have not succeeded in the larger world—on what Greene calls their secret meanness. I was quite satisfied with this, and she went back to her desk to work with the idea.

But in the evening Magda came into my thoughts and I realized that I had failed her. The randomness of life—how an act of fate may disrupt the planned progression of our quiet lives—had been her theme. But she gave it up to please me, who would rather not be a toy of fate, who has a plan for ordering our lives in that classroom. Satisfying her teacher had become more important than whatever she might be thinking, and realizing this I felt guilty, I had to do something about it. So I went looking for her the next day, and when we met confessed my error, told her in effect, "Magda, forget what I say and just go with your own thought." She was pleased and I felt much better.

Lately I find myself saying, "Don't do what I tell you! If you have something that works for you, then go with it! I haven't got the answers, I don't know your material." Jane, working as Larry's editor, called me over: "He's not doing what he's supposed to," she told me. "He's not writing about the Toughman Contest at all, he's doing something else!" "Oh, he was with me last semester," I said, "he knows better than do what I tell him." "So *that's* how it is!" she said. In this way I lessen the chances of my rejecting the unfamiliar or the unexpected, I encourage them to go on their own. Who knows what new thinking they'll do once they're moving, if we just go along with them?

But you're very much concerned that all this writing about individual experience may not lead young people to more serious thought, that perhaps you should turn to a "cognitive" approach. And by way of illustration you mention a writing assignment by William Coles concerning the distinction between an amateur and a professional. Well, remember that the students Coles talks about in *The Plural I* were all science majors—in other words, a select group. They may have been interested in such topics (although I doubt it)—they could deal with 30 successive assignments that begin with "Explaining a scientific law to a nonscientist." But this is not the sort of program I'm interested in, with students marching along through a sequence of clever assignments devised by the teacher, as if they lack all initiative and no good idea for the work will ever come from them. Some time ago you were telling me that a question arose among your students: Is the patron of a photo shop a client or a customer? That's an interesting question for them to work with because it's their own, and it might lead them to some understanding of how considerations of social class are part of the language. You don't need the "cognitive" approach and a series of "cutting questions" when you have discussions going on that provoke such questions as this.

Or what about this: "How can you take a ride to Cape Town with a white man?" That could be a difficult one to manage in the classroom but it might be worth a try. During the names project you didn't notice the students musing deeply on the use of names and labels in society, you say, and yet here's a use of labeling—when you're tagged "white man"—that could provoke discussion and perhaps further exploration into the subject. From out of their own experience we can draw our subject matter.

There are many academicians, however, who think that individual expression in the writing classroom is too self-indulgent, not demanding enough. And so you wonder if you have made a mistake by advertising that feature of the course and your emphasis on the expressive voice. I would say so. You should, like lecturers in other departments, advertise your aims not your methods. For general consumption you will talk about the importance of developing coherent expression, critical thinking, and the understanding of form—while of course you work for them in your own way. It was wise to change the description of your program from "personal experience writing" to "orienting students to the academic environment," which sounds much more serious and is in fact what we intend to do. Present the public image required, and then when you go into the classroom and close the door behind you, do your own thing. For we are beyond good and evil, but no one must know it.

Regards from Beelzebub

--- / / / ---

19 December

Dear Friend John,

It's been too long since I've written, but my time is taken up with resisting, it seems—resisting the derisive criticism certain colleagues make of the expressive, and their talk about the language of academic argumentation, of comparison–contrast, their insistence on cognitive approaches in the classroom, claiming Vygotsky as their authority. I can still hear a shrill voice squelching my plea for personal writing with the cry of 'voyeurism!' And what's more, they say we can't encourage that kind of writing because so many lives here are just too painful to write about. But I don't want to join them in this retreat from life.

My students tell me stories sometimes that show their lives have given them experience and opinions they could use in our work, but when they start to write they seem to hold back and I wonder how I can get them to use their strength. Then too, so many of them come to me hungry. What is the point of asking a poor kid from one of the squatter camps to reflect on his experience? His mind darts here and there looking for ways to survive, reaching out to grasp at any hope. The narrative of his life is all false starts and hunger.

Even so, there must be ways to help them draw on their strength. This term our talk about names has developed into a sort of research project, and that came about because of all the opposition from the students this time when I suggested we choose new names for ourselves, descriptive names that would express some characteristic we wanted to encourage—a power name. I know from experience that a power name can help a person in times of trouble because one helped my companion's son Matthew, who is 9. He wanted to give up during our hike to the Maltese Cross, a six-story rock formation in the Cedarberg Mountains where we took a 4-day vacation (of all madness, when I can hardly afford my children's clothes, and clothes these days seem to mean Rebock jogging shoes at R350 and another R120 for a Haka high-heeled shoe, and 'if I don't get it I'm going to kill myself!'). Well, after I told Matthew the story of how the Navajo warrior spoke his power name and then had the strength to outrun his enemies, Matthew gave himself the name 'Rocks'—and although his ascent was still heavily laden with sobs and moans, he did finish the hike. Then when we saw the Cross in the distance his pains seemed to leave posthaste and he *ran* the rest of the way. The young have such a reserve of strength.

So I gave that example and suggested we all choose power names for ourselves. They'd been listening quietly enough, but now several were talking at once—the opposition was immediate and strong. 'Are you asking us to change our names because you cannot pronounce the Xhosa ones?' That startled me and put me on the defensive. In fact, many of the African students resisted this suggestion and talked about the names they'd already been given by their parents, insisting that these names have actually determined who they are. Or some insisted that the given name imposed on them a duty they are obligated to fulfill—Gogo for example (Like Grandfather), or Themba (Hope for the Family). Well, this was interesting but time was running out, so rather than press the matter further I asked for a vote on it. 'We need more time to think about this', Musa said, so I left it at that. I found the whole discussion somewhat anxiety-producing but I'm trying to follow them along.

Later I remembered what Paki told me about being named 'Linen' so that the Afrikaner master could call his slave easily. It's a common story, of whites changing the names of Africans, so this matter of taking new names is definitely a political issue. I thought we had a relationship that would allow me to try this, but it was obvious that I'd have to go along with their resistance and try to find a way to use it.

So then I suggested we do a sort of research project: Go out and interview parents and friends about the meanings of names and how they're given, and write up the results. They thought this was a good idea, and perhaps we can extend it to include some library work. But just as we start this project and I'm feeling good about it, one of my follow lecturers tells me it isn't demanding enough, the subject isn't serious enough.

This was at the last department meeting, and I was saying once again that personal writing helps students become competent with language. That was once too often for my colleague Gretchen Hammersmith, and she explained to me the facts of university life. 'Academic work is what they need', she said. 'Academic literacy is the goal!' And she acts on this belief by attacking almost ruthlessly those students who would support their position on say abortion with references to the Bible, insisting they use arguments like those in academic journals, supported by 'appropriate' references. Of course I want to take a more Socratic approach, giving the students time to express those old arguments and expecting that others will disagree with them, and so we get a discussion going. But I suppose that's not rigorous enough.

In fact, the claim is made that because common language habits contain so many indirect put-downs of blacks (and women and gays), then personal writing in the classroom would result in students simply repeating the prejudices of the prevailing order. They need to become critically literate so they can recognize the social or class bias in what they read and hear. One of the strange thoughts behind this program for critical literacy is that students make cognitive leaps and do better work if they are given tasks that *do not* access their past knowledge or experience, because their past knowing has been shaped by archaic, absolutist forms of thought and best gotten away from. This sort of talk has enormous appeal in South Africa, where analyzing the language of the oppressor is an all-the-time concern. Which is why Fairclough's *Critical Language Awareness* is much talked about—another flash in the dark sky of language teaching. The idea is that students should be learning how language reinforces the inequalities of society, how the language of bureaucrats serves to perpetuate the system, for example. But I notice that you never seem to focus explicitly on such issues, as if maybe you think that running a democratic and nonsexist classroom is enough. (Or did you actually tell me that once?)

The fact is, I quite enjoy running a more open classroom, with students reading the minutes of our meetings and debating whether it's all right to eat in class. And as we practice these democratic procedures the students seem to become more self-regarding, so to speak—they're able to look at themselves from a little distance. I think there's a growing sense of irony. When we were debating whether the men should have the 'right' to choose women as their sunshine partners, for example, the men seemed to be taking a more amused attitude about their traditional view of woman as inferiors, as if it's more a matter of habit than a conviction they want to get strident about. Unlike last year, when there was a great uproar in class because some students wanted us to read the article 'Circumcision: The Cruelest Cut of All?' and many of the African men threatened to walk out if we discussed this in front of women or uncircumcised men. Then the women said that if we could not discuss this topic, they would not allow discussion of abortion or any topic related to a woman's body. So of course I went along with them and we dropped it, but this year when the subject came up we reached a different result.

Among the Xhosa and most other tribal groups here, the circumcision ritual is a rite of passage to manhood, and boys 12 or 13 go off into the veldt to initiation schools for the operation. There are various accounts of what happens there, some of which include the smoking of much dagga. Paki told me about the pain and agony, not so much from the cutting itself (done with a knife or razor blade and without anesthetic) but from having his penis so tightly wrapped in leaves for days afterward that every urination was an ordeal. You can often recognize boys who are attending these schools because they're covered with white chalk. Some say they should not be seen at all, but here in urban areas I guess they're not able to find the seclusion necessary. A hospital circumcision is not regarded as a proper initiation into manhood, but with four deaths this year and nine medical castrations because of infection after this primitive operation, the practice has become a hot issue in the news media.

So this year I offered 'Circumcision: The Cruelest Cut of All?' as one article in our course reader to write about, and several men chose it. While they were talking about the piece, getting ready to write, I sat down with them. Ogaufi (a Tswana speaker from Mmabatho, a large town) said, 'The people in the country do it there, and sometimes they come to town and cause trouble, they can even kidnap you and take you to that school. Sometimes the boys even die there and they're just buried in the bush'. Not having been to the school himself, there were things he wanted to know about it. 'What do they do with the piece they cut off?' he asked Sobantu (a Xhosa speaker). 'Sometimes they bury it under some leaves', Sobantu said, 'but also they sometimes eat that piece of meat because they fear the witchdoctors may get hold of it and use it for magic against them'. I asked Sobantu if he was willing to continue with this topic, inasmuch as we would be reading our writing to other students, including women. He thought about that for a moment and then decided we should go on with it.

Last year when this subject came up there was a great outcry, but now this year, after our discussions about men taking women as sunshine partners, and whether men should serve as class secretary or only women, the article on circumcision was taken as just another thing to read. It was important to them, but the men seemed to be taking a more relaxed, even ironic attitude toward their own uneasiness with the issue. Is this how we escape those so-called oppressive language forms, by developing a sense of irony and using language to further equality?

And by using language expressively in the classroom are we making an ironic criticism of the insistence on academic literacy? Well I'm trying, but the current of thought is against me. It's very difficult to convince others that nondirective procedures will work with our hundreds of language learners—oops, I mean academic literacy learners. One is expected to uphold standards. There is the constant demand that students produce papers which fit the academic notion of the well-referenced paper, so how much time is left for the 'provocations' you talk about?

Also, I think of writing as something done by a person, an individual self, but postmodernism tells us the self is unstable, changing—only a series of personas shifting according to the demands of the moment. So when I ask students to draw on their lives and tell about their experience, am I just asking them to construct yet another persona? And they'll put it on and take it off as they come in and out of the room? Anything to please me.

Well, I'd better put this letter to rest. The holidays are coming and I hope you enjoy them.

The End—Ed

- - - / / / - - -

January 23

Dear Ed,

Reading your letter was a writing experience for me: I wrote comments in the margin, bracketed passages, underscored lines, drew in exclamation marks, question marks—and as I went along composed all sorts of mental replies to those persons you contend with, as if I were there with them myself. Let's go through some of this together, and we'll begin with the names project you've been doing with your young people, for I need to begin calmly.

Many of them, you say, seem to believe they have been given their identities with their names, and so are reluctant to consider alternatives, as if they might somehow lose themselves by changing their names. From early in life we have this sense of the power in naming. Six- and 7-year-olds often believe they would not be the same people if they had different names, a belief all of us still feel even after we have learned to think of names as mere labels. Criminals in hiding usually do not stray far from their given names when inventing aliases, so unwilling are they to give up their old selves, while individuals who wish to change their lives will often change their names first. So when you ask young people to consider how they've changed and to select more fitting names for themselves, you are asking them to become aware of their shifting selves and take responsibility for their own naming. This must provoke some anxiety. We like to believe that our individual identities are quite certain and secure.

Then too you say that some are reluctant to choose a new name because their given name indicates a duty they are expected to fulfill, so taking another name would suggest a turning away from that responsibility. I was delighted to have this confirmation of my remark in *Provocations* that a given name is the first burden we carry in this world. You have ventured with these young people into uncertain or even dangerous territory perhaps, and aroused their anxiety. You can use it.

So you went along with them, you accepted their decision not to choose new names for themselves, inviting them to tell you more about the ways of naming among their people, among the various communities represented there in your classroom, so now *they're* instructing and you're following along. I've read that many tribal Africans are given three names early in life: a personal name, which may relate to circumstances in the family at the time of birth; a praise name, which may express a hope for the child's future; and a kinship name, perhaps one relating to an animal or plant or object held sacred by a group of families tracing their origin to a common ancestor. And many Africans may take other names for themselves as their lives change, so that a person one knew by a particular name some years ago might be known by a different name today. Is any of this true, I wonder, of the young people you're working with? As they explain their naming customs to you—and to each other, for they come from different tribes and different parts of the country—what had seemed commonplace to them may now become a matter of some interest. And as they talk and write about this, perhaps other questions about the life around them may arise that are worth answering. They might go a long way with this project because they're considering a matter a great interest to them: their identities, their very selves, in a country where individual and social identities are in a process of rapid change. Where else but with you can their stories be told?

"Mankind came to seek a name, and nothing more," as the Ghanan sage Opanin Kwame Nyame tells us. So you have joined in that seeking with your young people, asking for the stories of their names and suggesting they take new names for themselves—only to hear a shrill cry of "voyeurism!" from one or another of your colleagues. You stand accused! And furthermore, we should not encourage personal writing, they tell you, because "so many lives here are just too painful to write about." Well, those young people are living with that pain every day and it makes them serious. And we will draw on their underlying seriousness by giving them a place, a quiet room, where they can learn to develop their inner narrative voice, where they can tell their stories and know themselves. And where their concerns, their anxieties, may lead them to seek for patterns and meaning in a clamorous world, and tell us what they find. For by the gesture of the word they have the possibility of knowing who they are in this strange place.

Is this voyeurism on our part, to suggest that young people write about themselves and their communities? Suppose we say, "Well of course it is! I think you've touched on a very important point here, because after all voyeurism is surely a motive for much of the reading we do. That's why we read novels or biographies or histories—to find out what other people have been up to. The page is a window we can peep through. And by the way, aren't all writers exhibitionists asking for attention? So I think you're right. We should encourage our students to be exhibitionists—and then of course they'll need voyeur-teachers who are interested in what they have to say. Thanks for making this point."

I think we should agree with these people and go on to draw out the implications of their argument. Rather than be in a hurry to defend our own view, we will make do with theirs and improvise on it, hoping to give it a little twist. Just as we go along with the young people in our classroom when they become emotionally engaged with some issue, so should we here—for how else is anyone to learn from us? Let us be a mirror reflecting back to others their position, although in a certain ironic light sometimes perhaps. There's some fun to be had with this.

As when your colleague Hammersmith tells you this sort of research isn't demanding enough for university work. Well then, to please her you must give this work an academic name. You should not talk about the good time your students are having with it or the interesting information they bring to you. That's a mistake. You should say, "We are developing a project in onomastics." She won't know what that is (the study of names and naming), and will be properly impressed. Then mention the library research you're planning.

And speaking of irony, you're right to suggest that our encouragement of expressive writing is an ironic criticism of direct instruction in the forms of literacy. The young people who go on from your classroom where they've been active, to another where they sit for instruction in critical literacy or the forms of academic discourse, will have a certain distance on that experience. They may begin to realize that for all the talk about recognizing oppressive uses of language or gaining the power of literacy or understanding the text, they are being trained to be docile.

In the school cafeteria last week Janet called out to me, saying "Let me tell you!" About what? I wondered. She'd been with me the semester before—a black girl, short and heavy-set, who walked aggressively along a corridor, confident in her bulk, but who spoke circumspectly and not often. She had just come from the first meeting of her prose fiction class and she wanted to tell me about it. "He say to us 'This is tough! Only one two you gonna git high grades here'. So I say, 'How come you know that already, you only just meet us?' an he say, 'I'm being realistic'. So I say, 'You discouragin us already, you judgin us an you don't even know us!'"

I said, "Good for you, Janet! Tell 'im! But you surprise me, taking that chance, speaking up like that."

"You always tell me speak up," she said, "so I got the habit."

The mere existence of a classroom like yours is an implied criticism of the "cognitive" approach and hand-it-down-to-them instruction favored by so many others, and you need no stronger argument than the practice itself. To argue the issue would be to give up your ironic position, and pointlessly because there's no persuading those people by the force of logic or evidence, assuming we had any. They must hold to their views for personal or political reasons, and continue as representatives of those various social forces which contend for the souls of the young—as do we all. An ironist, however, hovers over this ethical reality, Kierkegaard suggests, and "It is this very freedom, this hovering, which gives the ironist a certain enthusiasm, for he becomes intoxicated as it were by the infinity of possibles." But a system for instruction, a preplanned sequence, is the reduction of possibles and so the ironist must be outside all systems.

And here you have invited those young people to organize themselves for action, and hovering there once they are moving along you have the pleasure of observing how they manage the opportunity. So they elect their officers, conduct the sessions, hear the secretary's report, and go on to the work at hand, perhaps wandering away from the task you've proposed to one of their own choosing. Your outsideness, your ironic position—your willingness to go along—has made a democratic pattern of interaction possible. And within this social context those young people learn to be alert to the cues that signal the need for another step in a sequence of thought or activity, and so develop more sensitivity to form. Within that context they feel encouraged to draw on their lives, their experience, their own thought and so in effect make something of themselves on a sheet of paper. And in time they will come to know each other and themselves as the individuals who have said and written these things.

But even so, something troubles you about this. You wonder if these young people are sincere in what they write, if they are reporting themselves as they really are. If perhaps they think you have really been "asking them to construct yet another persona" so as to please you. Well of course you have! But let me put this in a different way by asking a question: What social situation can we construct with these young people so as to give them practice in the skills it takes to present the persona of an educated person? Those skills are a major concern with us. In fact, ours is not the "pedagogy of disclosure" favored by some, in the accounts of which people sometimes get to nattering on so about themselves they become quite tiresome. Rather, in our classroom young people are often encouraged to express themselves by getting outside themselves, so to speak, by taking an interest in other people with other concerns, in events beyond the home and neighborhood—to extend their histories in some new direction.

In short, we work with them to build a situational context—a context of feeling and thought within which new moves are possible and new skills are learned. Within which young people may develop the ability to draw concepts from their experience with the text before them as it interacts with the text of their individual lives. The concern of all of us there in that room is not so much to relive the past as to have new encounters by which we modify ourselves and perhaps discover a new orientation to the life around us. As when Magda notices what happened to a bystander at the Toughman Contest, and to another at the bloody fight she witnessed in a bar, and so considers the part that chance plays in our lives. Or when Jesse, reminded by the Toughman Contest of a fight he witnessed in the street, remarks that "You don't see two men in business suits fighting," and goes on to talk in his own way about the social class implications of machismo.

Or when Malbia says, "It's all those people payin money to get in and see the blood, they're just shriekin and hollerin! That's what I like. They're lookin for the point of weakness." And then she read to us a few paragraphs about her struggle with another young woman for a man. I said, "So when you were having that problem with her you were looking for the point of weakness, is that it?" "Yeah, that's what I do, I'm lookin for it, I'm gettin right in there!" And she bent down in her seat with an insinuating wiggle of glee. "That's what everybody's lookin for," she told us, and the others smiled. I said, "That would be a good title, 'The Point of Weakness'. Will you tell us about it in a paragraph, and then use those two fights to show us what you mean? This could be good!" These people, Magda and Jesse and Malbia, not only have interesting stories to tell, they have ideas worth developing—and our task is to provide a context in which their ideas are important and useful.

But some of your colleagues seem to be more object- than person-oriented and have a quite different notion of what we should do with young people. Our students, they tell you, must develop "academic literacy," they must be "initiated into the specific forms and ideas that are acceptable in a university culture"—which means teaching them to write in the academic genres. To write descriptions, summaries, explanations, arguments, comparisons, contrasts and all the rest because that's what we do in the academy. But surely the forms of language used in a given subject area—psychology, chemistry, literature, whatever—are the business of those who profess that subject. What else are those people doing if not teaching a particular use of language? Of course it's so much easier to pass out facts than teach people how to think with them—than to teach writing, that is. Yet why should I try to do this work for them when I have my own responsibility to the young people who come to me?

Let me tell you about academic literacy. I read that Basil Bernstein's work in sociolinguistics has been "decisively overturned" by Scribner and Cole's "magisterial" study, *The Psychology of Literacy*, so I looked it up and what did I find? It turns out to be a study of language learning among a tribe in Liberia and contains no mention of Bernstein! Nor does it seem to contradict him in any substantial way. Then I read that William Labov has shown Bernstein's work to be a dubious proposition, so I looked up his piece on "The Logic of Nonstandard English" only to find that Labov is being critical of those who have made an invidious use of that work in order to denigrate the language abilities of lower status blacks: "Bernstein's views are filtered through a strong bias against all forms of working-class behavior . . . ." In short, it is necessary that Bernstein be misread and dismissed, for if he were understood his message would be persuasive but unwelcome.

By the way, Labov offers little support for "cognitive" approaches in the language classroom, noting that "in many ways working-class speakers are more effective narrators, reasoners and debaters than many middle-class speakers"—which suggests that even the latter would benefit from a narrative-based training. At one point he quotes the speech of an educated, middle-class black, asking if this illustrates Bernstein's elaborated language code; he remarks on the verbosity of this passage, in which "Words multiply, some modifying and qualifying, others repeating or padding the main argument." Sounds like academic discourse to me. As students move through college their speech tends to become more abstract, they learn to clarify an idea by repeating it or rephrasing it rather than by giving a concrete illustration in the form of a narrative perhaps. (I have in mind an interesting study reported by Dell Hymes in *Ethnography, Linguistics, Narrative Inequality*.) So this speaker, like the middle-class storytellers Bernstein tells about, seems less concerned with the content of what he says than with its form—with seeming to offer a logical argument, one thought after another. But as Labov remarks, "we do not know what he is trying to say, and neither does he," despite all those words. Perhaps he went through a training that required him to produce on demand so many words of argument on whatever topic was assigned—but when a topic does not arise out of an experiential context, or cannot be related to one, the student really has no thoughts about it and so makes a desperate effort to find something, anything to say, and having found something repeats it with variations, those pages must be filled. This is training in verbosity or pretense. For thought comes only with one's personal engagement with the matter at hand, it's experience that produces ideas.

How many young people sit in the classroom playing at being students, assuming the role, while their serious interest is otherwise engaged? But a university, as I understand it, is a place where young people should actively participate in the making of knowledge. I cannot give it to them, for what they learn they must appropriate for themselves—and that requires an autobiographical presence. That means modifying attitudes and habits of thought, and extending one's present skill with language, so as to come to terms with new experience—and new experience we can have together. It will require of them some reorganization or development of self, for here we're all working on another chapter in our life stories.

Of course this may not seem rigorous enough to those who say that "cognitive development" and "academic literacy" must come before narrative or individual writing. In fact, these people have told you that students "will do better work if they are given tasks which *do not* access their past knowledge or experience, because their past knowing is shaped by archaic, absolutist forms of thought and best gotten away from." The contempt shown here for those young people and their experience is startling! Although in fact it expresses a view rather common in this country among the practitioners of the so-called "critical pedagogy," who complain quite impatiently sometimes of the cynicism and resistance of students when presented with a program for radical social change, students who insist on clinging to their outmoded notions of "bourgeois self-fashioning." Perhaps we should refer all these unhappy professors to *The Pedagogy of the Oppressed*, where Friere remarks that

> As women and men, simultaneously *reflecting on themselves and on the world*, increase the scope of their perception, they begin to direct their observations towards previously inconspicuous phenomena. [Ordinary elements in their experience] begin to "stand out," assuming the character of a problem and therefore of challenge. . . . These elements are now objects of their consideration, and as such, objects of their action and cognition. (italics added)

But I fear that many well-intentioned teachers do not really believe their students are capable of thinking independently and cogently, so they hurry to give them correct ideas along with the information they expound. As Bernstein points out, the experience and ideas of students who come without middle-class habits of speech and thought "may be disvalued and humiliated within schools," or simply ignored as irrelevant to the educational endeavor.

What we have in much of this talk about the "culture of the academy" is an emphasis on the collective over the individual. Marx envisioned the inevitable goal of human development to be a homogeneous culture for one humanity, whereas in fact the energy of modern life is a drive toward cultural diversity. And what more diverse a place do we have than the university, with its population drawn from distant places and its catalog of seemingly endless specializations? You and I are there to help young people develop their effectiveness in written expression—in the expression of their individuality, the tendencies and understandings manifested in their experience of a changing world, so they may recognize their possibility and make their place at school, at work, in the world as circumstances allow. This seems to me a realistic preparation for modern life, where one's self is no longer given with a collective membership one is born into.

So it's the authoritarian stance of many well-meaning academics that I object to, not the knowledge or insight they offer. When the critical linguists you mention, for example, suggest that we should be looking with our students at how language is used to reinforce the inequalities in society, I can only agree, but as you mention I rarely focus explicitly on such issues. I don't need to because they will appear of themselves if the students are talking about matters that really concern them.

One quick look at the Toughman piece and Tanika said it wasn't for her. "I'm not doin this one," she said. "I'll thinka somethin, don' you worry bout it." So she went through a stack of articles I had there, from magazines or taken from books, and found Ralph Wiley's essay "Hair." It tells of a young black woman fired from her job as reservationist at a Marriott hotel because she adopted a rather striking hair style, and goes on to speak of how many people in the black community make a living catering to the concern of blacks for their hair. "The reason God gave black people our hair in the first place," Wiley remarks, "is that God always wanted us to have some business of our very own." And he suggests that whites have made African hair a symbol of their racist contempt for blacks, who sometimes come to feel that if only their hair were different they would be accepted in the white world. Wiley makes this point with some subtlety but Tanika saw it.

She titled her essay "What Comes Naturally." It begins, "In order to survive in the business workplace of the '90s, there are certain accommodations that must be made," and goes on consider how an individual's beliefs or culture may make those accommodations difficult. She refers to the woman who lost her job at the Marriott rather than change her hair to suit the employer, and speaks of braids, twists, afros, coiled cuts and other styles for African hair. She gives a brief history of these styles, remarking that some believe "your hair is the filter for information that your mind receives, and the way you treat it says a lot about the condition of your mind." She mentions how the slave masters refused to give their blacks "tools of personal hygiene, like a comb." She discusses white attitudes toward African hair and remarks that sometimes today "slave masters have the title of employer." With this she approaches her conclusion, which in the first draft began this way:

> Having a hair style that is natural for your hair has nothing to do with one's ability to master the duties of their job. Also, a natural state of hair is just what it says, "natural." This means [. . .]

and she goes on to explain that African hair styles are natural, sanitary, and attractive.

I said in effect, "Tanika, do you see that you're arguing with the honkies here, you're defending African hair as if what they say about it must be answered. But you've already shown the problem is not black's hair but white racism, and now here at the end you're leaving this on *their* ground, you're letting them define the subject. But the first sentence of that paragraph—I wonder if you could go on with that idea and get the argument on *your* ground." She came back later with this revision:

> Professionalism has not the slightest relation to a person's hairstyle, but pertains to one's ability to master the duties of the job. It seems that employers sometimes overlook the characteristics of their employees that are the most important to their business. They observe and demand change of insignificant features of their employees, such as a hairstyle or an outfit. Their focus should be on how well their employees perform their jobs. Still, there are people of color who are required to disregard their own beliefs or culture and conform or lose their jobs.

She understood the importance of what had happened here. Before she read this paper to the class she told us what she had gone through to write it, and she talked about her struggle to end the piece effectively. For the first time, I think, she had become aware of how the white viewpoint she despises had actually controlled her thinking and made her defensive. And this, by the way, from a young woman in a class for students at risk— young people labeled as weak thinkers, poor writers. Of course not all of them will write this well but now I have Tanika to help me with the others.

Such understandings, in this case of how the majority point of view is internalized even by those who oppose it, must develop out of the learners' lived experience. It is not to be added to their minds as simply another fact while their thought remains essentially undisturbed. So my task is to develop a context in which they can draw on their own experience and use it in the making of new thought—and where they may in fact have new experience to use in their self-appropriation. For they must in effect instruct themselves, I will not take that responsibility from them. But I will go with them as they work, and help along the way.

During every project we worked on, Richard kept asking me, "What do you want?" and I'd say, "I don't know, I can't read your mind—give us something good." But every week he would ask, "What do you want?" until finally I said, "Richard, you're asking me to tell you just what to do, and then you'll do it and you won't have to think." "But that's the way I was taught," he said. "That's the way they trained me." "Well then, just play along with us and you'll become a different person, you'll learn to walk by yourself." That was the help I gave him, to disturb his passivity.

The cognitivists, however, like the practitioners of a critical pedagogy, will tell their Richard just what they want from him, just what understandings he is to demonstrate—and they have so many good ideas or concepts to hand over to him! They cite Vygotsky as their supporting authority, you say, having in mind I suppose his remarks about the value of adult intervention in children's learning. Here they may have been somewhat misled by his translators, who took considerable liberties with his texts and cobbled together *Mind in Society*, for example, from various sources, adding the words of others to it and shaping it so as to make of Vygotsky a cognitive scientist very much like themselves. Yet he began, we should remember, as a teacher of literature and was inclined to think that literary texts provide more complex accounts for the understanding of mind than psychological theory. He was not interested in the development of abstract reasoning per se but in the development of *mind* or consciousness, which depends less on a series of cognitive advances than on a complex process in which emotion and reason are equally important.

In fact, the whole notion of teaching the forms of discourse as represented in textbooks and many college writing programs must be suspect in the light of Vygotsky's thought. As you said earlier, he remarks that "thinking is from the social to the individual," that "learning to generalize, to move from concrete language to more abstract language, depends very much on the 'social relationship' between teacher and student." So if the forms of thought have their origins in patterns of group activity that are subsequently internalized by the individual, as he suggests, then surely we need to consider what kinds of social interaction or group process we should develop in the writing classroom, rather than simply pass on the forms of discourse as preserved in textbooks or dictated by the teacher's outline.

James Britton was the first to see the relevance of Vygotsky's thought to the teaching of writing (*Language and Learning*, 1969), and even earlier Basil Bernstein drew on it to support his distinction between the restricted and elaborated language codes that would appear in *Class, Codes and Control*. So here we have ample basis for the kind of work we want to do in a classroom with young people—but even so, we are not to escape responsibility for the teaching practice we have chosen by saying that Vygotsky or some other authority told us to do it. Nor is there anything to be gained by arguing interpretations of his text with others. Let your colleagues have their Vygotsky and go along with them, talk about academic literacy and cognitive development and such good things, although you do so by reference to a private dictionary in which these terms have the particular meanings you give them, according to your idea of what young people may become.

Furthermore, it would not be healthy for a department to have a single philosophy of teaching, as if the truth were known at last for all time. Where a new way of life is developing, as in South Africa, there are many possibilities of interaction to be tried, and I've noticed that good writing is often produced in classrooms where methods are used I'm not comfortable with—so much depends on the character of the individual teacher. You wonder if the young people you work with are only trying to please you rather than speaking for themselves, and let's hope they do want to please you! Just as we ourselves want to earn the good regard of those we respect. What young people do in our classrooms they may do not only for themselves but for us—their work is sometimes a gift—and I see teachers who work very differently than I receiving a gift in words now and then.

We need those others who don't agree with us. Given the unsettled political situation in South Africa I can understand the concern of your colleagues to secure their positions, to insist on the authority of the teacher and its foundation in the work of other authorities. And as we all work together, their concerns, their ideas, their words, force us to clarify our own thought or reconsider our practice, and so help us complete another chapter of our autobiographies.

Well, I began this letter in anger because of what your colleagues sometimes say about our work, but now after this rather lengthy response I feel much better.

So I thank you for the stimulation—JR

- - - / / / - - -

January 15

Dear Ed,

Yesterday afternoon a young Wall Street lawyer called and asked if he could come for a counseling session after work, so I was busy with him from 6:30 till nearly 8—and I'll tell you the story because it relates a subject we've been talking about.

Dan had come to see me once before, so I knew his history. He's a bond trader for a securities firm and makes very good money, but now a big project he'd been working on for 9 months, one that could earn the firm a big profit, had fallen through. So all day he was depressed with the feelings of insecurity and unworthiness that have dogged him all his life— ever since his father told him years ago that he is stupid and will never be the equal of his brother. He has felt like an imposter passing as the brilliant young Wall Street go-getter, and now with this failure he'll be found out.

So you see the problem before me. We would talk and I would have to find a way to send this very depressed young fellow away smiling, perhaps even laughing. But after nearly an hour I began to wonder if my improvisational skill was up to the challenge. People will often hold tightly to their unhappiness as to a family treasure.

I listened for a long time as he poured it all out, tears welling in his eyes now and then, and murmured a few comments along the way. After all, the officers of the firm had agreed with him that the project was worth a try. They hadn't foreseen the unexpected event which rendered it hopeless. He hadn't lost any of the $5 million they'd given him to execute the project. Everyone in the office had been quite supportive. He listened, but consolation was not what he wanted from them or from me.

In fact, his gloom deepened. "In college you succeeded brilliantly," I said, "because you had your father to fight—you showed the old bastard what you could do. When you're fighting to prove yourself you overcome these feelings of inferiority. No wonder you're a good bond trader. But now on the job when the fight is lost and yet everyone is supportive, you feel infantile, as if the child must be consoled. They're trying to help but they're only making you feel worse." He nodded—yeah, he felt bad.

So I left that and went on to minor matters, stalling for time. When did he last speak to his father? When was his last vacation? Then I touched on another area of his work, where he supervises people concerned with legal issues, and spoke of how he guides them, how they need him, how they like him. It's good to work with them when he's feeling down. So far I hadn't told him anything he didn't know.

"Well," he said, "I guess there's nothing you can do." He had talked himself out and I felt the sense of an ending. By now I was tired of his self-pity and the tenaciousness with which he clung to his unhappiness, so I began talking with perhaps a slight edge of impatience in my voice, without knowing where this would go, just improvising.

"That's right, there's not much I can do. When we work with a person who has one of these complexes it's very difficult because he holds onto his problem, he doesn't want to give it up. If you took it away from him, he wouldn't know how to live without it. He'd be a different person, and who knows who? But he's comfortable with his complex, as with an old friend. You've felt this way a very long time, these feelings have been your companion all these years. So maybe we should give this companion a name. Now let's see—what should the name be? I wonder if—can you think of one?" Dan was looking at me somewhat quizzically.

I said, "Do you remember that cartoon character who used to go around with a little black cloud over his head? What was his name?" Neither of us could remember, but now he was beginning to smile.

"Well, we've got to have a name for this companion. No sense trying to get rid of him, he's going to be with you for a long time, you might as well use him. I've got it! This is Mumpy! Yes yes, now I know him—this is Mumpy!" Dan almost laughed.

"Now what I want you to do when you leave, is take Mumpy with you. For God's sake, don't leave him here with me! He's your close companion, you know each other so well, you have to be together. So on your way home, while you're sitting there in the subway car, I want you to think about Mumpy, this companion of yours. Think about what he's like and how long you've been together. And tomorrow at work if you begin to feel down, you feel unhappy, just pull over your memo pad and write on it, 'Mumpy is here!' Then write those words again, just cover that little sheet. Now you do this every time you feel unhappy. You never need to be alone in your unhappiness, you have a companion, you have Mumpy." And as we got up from our seats I said, "So let me hear you say it."

"Mumpy is here," he said, laughing.

So I walked him to the subway entrance, and as he went down the stairs called after him "Don't forget Mumpy! Take him with you!" He smiled and waved. Someday he'll pull the memo pad over and start to write "Mumpy is here," but then he'll say "Damn it all, I don't have time for you now!" It's so important that we find the right names for ourselves.

Hoping to hear from you soon—JR

CHAPTER 7

Of Narrative and Identity

3 February

Dear John,

The Dean of Education has created something of a stir with a paper in which he says that 'African universities will have to come to grips with the challenge of large class teaching', and I'm told that our program must take at least 150 students per lecturer or be disbanded. This has been an ongoing debate but now the tone is becoming acrimonious, with those who argue for small class size definitely on the defensive. We're accused of favoring a 'hothouse model' of teaching. And also the use of narrative writing is coming under attack even from some of our own staff, who insist that students need much expository writing and a course 'rich in linguistic theory'. It's time to get seriously academic!

I watched my colleague Gretchen Hammersmith shout or rather go hysterical in my class when she saw what we were doing there. Not rigorous enough for her! I'd invited her in so she would have some acquaintance at least with another approach but maybe that was a mistake. She has a high-pitched semi-scream and used it on a student who claimed that the fetus is alive by God's will and so it ought not be killed. Hammersmith burst out in her wild way with something like 'You'll *never* be able to discuss it that way in the educated community! That's not how educated discourse is carried on! And furthermore, not all Christians accept that view', and so on.

Then later she gave me hell for having this discussion in class rather than following the syllabus we'd all agreed to. It was developed with the thought that students should first experience the expository readings in our course reader—which is very polemical and politically correct with its selection of anti-racist, anti-sexist, anti-class exploitation articles—and only then, armed with facts and the forms of academic discourse, would they engage in debate. Yet there we were, plunging right in without a proper academic preparation.

The fact is, I'm giving grades for different activities entirely than students are doing in other classrooms, and I wonder sometimes if mine are keeping up with the others. I can hear Alistair now talking about the 'culture of the academy', and how students and lecturers who depart from common practices experience strong anxiety. Indeed I do, and often. I'm not sure about the students—I don't recall them ever complaining about not doing what everyone else is. In fact, when Alistair interviewed students for a research project he was doing, one of them said my course was different from others because 'I was asked my opinion, I had to think about things all the time. I had to react. That was different from all the other courses I took'. A few others made similar comments.

But you know, I get tired of arguing about the culture of the academy with Alistair or Hammersmith. I find that I'd much rather talk with lecturers in the social sciences or theology than in the writing program or English department, because their subject matter is interesting and so often about ethics. At a New Year's Eve party I found myself defending some fellow who had given up a successful career as an engineer and gone into the priesthood. That seems like a reasonable life choice to me. He's moved from an object-oriented career to become person-oriented (in Bernstein's terms), and he'll be talking with people about the moral decisions they have to make. Sometimes I wonder just what moral issues might arise in the provocative class you talk about, where students are not being instructed, they're acting and reacting. Or is it foolish to think that some sort of ethical awareness might arise there?

Among the Africans there's often an ethical obligation given in their names, as I've said, so individuals are constantly reminded of what they owe the family or community. In fact, one of the African lecturers told me that when students here write 'personally', they do not in fact tell about their individual selves so much as about the experiences of others like them in the community. They're more sociocentric than egocentric, and they describe themselves as living out one role or another the community has defined for them. As when Mjoli wrote that he was always troublesome before he went to initiation school, but after that he was completely changed—he was shown there what it is to be a man and he gave up all those ways that were always getting him into trouble. Such an account seems to me more generic than individual. And one girl wrote about being confused when trying to choose among all the courses at the university, but when I asked her if she was really confused she said 'No, but my friends are'.

So in their culture personal narratives are not a familiar kind of discourse, and here I've been asking them to write about their individual selves as if they understood that and could do it. Is what I've been trying to do with them completely misguided? I was really worried about this for awhile, and then the idea came to me that maybe personal writing is a way to help them give up their dependence on groupthink, so to speak—to teach them that they are individuals with experiences and thoughts of their own. So isn't personal writing a way to help them get beyond those 'archaic, absolutist forms of thought' my colleagues warn about, like tribal prejudice and rivalry? Isn't this a move toward democratic individualism?

But no sooner do I get that worked out in my mind than I read how postmodernism tells us the individual self is a myth, we're all socially constructed. So how much does one's self owe, I wonder, to social conditioning and how much to a unique individuality? I know you insist on the independent self despite the exquisite and I must say often enjoyable arguments of Barthes (in 'The Death of the Author') and Foucault (in 'What is an Author?')—if their essays mean what I think they do. The other day I was saying we should help students develop their individual styles, and Gretchen Hammersmith came back at me with a quote from Fredric Jameson, where he says there is no "unique and private identity, a unique personality and individuality, which can be expected to generate its own unique, unmistakable style". I guess I'm still out of touch with current theory.

This question of individual and society keeps coming up here. Alistair, for one, insists on the necessity of explicit anti-racist, anti-sexist instruction so that individuals are required to consider their social views and we counteract the subtle ways society has instilled repressive values. And I do wonder sometimes how best to manage the internalized racism among students, as when they move from blaming everything bad in their lives on apartheid to blaming themselves, describing their background as primitive, stupid, uncivilized. But I don't think they should be forced to give up what they are, their own heritage and personal histories, they should learn to use them. Maybe we need to get away from the big social issues for awhile and just produce some good individual, expressive work and get on with the story we're making.

But the fact is, I think I've been doing a very poor job of promoting the benefits of narrative and poetic methodologies to other lecturers. Maybe I should pass around this article I'm reading by Harold Rosen called 'Stories of Stories: Footnotes on Sly Gossipy Practices'—and here's a quote:

> Since narrative draws on any language resource that suits its turn,
> plundering every kind of discourse [. . .] it digs deep into the linguistic

resources of the narrator. Indeed, the teachers with whom I am working are persuaded that narrative, more than any other mode, produces the highest levels of linguistic performance.

Now there's a bit of music! But of course I'm going to be asked how students will ever learn the language of the academy if we stress the writing of narratives, how will they ever learn referencing skills? Here's a rather disturbing story by one of my students:

It is a sad memory and a memory that will never leave my mind. My best friend was murdered and I was forced to Avenge.

Mother has send us to the shop. The day before Sandile who was my Friend has quarelled with Dennis over Dolly who was now Sandile's girlfriend. We met Dennis while we were still on our way and we simple walk past him without encounting problems. We arrive at the shop and bought what we have been told to buy. I was busy paying for the grocery when Sandile left the shop. I hear him screaming and I rush to the scene to see what was wrong with him. When I got there I find that he was fighting with Dennis and he has been stabbed. I was not carrying a weapon so I have to use my hands for fighting. I send blows into Dennis's face and the knife sleep of his hand. I manage to grab it and he run away. I gave him a chase but he manage to escape. Sandile was lying down in the pool of blood.

I remember kneeling down and I notice a change in my Friend eyes. I call his name to see if he can hear me but he only say "Avenge for me best Friend" and he closed his eyes. By that time there was a mob surrounding us. I think it was the shop owner who had called the Ambulance. I was fifteen by that time and I was so upset. They put my Friend inside and after they have left I rush home to report the incident. Mother comfort me and she said that I must not worry my friend will be save. Sandile's mother came early in the morning to report that they have receive a call from the hospital that my friend was pastaway. I lock myself in my room and weep. Late that day New broke out that Dennis has been arrested. Rummours with their notorious Fact to trace their origin spread out saying I was responsible my Friend death. People also gossip that to show that if I was a true Friend I must avenge. To kill a person who has killed your Friend was taken as a custom in our society.

Arrangemants for the funeral were made and on the day of the funeral I was given a chance to give a brief description history of my friend. My voice box was as if was out in a deep Freeze and I can not talk so I was left speechless. Pain, sorrow and anger was embracing me. I was crying and not believing that I will never see him again. I look at he's girl friend and she was weeping and that was the moment when my friend last words rang and I decided that I will Avenge.

The day of the hearing for case came and I was the witness. I was young and I was not comfortable when I saw that Dennis's parents has hired a lawyer. I told the court what happened and it was the honest truth. The lawyer impose questions and they were tricky. I end up contradicting myself. I was so angry and feeling like bursting into tears. Dennis was sentence in to six month. I left the court trembling, I swear to myself that when he is set free I will do something.

After six months he came back boosting of being a hero in murdering my Friend, also claiming that I was the next victim. On hearing that I fail to wait and go out hunting for him. He was a alcolist so I know where to get him. I met him one night and I manage to gun him down and I ran away before I was noticed. I was the Firs suspect but I win the case because there was no evidence.

I have learn from these incident that I am capable of hurting. I've realise that if there is no evidence you can win. I will always hate this memory and wish it can leave my mind.

This was more of a confession than I wanted to hear, but when we talked about it he told me he'd gone looking for the guy and then turned back. And now the memory is still with him and he often wonders if he should have gone on, so in the story he carried out his wish. I believed him, and I thought he'd written a very interesting paper. Of course this is not the sort of thing other departments want students doing, they want papers that show evidence of research and referencing skills. But surely a narrative like this can be a step in that direction.

The English department has been hammering the English 101 students with up to five periods of work a week. Unless they're seen to be putting in as many hours as underpaid farm workers they're lazy bums, and the same is true in other departments. Continuous pleas from the masters class in applied linguistics to get their workload reduced came to naught, as the lecturers who have come up through the European or Afrikaner slave-driving system are determined to give new recruits the same treatment. 'We are being closely watched', one of them told me, meaning that we've got to maintain First World standards and then some.

Meanwhile, I'm forced to seek additional income as the salary here is seriously short of my rather modest needs, so in addition holding writing workshops for old ladies I've set up in the tutoring business. A teacher at Cape Town High School sent me her son, who's a nervous wreck. He dropped out of high school, and he's such a mess even the Red Cross Children's Clinic refused to accept him, so his father (a psychiatrist, divorced—this kid's unlucky) sent him to a counseling home in Mitchell's Plain full of youngsters with various horrifying histories. His roommate was an epileptic who would wake him up in the night sometimes having a fit, until one night he swallowed his tongue and David found him dead the next morning. His mother pleaded with me to take him as a writing student, as that's the one thing he really wants to do.

So every Friday morning he comes over to work with me, and we get on well together. Last week he read me a story called 'The Dictionary of Dirty Words', about a vicious bully named Stuie Gerwitz, the arch child bully of all time. His anger and the fear other children have of him are very dramatically described. Stuie, with his 'fat fingers and nails sharp as steel', tells how he vomited on his cousin and everyone hearing him 'knew just when to laugh, or else'. He knows so many dirty words that the dictionary of the title obviously belongs to him. The story hits a climax when Stuie senses the vulnerability of a boy already in some emotional pain and calls him a 'fuckup'—the worst curse of all at that moment, for it compounds the boy's feelings of rejection, inferiority, stupidity, and condemns him to be an outcast. The emotional force of the story continues with a contrasting scene in which another boy says to him, 'Let's be friends'.

It's a very affecting story, drawn from his own experience of course, and he told me how those curses seemed to affect him much more powerfully than the kind words. I thought maybe we should write about why that might be—to encourage some analytical thinking to go along with the story. That would be building on what he had brought to me, which is what I think you recommend. So we free wrote our reactions to this question of why curses are so much more powerful than kind words. And David came up with some interesting comments about how ego rules all, how selfish people are, how their pride is so important to them they make life 'a continual war' to keep it up, but sometimes they're beaten down until 'even misery is comforting, and they live for sympathy'. We talked about this—I felt it necessary to take his thinking very seriously.

Doesn't a lot of academic work simply ignore the life situation that students are immersed in, and so we lose the ideas that could come from it? On the other hand, I'm not sure how far into those lives I should allow myself to be drawn. I made friends with Mzonke Mpofana in my first year, and indeed he visited my home and I his. But I found my time being swallowed up by—well, the very needy situation his family was in. Could I give him driving lessons? Could I take his sister to the hospital? Could he use the office phone? Then there was Sister, who came back after nearly a 2-week absence from class to tell me the wind had blown the roof off her house (or shack?) in the Transkei and she'd gone to get it fixed, so now she doesn't have any money for food, so can I help her? I said that with so many needy students at the university, my helping her would be showing favor. She replied that she was no longer 'just any student but someone who has exchanged more with you in these personal papers'. Experiences like these keep me from being as sociable as I'd like to be.

Speaking of Mzonke reminds me that I stopped by to visit him last week. We were happy to see each other and began joking about how bourgeois we'd become. 'Hey man, you were always interrogating us about this Marxism', he said. 'And we were all Marxists in those days'. Which wasn't the safest position to take back then under apartheid, when the government had informers even in classrooms. For a time there was a ministry official with the title 'Liquidator' whose function it was to name communists, and anyone so named became in effect a nonperson and was permanently barred from public employment. I asked Mzonke what had happened to Eric, who let us know that he was a 'Classical Marxist' and therefore understood class struggle in South Africa. 'Hey Ed, Eric has become a lecturer in Port Elizabeth, and he doesn't talk about Marxism anymore'. I remembered him as the nattiest dresser in the class, certainly not favoring the peasant look. Talking with Mzonke brings back memories of other students and I wonder where they are, what they're doing now.

But here I am alone tonight with this bloody syllabus, the workbook and reader, looking at these exercises and articles, wondering if I should move along in the program in step with the other lecturers or are there thoughts among my students needing expression? An ironic moment as I reflect on the fact that I know nothing.

So *'Fudua!. . fudua!. . . fudu-a-a!* (Stir the pot! Stir the p-o-t!), the push-push yelling started as everyone, man, woman and child alike, strained all the muscles in their bodies to get inside' (the train that leaves Johannesburg for Soweto, yeah man!). Miriam Tlali's *Footprints in the Quag.*

So Fudu-a-a! white man—Ed

- - - / / / - - -

March 4

Dear Ed,

You have made many observations in your last letter that invite response, but first there is that story of a young man's sad memory. The setting in which this unfolds could as well be some section of Brooklyn or the Bronx, where people hear at night the sound of gunfire and in the morning send their children out to walk through ominous streets to school. It shows how in the culture of poverty a code of behavior develops, enforced by peer pressure, that defines quite rigidly and narrowly what it means to be a man. And how a woman becomes one of the few possessions a poor man can have, so losing her is like losing manhood itself. "I thought I'd forgotten her, but last night I had a dream. We were walking and talking and she told me her new boyfriend is a better man than me." (This from one of my students.) As white middle-class teachers we may understand all this in an abstract sort of way, but in these stories we have the lived experience. Without such expressions from young people we may fail in our understanding of them, for there is a natural tendency to ignore or dismiss, or simply not recognize, ways of thinking that are unfamiliar to us.

A high school class of honors students in Brownsville, Texas, read Gabriel García Márquez's novel *Chronicle of a Death Foretold*, in which a young man is murdered because he is thought to have violated a daughter of the local town. The students dismissed the story as unrealistic, the kind of thing that only happens in soap operas. It seemed preposterous to them that killing someone to avenge the loss of a woman's honor could be considered morally justifiable in any modern society. Yet in that class there was an Anglo boy dating a Mexican-American girl, and when he broke off the relationship her mother hired an assassin to kill him, and he was shot to death in the driveway of his home. Mexican-Americans and Anglos live in the same Brownsville neighborhoods, shop in the same stores and go to the same schools, yet hardly know each other. (Marie Brenner reported this story in the *New Yorker*.)

And in Rian Malan's *My Traitor's Heart* (you have me reading all these books about South Africa) we learn that apartheid held cultural differences between the races to be distinct and immutable, a consequence of God's will. So any expression of curiosity about African cultural values or experiences seemed to admit such differences and so give oblique support to apartheid, suggesting a patronizing or even insulting attitude toward Africans. Malan never asked his black friends about their beliefs and customs because then he would be setting them apart as different from himself, and consequently they remained strangers to him. In his very resistance to apartheid he had internalized one of its underlying tenets and lived by the law of separation. As you once said, the apartheid of the mind is very deep.

There seems no end of reasons for ignoring the lives our students actually have and denying the value of their individual expression—but with all those various cultures represented within the university and in your classroom is everyone to live there on some superficial level of politesse without really knowing or understanding each other? Obviously you think otherwise, for the work you do with young people encourages them to bring their histories with them. That story of a sad memory told by a serious young man takes us into the lives and culture of many young people—a region of disquiet that some of your colleagues would rather ignore in favor of "the culture of the academy," where life is neatly ordered and we learn to deal with each other abstractly, from a distance. The new workbook and reader you sent along are sound enough academically I suppose, but why not include such writing as this story, which reminds us of how difficult life can be for some of our young people?

There is so much one could do with it! I would ask the writer's permission to share this story with others, and I would ask him to assert its claim to be known by giving it a title. I would read it with students and ask for an immediate response in writing—and I might write along with them because I'd like to comment on what it seems to be saying indirectly about men and women. From these papers we would learn what other stories are suggested by it, what issues it touches on that are important to those young people. Then we might shape those papers into more considered essays. So from this one story other stories and essays would come, demonstrating once again that narrative is the basis of all writing. And by turning our attention to issues of ongoing life we are helping prepare the way for other possibilities of feeling and thought.

But do we really want to go into those grubby lives? By denying narrative we can ignore the sordid facts of everyday life as many of our young people know it, and deal instead with higher matters, with safe abstractions. We can marginalize dissenting voices. The problem with all this personal experience stuff—talking and writing about it—is that young people might not arrive at correct views or right conclusions. This seems to worry some of your colleagues. And perhaps they're uncomfortable with expressive work because they don't know what to do with it when they get it, so they hurry on to their own concerns. But your aim in working among such people is not to convince them they're wrong to reject a narrative methodology, for then they would resent you, but rather to help them satisfy their need for order and a predictable future while you continue on your own path. We must put the people we work with ahead of any "truth" we imagine we have, and keep quiet when they're talking.

One thing they talk about, and rightly so, is the need to help young people develop some intellectual grasp of how they're using language. So after all the work prompted by that story of a sad memory, I might raise this question: "Could this story be improved if its language were improved?" Now there's a problem—because the "poor" English puts us immediately into the situation. To "correct" the language would be to place both reader and writer at a considerable remove from the events, as though the person speaking to us in the story were much older and looking back with a mind now educated. And yet, are there some changes in language that would improve the effectiveness of the story? These are interesting considerations, it seems to me, and taking them up with young people would get them to thinking about language in a more sophisticated way.

They would be learning, for example, that there is a difference between the one who speaks on the page and the one who has written those words—words that may have once been spoken, many of them, when others were first told the story but now in writing have become a voice apart. And the writer is expected to be in control of that voice. So which sentences here need further attention? What, if anything, should be changed in the language of this story so that a convincing voice is heard speaking there?

Now even if they decide the language should remain entirely unchanged, they are evaluating it according to a different standard than that of their ordinary speech, a more formal or "academic" standard. And they are internalizing that standard even as they decide against it. However, to internalize a different or "higher" standard of language is to develop a feeling of dissatisfaction with one's present life situation (for a different standard of language implies a different standard for the way one is to live). What this will mean for young people as poor as these and with such doubtful futures, living in such uncertain times, is another matter. In any case, we can use such expressive writing to address many of the intellectual or academic issues that concern all of us who teach these writing courses.

However, such work is not part of the agreed upon curriculum, and you've already been given hell by Hammersmith for such deviance. It seemed to you that the students should move right into the action and begin debating, learning by doing rather than first reading various essays in order to acquire facts and the forms of academic discourse. Rather than position the students with a textual object, you would have them situated within an ongoing experience. And with this debate, with the exchange of arguments and reasons, you were developing with those young people a pattern of group activity that can be internalized as a form of discourse, just as Vygotsky suggests. So of course you set aside the material in the course guide for a time until it could be situated—and no need not feel guilty about that. Let it be understood that any such a guide offers only suggestions, not commands. And we will change direction at any time so as to take advantage of the moment as our class develops a direction of its own.

Although I wonder sometimes if they're going to move right away from me. In my 4 o'clock class last week Carlos was working with Angela, helping her find a theme that would draw her material together and give it meaning or significance. And they found one, so then he helped Roberto, whose editor was absent, and again he was successful. Pleased with himself, he said "You know, I should be teaching this class," and I said, "Well then, why don't you?" He looked up at me doubtfully, not sure I was serious. "Go ahead, get together with Angela and you two decide what our next project will be. And don't tell me about it, just bring your proposal to us and I'll go along with you if the others will." So next week, after this work we're doing is finished, he and Angela will tell us what they think we should be doing next. And I'm wondering what that might be, what provocation Carlos will offer us. He's a lively one, and tough—from the streets. A few months ago he was charged with assault, so he's on probation now.

I keep asking myself, What am I doing they could do?—and the answer is, Nearly everything, so gradually I shift responsibility to them. Which is one reason I don't collect, edit, and grade their papers. They should learn to form their own judgments about the work they do and respond accordingly.

Which brings me to your question about ethics: "Just what 'ethical' awareness might arise in the provocative class?" When we ask a group of young people to listen as someone else presents a paper and then tell that writer what was heard that's interesting, that's working well, or that suggests a question, we are encouraging them to take an interest in someone else's welfare. And this isn't easy for them, to set themselves aside for a time and listen actively to someone else. When we ask them to point out not the mistakes but the good words, good expressions, good ideas we hear in a paper, so the writer is encouraged to give us more, we are teaching them to practice upbuilding. When we ask them for their own experiences, their own ideas, we are encouraging their initiative. When we ask them to edit and evaluate their work, we are teaching them to be responsible for their own decisions. And all this, I think, tends to encourage the decisiveness that is characteristic of an ethical being making choices. Such are the considerations that arise when teacher and students develop a situational context in the classroom. Perhaps every teaching practice should be considered from the viewpoint of its ethical implications.

So what do we talk about when we talk in the academy? Well, that depends on what corner of the academy you happen to be sitting in, and over in your corner anyone using the workbook and reader you sent to me is talking about the hidden curriculum: "Here is another example of school practice, one which divides people" (referring to the practice of grouping students by ability level). Might students themselves report such practices and recognize their effects if asked to talk about their school experience? But then they might waste time in reminiscence, or perhaps get aroused, even angry and go off in who knows what direction? Let's be sure they get the right message first and this workbook gives it to them! So instead of teacher and student having a real relation to each other, higher instructs lower and

> their relation is rather one of indifference in which the schoolmaster and pupil discuss how a good school should be run. To go to school no longer means [. . .] merely to learn but rather implies being interested in the problem of education. (Kierkegaard, *The Present Age*)

So within the confines of this safe material the students take up as directed the matter of the hidden curriculum. And what, one might ask, is the curriculum hidden in *this* program? It seems to be saying to young people, "We are on your side. We will reveal how the authorities have manipulated and managed you, we will make you sophisticated—as we are! To understand the world as it really is you need our guidance!" Yet surely our first task is to learn from those young people what demands life as they know it has made on them so we may understand their world as they do. But rather than allow them to instruct us, they will be led through these various articles on the way to a correct worldview. This program requires a bowing to authority. (On the other hand, it's the work of serious people wanting to improve their program, and I respect them for developing their own course book. Their way is not mine but surely students can benefit from being with them.)

Of course you wish to free yourself of this preplanned program, to assert your autonomy—and so you find yourself "giving grades for different activities entirely" than those in other classrooms. With the result, as Alistair suggests, that you pay a price in anxiety, worrying that your students may not be keeping up the academic pace. Who knows what will come of this? For "Anxiety is the dizziness of freedom [looking] down into its own possibility" (Kierkegaard). So we feel this pressure to do the safe academic thing, to teach various forms and terms—what your colleagues call the metalanguage of thesis, assumption, literal/figurative and the like—while saying in effect, all this will be useful to you later on in other courses. But rather than promising future value, our work must have value in the moment if our young people are to be fully engaged with it, so we have very little talking to do and no promises to make. We work along with them, hoping to hear the unexpected voice.

We are not going to hear it, however, as long as students think of themselves as lower, as those who only do as another directs. Then our meeting is one-sided and alienates not only person from person but inner aspects of the single individual. The learner has no cause for drawing together various parts of the self, no particular expressive need—and yet the passivity of their attitude, following us along, fosters an illusion of growth. So let our meeting be a many-sided event, a meeting with individuals who make a difference for themselves through the decisions they make. Who learn to see themselves as individuals with *push,* and striving to unify their paradoxical, fragmentary selves, develop a narrative voice. A young man, one of my counselees, happy with a triumph he had just recounted, said "I want to go out and make a better story to tell you!" And that young man you once spoke of, who calls himself Searcher because he moves from squat to squat so as to stay in school, will be sustained by the thought of oh what a story this will make! We each become the person who has done these things, whatever they may be—we have our identity in the individual story we are making. So what are we going to *do?* is my question. While helping those young people you work with to make something of themselves in words and develop their narrative skill you play a meaningful part in their education and their lives.

Certainly narrative skill would improve much academic writing. I sometimes read a professional journal thinking that not individuals are speaking there but rather the lifeless academic language they have learned is speaking them. Is this confirmation of the postmodern view that we have no individual self, that we are only the constructions of language and society? You seem quite worried about this sometimes, citing Barthes and company. Of course it's not surprising if the postmodernists notice a certain lack of individuality in what they hear from their students, they've been so busy training them to speak the speech as given to them. Or in what they hear from each other, they're so often simply rehearsing their reading of the same texts and citing each other. In announcing this death of the self perhaps they are beginning to realize they have lost their souls.

When empiricist psychology in the early 1900s began to undermine the existence of the self—and the scientist Ernest Mach (who gave us mach numbers for high speeds) was announcing in Viennese coffeehouses that "The I is unsavable!"—a great unease was felt among writers and the educated populace, for if there is no such thing as a self then what basis can there be for decisions and moral choice? The new psychologists responded to the unrest their views were causing by writing reassurances, like William James' "Does Consciousness Exist?", explaining that life can still be lived happily despite the findings of empiricism. The postmodernists you talk about have inherited this problem, not discovered it—they've been brought up with it and often sound like the behaviorist B.F. Skinner come back to us: "Autonomous man . . . has been constructed from our ignorance, and as our understanding increases, the very stuff of which he is composed vanishes" (*Beyond Freedom and Dignity*). Although this time around the response has been to embrace the grim news as if there is actual joy to be found in the death of self. But that's only so much whistling in the dark, and may express a yearning for the comforts of mysticism to relieve the loss—a hope of finding refuge in something higher or more encompassing than the individual self. Who then will dare announce, "I am"?

A friend told me how as a child in the black ghetto he would sometimes be awakened late at night by his father, who had come in from his work pushing a broom along the hallways in an office building. And his father would say, "Let me hear it—'I am somebody!'" The boy would repeat those words and go back to sleep.

So let us resist the forces of massification, which are many and often subtle. For example, Barthes' essay announcing the death of the author is coming true in a way he hadn't anticipated. Freelance authors are now being reclassified by publishers as salaried employees who lose all future rights to their work, and so they become not authors but simply writers for-hire. Their published work is going into electronic archives owned by the publishers, who charge a fee for access to them on the Internet and of course keep the return. Even now the articles written by scientists belong to those publishers who own the scientific journals and print them for a very good profit. In short, the author as an independent thinker with rights to his or her own work may be disappearing. Jenny Bader (in a piece aptly headed "The End of Writing") describes how writers, who once worked alone, now "gather together with each other or with development executives to hone their craft [and] make their voices sound like one another." With so much writing now being done as a group project, "the sense of the individual starts to get lost."

It seems that Barthes and Foucault, who imagined themselves as intellectual revolutionaries overturning bourgeois certainties, were in fact preparing a climate of opinion that would accept this commercially induced disappearance of the author. And perhaps the general acceptance of such postmodern ideas among the professors is simply an indication of how comfortable they feel with things as they are.

In fact, although postmodernism is currently taken as the last word in sophisticated thought, its major tenets—that the autonomous self is an illusion, that an objective view of reality is an illusion, that unrecognized powers control us through our language—these were commonplaces among artists and writers of the last century: "'Identity'—it's an illusion.. . . We are poisoned by the superstition of the ego" (Ayn Rand's *The Fountainhead*). And William Burroughs, echoing Mach 50 years later, announced that "Your I is a completely illusory concept" (*Nova Express*). Of course the professors pay no attention to our poets, but let this stuff be recycled to them through the French and the academic sheep come baaing along.

Let me assure you that even if ego and identity turn out to be illusions, we still have our vanity and it will take us a very long way. No one is going to give up the first-person pronoun. In fact, one response to this threatened loss of self has been a determined assertion of self, an outpouring of memoirs. We seem to live in an age of self-narration where even an article in one of the professional journals may indulge in what's called "confessional criticism," offering an account of the writer's past self. For in fact the self is always dying—fading away, its remnants absorbed into another self that in its turn will also fade and die. A feature of autobiographies in our time is their speaking of the writer's previous selves almost as if these were other persons. I noticed this again yesterday in Ned Rorem's *Knowing When To Stop*. And Ben Hecht, reviewing his life in *A Child of the Century*, looks back "on the succession of graves, like those in a military cemetery, under which a legion of my selves already lies." Barthes, Foucault and company, having announced the death of self, are calling us to yet another funeral service—but I have no time to attend so many, except of course the very last one of all.

So long for now—JR

- - - / / / - - -

10 April

Dear John,

All right, maybe I can begin believing in the self again or maybe even in myself. But there's still a problem here. Right now I'm feeling guilty for making that remark about helping students move away from their dependence on groupthink and becoming more individual. I get a sense that Africans resent their culture being characterized as less individual, they think of this as a colonial point of view. To describe the move from a communal to an individual identity as a 'development', implying an advance from the primitive, only disguises the exploitation or destruction of local cultures. 'All our action is usually joint community action rather than the individualism which is the hallmark of the capitalist approach. We always refrain from using people as stepping stones'. Those are the words of Steve Biko, a leader in the struggle, speaking about African culture. But then he goes on to say that 'We are prepared to have a much slower progress in an effort to make sure that all of us are marching to the same tune', and of course I immediately think of Thoreau: 'If a man does not keep pace with his companions, perhaps it is because he hears a different drummer. Let him step to the music he hears'.

Some Xhosa students were telling me the other day how they grew up sharing with each other, and they said this sharing model should be the basis of the South African economy. From their point of view the local economies are being exploited or destroyed, and people are set against each other. How long will it be before my students realize the individualist direction I'm leading them in and revolt?

In fact, there's a growing movement here to keep the local customs and languages alive. One of the professors at the University of Cape Town, a thoroughly Westernized African, has begun making animal sacrifices in his backyard—and other people are also returning to this traditional practice, judging from recent reports in the newspapers. The purpose of sacrifice is to honor the ancestors so they will continue to watch over their living relatives, or otherwise they will send misfortune. The animal must be made to bellow or cry out in pain as a sign that the ancestors hear and approve. In the old days the missionaries fought against this practice but now many Christian churches allow it.

I feel very uncomfortable talking about this because it's the sort of thing that can be sensationalized to sell newspapers, all to the detriment of African culture. Also, the postmodernists tell us that reporting or commenting on African customs or poverty is itself a form of imperialism, a way of treating those people as the Other and exploiting them for one's own purpose. We can't know them as they really are because in reporting on them 'objectively' we actually construct them according to our Western bias. So we should just let them be, I suppose, but as a teacher I'm dealing with people who keep bringing these living issues into the classroom and want to talk about their individual concerns. Or should I say communal concerns?

Well anyway, it seems that I'll be getting farther and farther away from those individual selves in the classroom as our program moves to large group instruction. The dean bird has passed on the news: rising enrollment and no money for hiring more staff, so get ready for sessions in the lecture hall with 150 students or more! A positional context, as you would say, with me standing behind a lectern. I'm looking at the syllabus, hoping to save something of our program and keep the conversation going.

The desks in most of those lecture halls are in tiers rising away from the lectern in front. Students will go there for a double period each week, taught by one of us senior staff, then each of these large groups will be broken into five tutorials of 20 students each, taught by student assistants—masters and honour students. (Note: university study for a B.A. is a 3-year course here, followed by a 1-year honour's degree, and then a 2-year master's degree course.) So it seems to me that the student assistants are going to have all the fun and the lecturers are going to have all the headaches. Surely Socrates would have had difficulty in these circumstances.

And here we are, all seemingly bent on changing the program entirely and making it 'critical'. This means, as best I can make out, that we're going to help students improve their abstract thinking process by training them in some theoretical mode of analysis such as critical linguistics or Marxism, and having them write academic essays that apply it to a text. The first reading is an excerpt from Pepetela's novel *Mayombe,* which tells the story of guerrillas in the Mayombe forest of Angola. They call each other Comrade but they have various ideological views and various reasons for being guerrillas—it's not a simplistic novel. Here's New World, the revolutionary theorist, telling Struggle he's got to go to school if he's ever going to be really free, and perhaps that gives an opening for me to do my thing with the students. They can start off by writing about their own experiences in high school, about friends or problems they had there. And will they agree there's a connection between going to school and being free?

I have another idea but maybe it's a little too far out. All those students will be sitting there in the lecture hall, in the lonely crowd, and I thought they could write letters to each other, to the person sitting on the right or left, ask questions and get acquainted that way. And maybe something more would come of it. What do you think of that idea? There has to be a way to save something of our program and not just have them all sitting there passively, looking down at me speaking from behind a lectern.

Well, let's leave the lecture hall and talk about something else. Had the one and only Alistair Vonkeller for lunch today—butter beans with tomatoes and onions, brown rice and other good things, along with some white wine because poor Alistair has to finish a paper about language policy that he's not interested in any more. I thought maybe it was time for me to listen to his problems for a change, I've handed so many of mine to him. He went on to tell me about his latest interest, which is narrative therapy. Now that sounds promising, doesn't it? Seems that it's all about the life story the patient tells, and by using various linguistic means you might be able to give that story a new direction. For example, you can look for the key words in the life story. He thought that in his own story 'consume' was a key word, which for him means women as man-eaters. So that's the story of his involvement with women, you see—they eat him up. With a bit of soy sauce. But once you know a few key words in your story you can exchange them for others and live a different story. That's the essence, as I remember. Then I offered him the baked potatoes and he took one.

After lunch we walked up Norfolk Road, lots of trees and shrubs, and Alistair was talking about Eastern thought and meditation. He speaks very deeply about such things, you might say, and I do think that some of the koans of Zen Buddhism are fascinating—they seem to help the disciple move beyond the distractions of daily life and even give up his or her very self for a time at least.

As we turned to go back Alistair said, 'Well, I've got to get on with writing my paper. I'm just tired of saying that language policy has to be taken seriously, and the fact that English is being used as the only language of academic discourse in this country ought to be questioned'. It seems there's a Xhosa word, lilwimi, which means 'many tongues', and now there's a growing lilwimi movement, you might call it, to keep the many languages in this country alive. Multilingualism should be seen as a resource, not a problem—that's Alistair's position. By now we were back at the house and he went on his thoughtful way. It was a pleasure to spend this time with him, he's been very good to me.

Speaking of language policy, I got myself over to the University of Cape Town for a huge conference where representatives gathered from the English support programmes of almost every university in South Africa. We heard talks about English for Academic Literacy ('the ability to integrate your voice with the voices of the academy'), about Practical English and also Terminal English, as one delegate called it. She argued fervently that we should move to discipline-specific programmes and abandon the attempt to teach a general literacy, for language is learned within a Discourse. Students should be able to select a beginning writing course in law or psychology or economics or whatever their interest. In fact, the conference itself was a big push in that direction—to make the writing program *practical,* because students want to get on with the 'real' work of the academy. There's already talk at UWC of making our writing program discipline specific and that worries me. People cite James Gee's *Social Linguistics and Literacies,* and also Brian Street's *Social Literacies,* as showing there's no such thing as a general literacy that can be usefully taught. So there's another threat to our writing program and the kind of work I want to do.

By the way, except for our Sinfree Makoni and the fellow he brought with him, all the representatives at the conference were white. And here language policy is being decided for South Africa? No wonder Alistair is tired of the subject.

Two days later I stopped by to visit Mzonke, and the two of us held a mini-conference of our own on language teaching. When I first knew him he lived with his parents in Guguletu, at NY4 #57, and I was always curious about that address because many of my students lived at NY1 or NY2 and so on. I had the idea that maybe NY meant New York, that here was another example of the influence of American movies. Finally he explained to me that NY means Native Yard. This was very surprising because the word 'native' is certainly a despised colonial designation, and one might expect these areas would have been renamed by now. But then, some of the renamings have their own weirdness, hiding certain realities, projecting a nicer image. Like 'Valhalla Park', the coloured slum I pass on my way to work, given that name by the apartheid government during the removals from Cape Town. And Grassy Park, where there is no grass.

Well, at 1:05 p.m. I arrived at Mzonke's posi (place) on Seth Drive, Hazeldene. We sat in his living room looking through the security gate at the grassy rubble-strewn field across the way. Port Jackson trees are growing up all over there, and I was surprised to see any at all since only 100 yards away is a huge settlement of shacks and the people living there use the trees for firewood. The small but neat one-story modern houses along Seth Drive stand in a contrasting line to the rubble across the way, while erratic trails of smoke drift up from the squatter camp beyond the rubble and trees.

'Hey Ed', Mzonke said, 'it's nice to see you, my man', and soon we were deep into a discussion of how he should go about improving the writing of students in history classes at Fezeka High School. 'Already you've challenged my ideas', he said. 'The first thing I wanted the teachers to do is point out all the errors that students make, and here you are contradicting me. But how are they going to learn correct English if we set them this example, if they are allowed to do anything they want to?'

'Hey, I'm only saying let them get their ideas on the page first. Then later we'll talk about making it beautiful'.

Mzonke's friend Sandile arrived, slightly tipsy. He works for the 7-11 chain of corner grocery stores, or cafés as they're called here, trying to get other black businesses to join the franchise. Soon he was talking about the 'jew-boys' who are his bosses. I've known that many people in the African community have this prejudicial attitude, and here was a chance for me to explore it firsthand. We had quite a discussion. I asked them if the English people they've met were more generous than the Jews, and Mzonke said 'That's hard to say. But you know there is this story. They say the English are so polite to their workers. It's "Please John this, and thank you so kindly John." And when it comes to lunch, they invite you to eat, but they only give you very very tiny meat. But now the Boer. He kicks and shouts at his workers, curses them, but when it comes to supper he shares a great piece of meat with them'.

I asked if stories like that really tell us the truth about people, and he said 'Well, maybe not, but that's what we learned about Englishmen. You know, in our school the English teachers were always so polite, with thank you and please, always telling us we were doing fine. But then come the end of the year and all you can find is a little, little mark. So whenever we would pass them in the hall they would always greet us very courteously, and we learned to do the same—"Good morning, Miss So and So"—but when they had passed, we would curse them'.

More friends were about to arrive, so Mzonke left the room to prepare for them and Julianne came in from the kitchen to sit with me. The conversation turned to names. 'And why is your son called Ayanda?' I asked. 'That means Love, doesn't it?'

'No, it means, And more to come. Mzonke thought of it'.

'Oh, I see. So you wish to have more children, Julieanne?' I was annoyed to find so little regard for family planning when this country is already so overcrowded and hungry.

'No, it's not me—it's Mzonke who chose the name. I don't want any more children but what could I do? It's the custom for the man to name the boy'.

These little exchanges at Mzonke's give a peep below the calm exterior of daily life here. Seething struggles between men and women, ethnic rivalries, fear and envy and yearning, writhing and sighing in the depths of our minds.

Salo Kahle (So long)—Ed

- - - / / / - - -

May 4

Dear Ed,

Your Xhosa students who speak of how they grew up sharing with each other, and want the new life to be much like the old, are "Wandering between two worlds, one dead,/the other powerless to be born." For having left the old world of the village behind, they're after the good things Western economies have given their peoples, but to have those things and still live in the old way—that's a world which can exist only in hope. So now they feel disoriented in the strange, half-way place they find themselves, as you've said. But then, that's one reason they're at UWC, to make a comfortable place for themselves as the country moves from a subsistence economy to an open, large-scale market system. In this new South Africa many of the traditional customs may still be followed, but perhaps in a self-conscious sort of way as with that professor who has returned to the practice of making animal sacrifices in his backyard.

Speaking of such African customs makes you feel uneasy, as if the mere report implies a criticism. But we in the U.S. are certainly in no position to be critical of African ways or beliefs. I mean, here's a country where a Harvard professor holds therapy sessions for people abducted by space aliens. Where a University of Virginia professor, the head of a department, investigates reincarnation—with positive results, as you would expect. Where a chemistry professor at Texas A & M is reviving the practice of alchemy and attempting to turn mercury into gold, with some initial success he tells us. Where some nursing schools teach the laying on of hands, or "therapeutic touch," as a healing procedure. Where newspapers carry astrology columns and psychic hotlines pull in dollars for their operators. I could go on, for there's no end to irrational belief in this country.

And as for the postmodern notion that to report or even comment on African beliefs or customs is a form of imperialism, that seems to me in itself a contemptuous attitude—as if those people are not worthy of attention or have nothing to teach us. I'm reminded again of how Rian Malan hardly knew or understood his black friends because he had internalized apartheid notions of racial separation and so could not express any interest in their beliefs or experience.

Also, as Africans move from their villages into the urban environments where they will assume a variety of specialized roles and become more individualized, you can expect not only an increasing concern among them for preserving the traditional customs but also a resurgence of tribalism. The development of individualism, it seems, encourages an emphasis on group identity:

> There is more individualism—more choice, more of a culture of personality, personal satisfaction, and self-realization; and yet group identity seems as virulent as ever, if not more so—we see greater tribalism and more nationalism. The world is thus fragmented into a herd of clans, nations, solidarity groups, religious and ethnic groups, clubs, cabals, and so on ad infinitum.. . . The point is that all this tribalism is a *consequence* of individualism and is not in contradiction to it. The individual, let loose from traditional moorings, does not float aimlessly in a sea of products and decisions. He or she looks for new moorings, *has* to look for new moorings. . . . Some [of the new

affiliations] lead to conflict or even take people down the dark road to war. Some are politically neutral—most of them perhaps. Others lead to a demand for multiculturalism in its various guises. (Lawrence Friedman, *The Horizontal Society*)

And what is multiculturalism but an insistence on the uniqueness, the *individuality* of each cultural group? Which gives us identity politics. This is part of what may be the central problem of our time: the conflict between an individualist way of life and the desire for the spiritual comfort of community.

And where other resources fail, those seeking spiritual comfort may find it in mysticism or in therapy. So there is an endless series of fads in therapy, for none of them seems to satisfy for long—and our own field has supplied a number. We've had drama therapy, poetry therapy, bibliotherapy, and now here is Alistair sitting at your table with a baked potato, talking about narrative therapy! For a moment I wondered if perhaps he was about to give up the structured classroom in favor of a narrative pedagogy, but no, this seems to be all about himself, really, and not about others. I shook my head, saying "Oh no, oh no!" as Alistair sat there consuming his potato and talking about the all-consuming woman!

What bothers me about the therapeutic personality is the constant self-regard. As teachers, however, we learn about these things, about narrative and story-telling, names and naming, for the help they give us with others. For instance, the concept of the key vocabulary, which Alistair mentions, was developed by Ashton-Warner during her work with Maori children, and was used to teach them how to read. In listening to their stories she found that for each child there were certain words more interesting, more meaningful than others, so nearly every day she wrote one of those words on a card and gave it to the child. Children who had labored for weeks over "See Spot run" took one look at "corpse," "beer," or "hiding" and they could read: "The word cards became as personal and precious to the children as the imagery they represented." I'm drawing here on Lynley Hood's *Sylvia*, which has this account by one of the pupils in that school:

> One day Gilbert Nuku threw a ball inside and broke the window. He was sent to get the strap and when he came back Mrs. Henderson gave him the words 'ball," "window" and "glass," and made him write them down. Gilbert was a bit of a dunce but when it came to the word "window," he knew it. After school when we went home and played marbles in the dirt we used to talk about our words [. . .] and Gilbert used to say, "My word is window." I thought—Gee, Gilbert got a big word. I wonder what word I could learn next?

So it seems to me that Ashton-Warner's contribution to the mental health of those children was listening to their stories and teaching them to read— that was enough for her. And in their success she found her own momentary happiness, for she was a very troubled person.

Like Ashton-Warner, we too are concerned with helping young people learn to read and write, and so one thing we do is help them learn what stories there are for them to tell, encouraging them to develop a narrative skill. And the stories they tell us will often be about the life around them as they are coming to know it, and their adventures with the ideas suggested by it. The narrative therapist is much concerned with uncovering the story of one's past (as the Freudians are—and Freud has been called the first narrative therapist), whereas you and I are concerned with the story yet to be made. The thoughts our young people need are not to be found by introspective navel-gazing but rather by turning their attention outward—so let's get on with our work and the stories they're making.

Of course one story these young people are living is the adventure of their entrance into the symbolic system of the academic world and learning there the language of academic discourse, which is mainly expository. So what's the point of their practicing narrative skills? I have before me the current issue of *College English*, and note that every article begins as narrative. For example: "In one of my basic writing classes two years ago, we were discussing an Algerian text." Or consider this: "The three books under review represent the climatic phase of the process of grooming Willa Cather for her place among the greats of American literature." In other words, here's the story of Willa Cather's literary reputation—and much academic writing is the recounting of history. Or an academic article may introduce the work of some writer, then another who contradicts the first, and a drama of ideas is set in motion, often with anecdotal asides. In fact, much writing that is not ordinarily thought of as story has a narrative progression which provides a frame for the inclusion of facts, analysis, and commentary. Academic discourse in general is a specialized kind of narrative.

And the development of narrative skill begins with the stories people can tell, with what they already know about the world around them. But very often young people are urged immediately into the expository rather than encouraged in their telling. To be considered academically literate you must learn to lard up your text with multiple citations and explications of various authorities, never mind what it all means in the personal experience of individuals. Otherwise you invite the charge of being unserious, anecdotal. But has anyone in composition studies noticed how important personal narrative has recently become in the social sciences? There has been a dispersal of authority, so to speak, and research reports often include the voices their subjects, who become participants in the study rather than simply exhibits. In education itself research into narrative and its uses is changing the character of inquiry, and we find James Gee, for example (who is admired by your colleagues), reviewing the narrative told by a 7-year-old in a study of how children construct meaning in school.

We might also consider the importance of narrative in the ongoing work of business and the professions. Every morning on my way to school I read the *Wall Street Journal*, keeping watch on the capitalists, and today I find it advising executives that "Your job is to tell a story." In fact, there are consultants who help them do that, who teach corporate leaders how to choose stories that reflect their company's core values and to be good storytellers—although I suppose we must listen to them with a skeptical ear. But then, I've read that narrative is also being used by social activists to critique irresponsible activities in the community. They are exploring ways in which personal narratives or "testimonies" can help researchers and others advance environmental causes by bearing witness to the ecology of neighborhoods. A good story can be a formidable defense against bad law or the rapacious corporation.

Then too, the legal profession's concern with narrative seems obvious. But the movement called "narrative law" goes beyond the traditional presentation of facts to promote storytelling as a reformist alternative to traditional legal discourse and debate—a way for "marginalized voices to be heard, to challenge the status quo, and to move away from increasingly abstract forms of modern law." (I've been reading *Law's Stories*, by Paul Gewertz.)

In fact, narrative is a primary and irreducible form of human comprehension, a rival to theoretical explanation. Narrative is the form in which we make comprehensible the many successive interrelationships that are implicated in the making of a situation and the elements it includes. (I'm drawing here on an essay by the historian Louis Mink, "Narrative as a Cognitive Instrument".) The cognitive function of narrative form, Mink remarks, is not just to relate a succession of events—in fact, *narrative defines what is an event*—but rather "to body forth an ensemble of interrelationships of many different kinds as a single whole." He insists, and rightly so I think, that more attention should be given to narrative as a cognitive instrument. For narrative logic is universal and all other logics derive from it. (Check out Richard Brown's *Society as Text* for an interesting discussion of this point.)

Of course once we have a narrative we have a text to be analyzed or interpreted, and it seems to me that with this current plethora of narrative the need for analytical intelligence and critical thinking has never been greater. Every narrative should be interrogated—and the skills required are also necessary in the making of more useful narratives. In saying this am I complicating the issue? Well, considered theoretically the activity of a classroom becomes very complex, with any number of aspects to be considered, and I suppose we'll have to return to the narrative of what we're doing to make it all clear even to ourselves.

But now you're worried that the narrative you and your students have been making together of your experience in a classroom is about to be disrupted, to be replaced by a series of lectures. But even with more than a hundred young people in one room you think perhaps there's a way to maintain a situational context and keep the narrative going. Would letter writing be useful here? you wonder. If you think it might, then give it a try—it's worked for us. Who knows what those young people will write to each other and what might come of it? They could bring their letters to the tutorials with the teaching assistants, where some might want to share them with the others. And they could have an editing session. Later you could meet with the assistants and talk about what they heard in those letters, and from this discussion might come your next step. This sounds to me like a way of continuing the narrative, for with all those people exchanging letters surely someone is going to raise an issue that matters to them.

Some time ago you spoke of preferring conversations with scholars from other departments than your own because their subject matter often deals with living issues and so with ethics. Those issues will arise in the narrative classroom too, and not because students are given them to write about but because of how they must live there—not simply acquiescing but developing for themselves patterns of behavior. You are moving away from the usual pattern of academic control, with the professor giving directions at every step along the way from his position as head of the class. You are developing a more flexible way of working with young people and so behavioral issues are bound to arise—in fact, you were asking a while ago for suggestions about discipline. Because when you have young people organizing themselves into the Dynamics, say, and selecting activities for themselves and working together, you have abandoned the idea of a fixed behavioral code to be enforced, and opted instead for a much more complex moral situation. You are asking, in effect, that young people not only live there with each other but for each other—that instead of relying on rules that define how they are to relate to one another, they must now begin to take each other into their personal account as individuals. You have refused to substitute a code of behavior for morality, and in that room ethics are in the making. That's why you're not a true academic but rather a teacher, because you're more interested in individuals that in subject matter.

And so your work with them depends on their developing shared ways of doing, rather than on directives from above. You are helping them develop what has been called "social capital": the social and political habits on which democratic self-government relies—habits of self-reliance, along with the skills of cooperation and skills of leadership that make for a strong civil society.

But the move to a discipline-specific writing class, which you say is now being promoted, would put an end to this. The emphasis would be on vocational training and a restricted literacy, with language fragmented into mutually exclusive discourses. No wonder you're worried! Of course the writing program at UWC, as you've described it, has been dominated by the literary concerns of the English department, so I suppose the other departments now want some attention to their particular concerns. But surely it's important to bring young people into the shared discourse of the polity, to develop cultural literacy and a reserve of social capital. But rather than continuing to build social cohesion and a democratic ethos by the participatory means you favor, young people in a discipline-specific writing course would be sequestered within the confines of a discipline and no longer have access to a classroom where independent thinking will be encouraged.

At present you are helping them create a counternarrative to all this. When they are sitting in that lecture hall writing their letters to each other, who knows what concerns, what ideas about the life around them they will bring in for discussion? Of course they'll be talking about themselves at first but soon the conversation will lead to other subjects. And that's how we're going to go beyond ego, so to speak—by using it. Or are you still looking to the Eastern way you mentioned, to the contemplation of a Zen koan perhaps, which you said in your last letter moves one to give up his or her self? Why give up something that's so useful? Unless of course you're tired of story-making and wish to withdraw from the world into meditation.

You'll have plenty of company. I have before me an article (in the CCC journal) that explains, under the subheading "Zen and the Critical Writing Teacher", how useful koans are in helping one transcend ego or self, and how they "challenge logical and dualistic thinking." Who wants to be confined by logic, after all, when there's dreaming to be done? And I could mention other such articles. This interest in Zen you share with so many in our field reminds me of an experience I'd like to tell you about, and you may feel free to draw from it whatever moral you wish. It concerns a roomful of academics, and there's ego enough! Including my own of course, although on this occasion I contented myself with being simply an observer.

When Ming Shui, of Brooklyn College, whose translations of Chinese poetry I edited, invited me to his home for a dinner party I brought Mrs. M along. A high school teacher among the professors, I thought, would make an interesting mix. There were eight of us there in all, and as we sat in the living room getting acquainted before dinner, cocktails in hand, Mary—a professor of history—mentioned how surprised she was to find that most of her students were believers in astrology, taking it quite seriously as a source of insight into life and character. Brenda, Ming Shui's wife, said "That sounds sensible to me." So it was explained to her again: these kids actually believe in astrology, they think it helps one plan for the future. Brenda said, "But that's better than leaving your life to chance." Her husband turned to her: "Do you really believe that?" It was an awkward moment. "How long have you two known each other?" Mrs. M asked, and the moment passed in laughter.

Mary went on to tell how her department, in selecting a new chairperson, had passed over a very well-prepared and dynamic young woman to select a candidate whose application included newspaper clippings from his military career. "Well, he understands the chain of command," Mrs. M murmured. "Oh those men voted for him fast enough," Mary said. "They hardly took 10 minutes." "Were you late for the meeting?" Mrs. M asked. "Yes, about 10 minutes." And again there was a momentary silence.

Broken tactfully by Ben, a philosophy professor, who pointed out a ceramic figure of the Buddha sitting on a stand in one corner of the room. "I found that in Japan," Ming explained, which reminded Jesse from the math department of his experience with Zen Buddhism and the sound of one hand clapping. He had never solved the koan given him by his Zen master. "He gave me this one: 'Medicines cure diseases, and the whole earth is medicine. But which is your self?' I think he chose that for me because it would pose a real problem for my Western mind, and it did. Am I the disease or the cure? We should meditate more, you know—there's a wisdom that lies beyond words."

"Well if I may," Mrs. M said, "offer you one of the koans of my own people, although we have another name for them." She was raised among the Navajo, you may remember. He looked at her expectantly and we waited to hear. She said, "Consider: what is the difference between a duck?" Once again we sat in silence, wondering how this should be taken. Someone said, "Are you sure that's . . ." and then reconsidered. "This is very puzzling," Jesse said. "I'll have to think about it." "Yes," Mrs. M replied, "the path to enlightenment is a long one." "You know," Ben said, "as a philosophy Zen is very much like deconstructionism, very postmodern. It recognizes language as a prisonhouse, and it would take us beyond ego or self, it—" but he was interrupted by Brenda calling us to the dining room.

She had prepared an elaborate Chinese feast, and there was little conversation at first as we enjoyed it, turning the lazy Susan in the center of the table to bring around one dish after another. "This proves," Ben said, "that the Chinese is one of the great cuisines of the world." The others nodded appreciatively. "And I'm sure you know," Mrs. M told him, "that the Chinese also have a great store of folk wisdom. For example, they say a woman is like an umbrella." We waited . . . and waited. Ben said, "And why is a woman like an umbrella?" "Because sooner or later you'll have to take a taxi." Mary looked over at Ming: "The Chinese don't really say that, do they?" "It's a very patriarchal society," he answered. "How true," Brenda said. "You know," Jesse said, "my Chinese students are the best. They're the bright, hardworking ones." "Oh that's because they're Jewish," Mrs. M told him. "I'm surprised you don't know that." Ming laughed.

Later as we were all preparing to leave, putting on our coats, Ben the philosopher turned to Mrs. M. "Now about that koan you gave us," he said, "I've been thinking about it. Could you give me a clue perhaps? What is the difference between a duck?" She smiled: "One leg is both the same." He nodded. "Oh that's marvelous! The answer is another play on words and we are caught within the emptiness of an infinite circularity—a prisonhouse of language that contains no truth, as the deconstructionist would say. And Zen would have us recognize that. I think I can use this in my class. Thank you." "You're welcome," she said.

In the taxi on the way back to Manhattan I said, "You're a sly one. I think you puzzled a number those people. Now that koan you gave Ben— you said your people have another name for those things." "Yes," she said, "we call them jokes." And she went on talking about Navajo humor. "Here's an example. A few men were sitting together talking and one of them said, 'I dreamed I was hatching four eggs. And only one of them was mine.'" So let's meditate on that—it's hilarious, you understand.

Hoping to hear from you soon—JR

--- / / / ---

19 June

Hey John,

I don't have much time for meditation now that the lecture program is in full swing and I go in there once a week to address the multitude. I plan for the sessions, but then on the way there I feel nervous running the details over in my mind. Is this going to work? I wonder. Are they going to be sitting there completely silent, watching me, waiting for it to be over? Sometimes it seems better to do it the Zen way and just stop thinking about it, go with the flow.

So the first day I went in with my guitar and taught them a song I'd written to the tune of 'I Can't Help but Wonder Where I'm Bound' (by Woody Guthrie, I think). I called it 'The Road to Success'. Here's the first verse and chorus:

I've been to many a school,
I've talked to many a fool,
I've studied maths, science, history.
But the road to success appeared
And banished all I feared,
And now my mind is altogether free.

> O the Road to Success is long,
> There's many a turn that's wrong,
> But on that road is where
> I belong.

I sang a few words of that and they picked them up, then a few words more and so on till they'd learned the song and we sang it through together. I didn't do it solo because their own songs are never for individuals, they always sing together.

When I asked if they could write a verse, 'Perhaps in your own tongue, if you wish', it was only about five minutes before one student came up to the podium with this verse in Xhosa, and we sang it too:

No mhla sesiphinda	Today we again
Sibanana futati	See each other
Emva kwesikhathi eside.	After so long.
Ngethemba lokuba	Hoping therefore that
Suknowabusana	We will delight one another
Kamandinje nqakuqala.	As wonderfully as the last time.

The student also provided the translation. This verse is not on the theme I started with (success), which may reflect the divergence between the American and African patterns of expectation, but I was happy to have it and we had a good time singing it.

It was important to me that here in this first session the students take an active part. And there were others who also wrote verses, but unfortunately I did not collect any of them. I'm always in a hurry to move on to God knows what academic destination—which I suppose is also the American way. So we went on to consider *Mayombe,* and that passage where New World tells Struggle he must go to school if he wants to be really free, and they began writing about their own experiences in school. I'll share some of this with you later.

I was a little worried, wondering what the dean bird would think of all this when he heard about it. Not academic enough, he might say, but so far there's been no word from him. What encouraged me to go this way was Steve Biko's piece on 'Some African Cultural Concepts', where he says that 'tunes were adapted to suit the occasion and had the wonderful effect of making everybody read the same things from the common experience'. So I thought this would be a good way to start us off and bring us together. The African love of song and rhythm, Biko says, dramatizes as nothing else 'the eagerness of Africans to communicate with each other', and I'm trying to open new paths of communication for them. I'll let you know what they have to say.

Over and out—Ed

CHAPTER 8

In Africa
When the Sun Comes Up

28 June

Dear John,

Shorter cold winter days now, and I'm sorry not to have written sooner but I have all these folders full of writing from the tutorials taught by the undergraduate assistants. One hundred and twenty folders, each with pages of free writing, reactions to stories, a finished essay on high school memories along with the earlier drafts, and much more—hours of reading. This is madness!

My tutorial group decided on the name Perfect Strangers (last quarter another group chose to be Club Nightmare). And what did they remember from their high school days? They were responding to that passage in Mayombe where New World tells Struggle he'd better go to school if he wants to be really free, and one said, 'If life were something rewindable I would never return to that wooden hell'. A few reported good experiences but many others told about beatings, arbitrary rules, absent teachers, student boycotts, and one school called The Holiday Inn because the principal would grant any request for a day off—not a bad lot of stories, actually.

> It was something build of rusty porous corrugated irons. It was typical of a primitive shack in the informal settlement. The desks were not enough for the students to such an extent those who stayed in the vicinity of school would bring their own chairs from their homes. . . . It was not strange to hear hues and cries of violance while we were busy studying in our 'shack'.

> On the rainy day we would not attend school because the classes were raining inside. Or sometimes we would have to leave school before time. I remember some windy day when we were writing June examinations. We could not concentrate on what we were doing as the loose shets of corrugated iron were tattaring miking monotonous noise. When the political violence was taking place we would not dare go to school.

Here's part of another:

> The teacher asked me to stand in front of the class with one leg until the end of the period. The reason why she treated me so, I was coming late during her period, that was the punishment I got. During the time the teacher taught the others she sometimes came to me and beat me at that one standing leg, she liked to beat the ankles because she said they are painful. When I tried to change the leg because I felt pains and my leg so tired, she beaten me on a head and said 'I want to beat this knob top because its just big and empty. Then I stood until 30 minutes gone.

This is what the school experience has been like for many of these students, although corporal punishment is supposedly illegal now. I asked them to follow up these stories with their thoughts about why such things happen in schools—to move from the narrative 'what happened' to the expository 'why'. They could put their stories into the context of politics or economics or personal philosophy or tribal beliefs or whatever. A few wrote the usual diatribe against apartheid education, or what remains of it, and many of them, especially the bush Africans, came back with sometimes interesting discussions of tribal beliefs like the importance of respecting one's elders but having no bearing at all on the events in their essays. And one offered this thought: 'The roots of education are bitter but the fruits of it are sweet'. When these papers about school life were read to the whole class a thoughtful atmosphere prevailed. But the TAs I supervise seemed to have trouble getting their students to read their work to the others. And I keep wondering if any of this is really helping them get into the expository mode required at university.

The students who meet with me in the lecture hall—more than 100—scanned the new course reader and voted to work with Camille Paglia's 'Do Women Ask For Rape?', so in the training session with our TAs we tried a reading of it and when we paused for discussion after just the first page the roof came off! I thought maybe we should go through the whole article this way, pausing to talk about interesting points that came up, but Jane Wiley said the discussion should be brought to some conclusion first 'because that's what academic literacy is all about'. So we tried that and gave the TAs 5 minutes to write out any conclusion they could come to after our discussion but they said this was too soon, they'd just started thinking about the issue. Even so, another lecturer wondered if all this talk would simply 'go up like so much smoke' if they didn't write down what they'd discussed, but the TAs said they wanted to read more of the article first.

Later they read it with students in their tutorials, and also 'The Story of Lulu Diba', which tells of 'test matches' at the University of Zululand, when a girl thought too stubborn or haughty is lured by a boy into a place where she will be gang-raped. Then each tutorial held a mini-debate on the issue, prepared position papers afterwards and elected representatives to present their arguments to the large lecture group. But the representatives complained that they didn't have enough say in how we were organizing all this, so we left the planning of the presentations entirely to them. Some of these students are older than the others—in fact about 25% of them are second- and third-years students sent to us from other departments and they want to assert themselves. I like this mix of ages because the older ones bring ideas and information into the classroom and that encourages the others to work up to their level.

When we gathered in the lecture hall the first to speak was Mandilakha Philemon Zenzile (who insists on being called by his last name, although he is also known as Tower of Strength, the power name he chose for himself). He started out with a brief disquisition on the short skirt, telling us that 'Some people cannot control their sight of it', but women are aware of the risk. In an earlier time, he said, they used to follow after their mothers but now 'they drink like their fathers'. This was greeted with loud but rather cheerful jeering from the women among the hundred and some students assembled there. After a slight pause he continued:

> Now take the situation in a shebeen. People have to know what is expected. Here a woman goes to a shebeen to meet so and so. And she arrives without even a blue cent. She asks a man for a drink. He knows he can buy her a drink. Then we all know what is expected. She cannot say no.

The hubbub increased, and he paused dramatically like an actor, then began telling us about the situation between prostitutes and their clients who cannot afford to pay. At one point this rebuttal came from someone on the floor:

> Women do not invite rape just by wearing short skirts. In olden times there were no rapes, yet women wore very little. Our society today is a criminal society. We all recognize that. So a woman is responsible if she is raped because she has not taken precaution.

And someone else made this statement:

> This question can only be answered in respect to a context. In a patriarchal society there is a sign saying 'Enter at your own risk'. There the woman must know that rape will occur. But now, we are in a post-

patriarchal society, and rape is wrong. That is to say, if everyone is equal, women can do what they wish and are not reponsible for rape.

Well, it was a lively session. They debated these points right up to the end of the period and then shouted that the debate must go on 'For at least 10 minutes more, Mr. Katz!' And on they went, with much good-natured exchange. One thing interesting to me in these presentations before the lecture group was the way narrative was used, sometimes to illustrate a point and sometimes to carry the argument along.

I opened my tutorial the next day by asking if anyone had a song for us this freezing cold morning, and Margaret began singing in Xhosa, inviting us to join in:

Musab'ukwenza negenkohlakalo xx	Don't do that
Kuba lent'ilivili liyajika-jika	Because the wheel is turning
Ngomoso nguwe	Tomorrow it's you
Namhla noimi.	Today it's me.

That was the refrain. It's a song that warns us to be careful how we treat others because what goes around comes around, as we would say. This theme has often come up in my conversations with Africans and most everyone joined in the singing, they all know this song.

Then we went on to write our reflections on the debate, and Zenzile revealed that he does not hold the chauvinist position he had argued for (although who knows which of his multiple selves he 'really' is?), he just wanted to be sure a good discussion got going. Well, he certainly provoked one of the most amazing furors we've had in that lecture hall.

Since then we have moved on in the lecture meetings to writing letters, with the students asking each other to explain themselves, so to speak, and that's developed in a very surprising way. The first read-around we had of these letters in my tutorial group did not bring us anything unexpected, but many of them had a certain charm, I thought:

> Thank you for your letter I received last week asking more information about my family. I write with pleasure about my family. I am very glad to tell you that friendship is formed through communication and understanding each other.

And he went on to tell the history of his family. In reply, his correspondent told about the removal of his own family from District Six by the apartheid government, then added this:

> I want to tell you about the history of the so-called Colourds as I know it. It was the colonizing of this country that destroyed our heritage and culture of

our forefathers. It is so, because it is said that the so-called colourds have not culture, but we know what we are and where we came from. My people were generated from Griqwa, Sun and Bushmen. I do not know how you see this as a person, but it is true.

This question of whether the coloureds have a culture of their own is a contested issue here. I suggested the students should feel free to bring into their letters anything at all they wanted to talk about, and as we went on they began to speak about an amazing variety of other issues. Not the usual and endlessly regurgitated topics of abortion, capital punishment, bride price, etc., which teachers give and the whole class writes about because supposedly they're of general interest, but rather issues alive in the community right now. One student shocked the others with an account of her decision to have no boyfriend, as she was satisfied with Christ until she married. At first I hesitated asking if she'd like to write a paper on this, thinking maybe she'd be a little shy after all the commotion, but in fact she jumped at the chance.

Another person in my group—we were reading these letters in my tutorial, in small groups of five or six—had written a letter exhorting the other to attend church services, and the girl who received it wrote back that church is nothing but a fashion parade. In a neighboring group there developed a helluva controversy over a student who considered himself a member of the Hlubi tribe, which he claimed is not a Xhosa tribe. The other students, Xhosas, were absolutely irate and insisted he was wrong.

So these letters did bring in subjects that are important to the students, and I'm hoping this will lead to some serious work. I'm thinking of asking them to write the comparison–contrast essay about themselves and their partner (since I still feel obligated to meet the requirements of the course outline). Or should we write about these new issues instead? Oh dear, then I'd be breaking all my agreements with my colleagues and pushing off in this different direction.

And I have to admit there are times when I feel uncomfortable with what some of the students say. One of them wrote about a bergie (the Afrikaans term for a mountain person, but used to describe any bum at the door) who told a white family he would be happy when he got their property, which was rightfully his now that black rule had come in, and 'he eyed their youngest daughter lasciviously'. I found myself saying, 'Well, parts of this work but the way this bergie talks seems a little unconvincing'. The piece made me uncomfortable. I've noticed that when I leave a group they become freer and more voluble, so maybe I reveal too much of myself.

My younger daughter Jessica (15) called me just now while I was typing this. She seems to be coming into her own, breaking out of the shyness that has characterized her entire life. It's curious however that she seems to have adopted mainly coloured friends and has all but washed her hands of the so-called white culture. As we drove into Rondebosch she asked me, 'Do any real people live here?'—meaning coloureds. The times they are a-changing.

Yours—Ed

- - - / / / - - -

July 27

Dear Ed,

Having reached an age when nostalgia is the principal emotion, I was interested in your account of how those young people with so much before them enjoy looking back on their short lives, telling each other stories of their school days. I suppose that's been their one big experience in life so far. A young man, a musician, recently came visiting with his young woman, and I asked "How long have you two been together?" "Five years," he said, and then looked up as if surprised: "Why that's longer than high school!" He was measuring out his life in school years. So when you ask your students to write about those years, you've given them a subject about which they have plenty to say.

My students have spent their school years in relatively comfortable circumstances and they take education as a given, so to speak. Of course many of them work to help pay their way, but they have the self-satisfaction of the well-fed and some of them drive to school in their own cars. They enjoy such privileged lives that I sometimes think 6 months on a farm would do them good. Most have English as their first language so they usually write more fluently than yours. I mention all this because I'd like to share with you some of what the students in my prose fiction class have written about their high school days.

After we had read a number of short stories together, I said "You must have met people a writer could use in a story. Who do you remember from your days in high school? What happened there that's worth telling about? Let's take a few minutes right now and put down whatever comes to you, whatever you remember that a writer could use." Within 15 minutes everyone had produced a little character sketch or an anecdote, which we then filled out with more details without trying to do a finished piece of work. It occurred to me that rather than try to make these into short stories, we could condense them into finely wrought little pieces. I passed around a few excerpts from William March's very good but now-forgotten World War I novel, *Company K*, a kind of roll call with each passage of half a page or more headed by the name of a soldier. I thought we could tell the story of a high school year this way, as March told the story of an infantry company.

As it turned out we had many interesting characters and situations to use. A young woman on her way to the grocery store is spoken to by a stranger, an older man, and they go to a park together, where they sit on a bench and talk of life and love. A group of young women are cutting each other's hair, one of them putting weed into small plastic bags, when there is a knock on the door and the police come in to arrest four of them for using stolen credit cards. Here are two of the finished stories:

Eric

Look kid, you wanna know the best way to get through high school? It worked for me, it'll work for you. I've been doin it the last three years and now this is my last year in this hell hole. You see, you have to be—well, not a teacher's pet, you have to get in deeper, you have to be sort of like their lover. But watch out for that gym teacher Jones, she's too tough. I figured I was doin her a favor givin her the hungry look, she's such a dog, but she put me in my place, made me sit in the bleachers all the time. I failed her class, you know. Only course I failed in all three years. Because I wouldn't change into my gym clothes. I didn't want to mess up my threads, I gotta keep my look goin. Figured I'd get to her but she was on me all the time. See, you have target 'em all, the fat ones, the mean ones, the ones with losing personalities, the old hags, and the pretty ones but they can be hard to manipulate because they already got guys after 'em. But that never stopped me. I asked Mrs. Ross to marry me, leave her husband and marry me. It was a joke, I was smiling, but you put ideas in their head. She was happy to have my around, an end of the year I got my A. So just let your charm do all the work. Hey, and don't forget the threads! Tight jeans always worked for me. (Eric Ugaz)

The Stranger

The first time I noticed him was junior year. He was overweight and quiet, and no one knew him very well. But during the summer he lost weight and gained muscle, and during senior year he was quite popular, although no one knew him very well. We were study partners in English class—we read Camus' The Stranger together, and he explained it to me. I didn't understand how someone could think life isn't very important. Then one day when we were going to give our report he wasn't there. And he never came to school again. I heard someone say he'd been arrested, and so after awhile I called the police station and asked about him but no one would tell me anything. The next day I tried again, and this time I cried a little. So then the officer told me he was the leader of a gang and he shot somebody. So I wrote him a letter and sent it to the jail. Days went by, and weeks went by, and I wondered if he got the letter. Then finally he sent me an answer. He said he did shoot a man, and he asked me not to show his letter to anyone at school "because I wouldn't want them to ban the book. It was a good book." I folded the letter very carefully and put it in my copy of The Stranger to keep it there forever. (Carol Castrovinci)

With many of these stories I was surprised at how much thievery, fighting and other violence there seems to have been in the lives of my youngsters, most of whom as I've said come from quite stable backgrounds. Of course they would choose the more sensational events to write about, but it seems they had an ample selection. Although there were some reflective stories too, like the one that ends our book. It tells of a powerfully built and quiet young man called Grandpa because he's older than the others, having failed a grade or two, but they like to be with him because he listens to them when they're unhappy, and doesn't talk about himself. The end of the story tells us that "He may have been lazy in school and not too smart, but he made one smart decision. He married a smart girl."

These stories are more impersonal than the ones written in your class, which seems to me the principal difference between them. Your student who tells of the school where youngsters brought their own chairs, and rain came into the classroom, is back in that school as he writes about it and we are there with him empathetically. Put his description into the present tense and it would sound much as if he were telling it to someone at the time. But with "Eric" and "The Stranger" these writers have managed to get enough distance from their earlier experience so they can use it effectively in shaping an experience for a reader, and the feelings involved are those evoked in the reader. The writers themselves, although they write in the first person, have joined us as readers of these stories, and this objectivity is a habit of mind that will be useful in other, more expository courses. I'm planning to give them copies of this little book they've done so that later we can read it as a literary text along with the others we've talked about, and consider what it tells us about coming of age in this society.

Your students have also produced interesting accounts of school life—of student boycotts, schoolroom beatings, the school like a Holiday Inn—and now you would like to turn them from the narrative "what happened" to the expository "why," but you say they find this a difficult move to make. One reason may be, as Bernstein suggests, that for them a shift from narrative to reflection calls for a shift from we-centered to individuated experience—from this-is-what-we-went-through to here-is what-I-think-about-it—a shift many of your students are still learning to make. They know the school simply as a place where they lived with others for time, unhappily many of them, and have trouble discussing it abstractly as an institution. They have neither the inclination nor the information needed for doing that.

But they are interested in talking about church as a fashion parade, and whether the Hlubi belong with the Xhosa, and if the coloureds have a culture, so let's set aside any concern about their learning to write comparison–contrast essays and go with whatever work the ongoing movement of the class seems to call for. Just as the literary artist sets characters in motion without knowing what they will do or where they will go, so we will follow the youngsters along and take our chances as they come. In short, the activity of a class should have a narrative structure—a movement, a feeling of expectation that carries us along toward some as yet unforeseen destination. And that means making room for the unexpected and going with it when it appears: the uncovering of a division among us, perhaps, or an unexpected voice bringing us some new or even disturbing thought.

You're beginning to develop this narrative structure when you encourage students to give their class a name, which like the title of a book suggests a story, in this case the one *they're* going to write. And the names they've chosen—Perfect Strangers, Club Nightmare—suggest they've already taken an ironic stance in this situation, living within it from a distance so as to make something of their experience together. And as they move along there will come a moment when everyone will feel the sense of an ending and we make our conclusion.

It's interesting that Jane Wiley wanted the TAs, after considering only one page of the rape-on-campus article, to draw some conclusion "because that's what academic literacy is all about." Her narrative sense is faulty. Or perhaps she felt insecure, not knowing if all this talk would come to anything without direction from her, and so she invoked an exterior standard, academic literacy, to justify her demand, halting the flow of narrative. But the TAs wanted to get on with it and they felt secure enough with you to speak up. Someone should be taking notes during the discussion so their good ideas are not lost. It seems you have begun a journey with those young people, and I wonder where they'll go.

Bye for now—JR

- - - / / / - - -

2 August

Dear John,

Greetings. Another cold winter's day and again I've got 150 exam scripts in the boot of my car waiting to be marked. But I have something else to think about as well. There's a permanent post to be filled, so I'm hell-bent on acquiring it. I'm even writing an article, 'Constructing Tutorials as a Young People's Club', for the university's magazine, *AD Issues,* so I'll be able to list another publication on my resume. It's going to draw on events in my 8:30 a.m. class, which I'll tell you about. We've been having a good time.

On Monday Tina was reading the minutes of last week's meeting: 'One of the wise sayings we heard from the late people was Akukho nkanya idubula ingethi, or after the bush-flower blossoms it dies, which means that all things come to an end. The next was Akukho kwali iphandela enye, ephandela anhye

ngenethole, and that means no person is working for other people, you work
for yourself and your children. Also last week we debate in group about the
lobola article that we read. One group's view proposed by Lucky was that
lobola must abolish because it is a business. We debate about that. The other
group said apartheid had an effect on lobola, destroyed it, because lobola is
important and has its place, it shows love'.

Just then Phumza opened the door and came into the classroom. Tina
looked up from her reading and said, 'Oh Pumza, you're late and you can
now give us a wise saying'. 'All right, but I have to think of one', and she
went on to her seat.

Tina soon finished reading the minutes, so I turned to Elizabeth and
asked if she and Abel were ready with their reports on church-going as a
fashion parade—but then Phumza raised a hand. 'I have a saying', she said,
'but I have to write it', and getting up she went to the chalkboard and wrote
'Inkungu ilala kwintaba ngentaba'.

'And what does that mean, Phumza?' For a moment or two she
looked at the board silently. 'I can't translate it, it's too difficult'. There was
some stir among the Xhosa members of the class.

'I'll translate it', Lucky said. 'You see, it means that today it would be
me and tomorrow it would be yours'. Everyone not Xhosa looked puzzled
by this. 'I don't understand that at all', Felicia said.

'In other words, what happens to me today might happen to you
tomorrow. You see?' Felicia still looked puzzled, and I said 'Well, that's
something to think about, but what do those Xhosa words on the board
actually mean, literally?'

Bulelwa said, 'Here, I'll show you', and getting up he went to the
board and wrote English words under the Xhosa:

Inkungu	ilala	kwintaba	ngentaba
mist	lay	mountain	in all mountain

'You see', Lucky said, 'the mist that lies on one mountain will lie on
all mountains. That's what it means word for word. So what happens to me
today happens to you tomorrow. Maybe it's sort of a metaphor'.

'Well', I said, "it's interesting how the words give us the meaning
indirectly, so we have to interpret them'.

Then we turned back to Elizabeth and her report. She opened her
exercise book and as the group settled into quiet began reading to us.
Church, she said,

is for poor and rich, ugly and beautiful people. As it is said that all people are
equal in the eyes of God, but these days it doesn't go that way.

If someone don't have a beautiful dress or sit she won't go to church at all.
Sometimes you hear someone saying "I had bought a nice dress for church".

Even small children don't go to church unless their parents buy some special clothes for only going to church. That is why other churches have a common uniform for all members. They want everyone to be equal and feel free to go to church without thinking first about what to wear.

I think uniform is a very wise solution for this fashion in the house of God "church" because no one will fear that he or she didn't were a beautiful dress or suit. All churches must take this church and fashion matter under consideration because it is the main reason why people are not attending churches.

Well, this sounded like a good beginning, and maybe the others would have reactions to this she could use or respond to. 'Would anyone like to comment?'

'You want us all to wear uniform?' Norman said. 'Hey, that's another thing altogether'.

'But you know the Bible says you must come as you are to pray', Felicia told us. 'You shouldn't have to get dressed up special'.

'Okay, but we have to investigate this meaning further, by what it means to be a Christian. A Christian has to share. If you have many clothes, you are supposed to give to the poor'.

'Once I went to church', Lindiwe said, 'and there was this fellow wearing a brand new suit. I mean, a really fashionable one. And this brother next to him said, "Hey, why don't you give me that suit?" It almost ended in a fight'.

'We have a uniform in my church but we only wear it for certain occasions', Lucky said. 'The church practice is based on the culture of its own community'.

'Then Elizabeth is right, you see', Nontseka said. 'The problem is based on tradition. We need to wear uniform, especially us blacks. Because blacks are used to gossip. And if they dress up, they gossip. Maybe the coloureds can come dressed as you are but we blacks like to gossip too much'.

This aroused some dissent—and perhaps I should mention that in village culture gossip is an important social activity, but less so in the more urban environment most coloureds have known. So Nontseka started quite a discussion with that remark and I'm thinking of putting all this into the article I'm writing because it shows how such talk can be a move towards a more elaborated language. The students can't rely simply on common understandings but are having to give reasons for the positions they take and work up arguments to justify themselves.

However, the big worry here at UWC is that this ordinary out-of-school-from-home kind of talk is only 'gossip' and will not move the students to academic discourse. Elizabeth's paper, the argument would go, relies on what she already knows and on discourse strategies from her social background, it's not academic enough. So maybe I should include

Shepherd's paper on the Hlubi-Xhosa question in my article. When he finally had a draft ready—it took him 3 weeks—I asked him to speak to his essay (a common practice here), rather than read it to us, and he did so, amplifying many of the points, providing information he later put into his rewrite. Here's a bit from that first draft:

> It is difficult to trace the origin of the black society because the missionary and Historian made History according to the tribes that first in contact with. I will divide my argument into subtopic or phases. First will be some historians in my research, secondly my own analysis, thirdly will be interpretation by some historeans.

And he goes on to cite several sources. This has many problems with language, as you can see, but it's a good start in the academic direction.

Shepard is a second-year student, so he can bring into this what he's learned in history or sociology. Which seems to suggest that our course can provide the expressive space while other academic subjects provide the information that will be used to develop individual concerns. After the passive social positioning they've experienced through much of their schooling, these students need a much more open social arrangement in classrooms—a situational context, as you would say, with less passive reception and more active discussion if they're to develop their ability to think for themselves. Then they get a chance to experience their own power to make meaningful statements to the others, and that's something beyond gossip.

And guess who's in town—Basil Bernstein himself! But when I asked if I could join the select group of scholars who would be meeting with him, I was informed that only those with a special invitation could attend, and eighty people were on the list before me. So when the scholars gathered I drifted around into the neighboring room, a laboratory, and found an unlocked door opening into a short vestibule between the two rooms. So I relaxed on a lab chair and listened to the disquisition from there.

He gave a general sort of talk on various matters of linguistic interest. At one point he made an interesting distinction between 'vertical discourse', which deals with organized knowledge built up and learned one step at a time, as in physics or math, and 'horizontal discourse', which uses local, context-specific strategies to develop knowledge and share it with others. Vertical discourse empowers the teacher, whereas horizontal discourse invites the expression of other voices and creates the participatory acquisition of knowledge—it depends on a structuring of social relations. So there's a name for what I'm doing with students: horizontal discourse—while others are trying to systematize our work as vertical discourse and teach a specialized language from linguistics or rhetoric or whatever to go with it. Bernstein also made a sharp distinction between the production of knowledge by specialists and the recontextualization of that knowledge for teaching purposes. And one thing he said is neccesary for the production of knowledge is 'thinking the unthinkable', which reminded me of your definition of sin.

Afterwards I was wondering if I should be doing more recontextualization of knowledge for my students, but then I decided we should just go on producing knowledge for ourselves, since I don't have much information to give them. All these subjects come up that we talk and write about, and the classes can get pretty loose. Which means I can't always bring in the readings from the text we lecturers agreed to use. In fact, I guess I've been trying to run a two-track course, my own and the official, more academic one, but they don't quite mesh.

It was interesting that my tutorial group named itself Unity in the first quarter, and then when we chose a new name this quarter decided to call themselves Perfect Strangers. We were talking about the power inherent in names, and at first they wanted to be either the 'Revolutionaries' or the 'Hard Livings', but someone objected to 'Hard Livings' because that's the name of a Cape Flats criminal gang and the gang wars have been escalating. Feelings ran so high about this, with so much disagreement, that in the end they decided they're Perfect Strangers.

A good Bernsteinian sequence, this move from Unity to Perfect Strangers—if, that is, he still emphasizes the individualizing that may come with the elaborated language code. But then I hear from one of my fellow lecturers there's no such thing as the individual self, that every utterance is determined simply by a particular moment in the class struggle, social conditions, the time of day, what you ate last night—in short, whatever forces one is caught up in at the time. Well if he really believes that, then I suppose he considers himself one of the forces students are caught up with and he can just give them the facts or explain the reading without expecting anything original from them. Perhaps as Kierkegaard would say he's renounced his personal passionate interest in them in order to become objective. (I've been reading the *Concluding Unscientific Postscript*.)

Now I recall why I've been dissatisfied with my two-track approach. There's such a contrast between the intelligence students show in their talk and then their misreadings of articles in our course reader. They have a passionate interest when they read about lobola say, or women who kill their husbands, and they come up with reactions or interpretations that are expressive, yes, but which often have nothing to do with the text. I feel the need to go over at least a few paragraphs with them and ask some pointed questions. How much emphasis should I put on accuracy of reference?

Talking with Alistair today, and he found fault in my letting all this talking and writing go on with so few intercessions, and he insists I should do more direct teaching about the forms of academic discourse. My pedagogy, he says, is much too indirect, the students don't know what they've gotten. It's the job of the lecturer to point out key words which indicate the meaning of a text they're reading. And 'You can point out how cause and effect are handled in a student's paper', he says. Well, I agree with him so long as these intercessions don't destroy the sense of inquiry, of adventure, and of—well, let's call it the sense of ironic perception that can light up a classroom. I'm letting them go on to see where they'll go, I told him. And if I tried to teach all those language patterns that make up academic discourse as described by genre study, I'd be spending the semester just naming them. I mean you ought to see the preposterous questions which are asked of students in the English department about discourse markers, ellipsis, mode, tenor, field, and all the other secrets of academic discourse, while seventy percent of the class sit there in silence wondering if they'll ever get it.

Alistair objected to my assertion that giving students the opportunity to choose their own topics to discuss and write about would lead to more sophisticated thinking and writing from them. 'Don't they discuss those things, like what to wear in church, outside the classroom?' he asked. But surely the classroom context makes a difference, with the different cultures taking part and everyone using the English language. For the African men, discussing some of these things with women would be forbidden in their neighborhoods, so they haven't had to deal with a contrary view. Here's an obvious case of how the primary language code used in their familiar surroundings is not adequate, because when they go in among the Perfect Strangers they have to reach for the language that will explain or justify.

But now for that most painful time, marking the exam scripts. I come upon the work of Nontyatyambo Luzipo. She's no doubt a recent immigrant from a rural area, perhaps a village in Transkei. She writes in answer to an essay question asking if English and other school subjects are destroying African culture:

> We are coming from rural areas searching for education from urban areas. We were coming here with different cultures. I am agree that language like English destroy our culture and urban changes rural beliefs. in our tradition a Xhosa woman will not suppose to ware trousers but now we see if it's right to ware trousers the only thing which discribes you is the ring that you are a wife. [. . .]

This from a woman whose attendance has been good, she hands in her assignments on time, and she joins in small group discussions, probably when they are talking in Xhosa. She never dares enter the general class discussions. I'm sure that she will fail all her other courses. Shall I fail her essay here?

Feeling hopeless about her position I've made no overtures to her, and she has said very little to me, so this gives me a sense of guilt and I'm squeezed into this impossible dilemma. What if the law department finds that we are passing students like this? They could well abolish the requirement that their students take this course—and in fact their dean refused additional funding for us at one point (he's a senior member of the Funding for Posts Committee). Later he was pushed by concern all through the university with the language problem into releasing funds for the new permanent post I'm after. All this I have in mind as I read Nontyatyambo's paper. But maybe her answer isn't so bad—I understand the assertions she's making, after all. Yet her answers to the reading comprehension questions show that she missed the point of the exam text. Well, hardly twenty percent of the students understood it as a defense of men against feminist theory, so I suppose the choice of text (not my selection) was inappropriate. How do I rate an exam script like this?

But let me tell you I'm tired of worrying about what limits to impose on myself or others and feeling guilty. I had the final session with my therapist, dear Dr. Jean Sperling, this past Friday, Am I ready at last to take on the world without her? And she without me, poor thing? I'm up and running for my life now with the Harrier's Running Club, which is just down the street. Six to 20 of us rumble out of the clubhouse twice a week, do our stretching exercises and go on the run for about an hour, down the streets and through the parks of Claremont and Rodebosch. The leader tells us to 'Stop before you get tired', and that's the kind of running I like.

If you don't mind I'm going to list you as a reference on my application for the new post. With two teenage daughters and life getting more expensive it's very important that I get full-time work. I've got some good local support but the big problem for me is the push for affirmative action appointments. A chap arrived today looking for a post, a Cape coloured with no less than two Masters degrees, one from SUNY, and he speaks Xhosa. So I'm going to show him around, give him a tour of the old deserted residences and that very nice elevator shaft over there.

Keep the pot boiling—Ed

- - - / / /- - -

August 20

Dear Ed,

I read and re-read the story of your morning class, and wanted to hear more. What an exciting and good time you're having there with them! And the beautiful words you're hearing: "The mist that lies on one mountain will lie on all mountains." Perhaps those young people might go out sometime and gather from parents and grandparents the traditional sayings that perhaps now are beginning to fade from the collective memory. The folk wisdom they might bring to you from the different cultural backgrounds represented in that classroom would make an interesting study. And then there was Elizabeth's paper about church-going, and the discussion it provoked—I'm really looking forward to reading more about these people when you've finished your article.

All this activity is happening in your classroom and then you have to hear from someone that it amounts to little more than "out-of-school gossip"! Or Alistair faults you for not interceding often enough with direct instruction, for not leading those youngsters through the rhetorical forms he thinks they should know. And he wants you to point out the key words in a text they read, so they'll get it!—but I say, let them pick out key words for themselves and compose their own readings of the text. As they gain experience doing this they will gradually mature in their understanding—and also you'll know how they're thinking and so can decide what your next move with them should be.

What you *will* point out to them are the beautiful and good things they've said. Among all the words we hear or read in our sessions, one after another, there is sometimes beauty and even wisdom that will be lost or go without effect if someone doesn't point it out. There's a music in their minds that carries ideas flowing along, and we want to encourage the singing.

One morning I came into the classroom early and sat down at my desk. Four or five young women were already there, and as we nodded good morning the door opened and Matt came in. He's a baseball player, with a lot of charm but not much push in the classroom. As he went along a row of desks toward his seat in the far corner behind the girls, I called out to him: "Hey MATT! I hear they call you—LOVERBOY! Is that right?" He sat down and sadly, almost mournfully, said "No, no—I'm not for women, they'll break your heart."

We thought about this for a moment. "Well, if that's true then another woman will mend it. Right, Rachel?" She nodded. "Rachel, have you ever mended a broken heart?" "Oh yes!" she said. "Well Matt, I'd like you to meet Rachel."

Sometimes I can't resist provoking the youngsters in this way. And notice that what Matt said—"I'm not for women, they'll break your heart"—is a line in iambic pentameter. He has the music. And he has a quick mind, he can spar with me. Another day, there were four or five of us sitting there chatting casually when the door opened and Matt came in. I said "Matt, we've been talking here and Demitri tells me you have another name."

"Yeah? What's that?"

"Well, Demitri says they call you—the Careless Kisser."

"That's Demitri's name!"

"Oh no, Demitri's the Careful Kisser. *You're* the Careless Kisser."

"Nope—I only kiss my mom!" And there's the iambic rhythm again, three beats in the line this time. "You're quick, Matt," I said. "Come over here and sit with us."

You and I are listening for the rhythms, the images, the ideas—and we will pause with our youngsters to look back at the work we've done, and savor those good things. Sometimes among the Perfect Strangers you too have heard singing, and now as their current work draws to a close you will tell them some of what you've heard. When Lucky suggests that a folk saying about the mist on the mountain might be a metaphor, he's a long way from gossip. In fact, these students have a natural tendency to move away from the clutter of particulars to a more general level of abstraction in order to manage the matter at hand: "The church practice is based on the culture of its own community," for example. They haven't had to be prodded or instructed to move in that direction, their talking about the issues raised by Elizabeth's work takes them that way. And you will point out afterward what they have done, how they have moved, and so confirm them to themselves. I take notes as we go along so that when the time comes I'm ready to comment on this text—on the story we've been making together—and of course I invite them to do the same. We'll evaluate ourselves.

Now about those essay exams you're reading and grading for their "academic" quality. There you sit in judgment alone, suffering your conscience—feeling guilty if you pass some youngsters and guilty if you fail them. Yet consider this: If the authorities were really concerned to pass only those who can write academic prose, then you would not be allowed to grade your own exams! A set of outside examiners, from the English department perhaps, would read those papers and pass judgment (as they do in my school). But now you're left to be the bad guy who will fail Nontyatyambo. Don't do it! If the woman has done the work and shown progress, then she has earned her pass in this subject at least. Skill in writing is a matter of slow growth, after all. She had an active part in the work of that morning class, where people went their various ways following their interests—coloured culture, church going, the Hlubi question—and what she learned from living for a time within that inquiring culture will be useful to her later.

My own students seem to feel they have to push me out of my place as leader if they're going to go their own way. They begin to think they don't really need me any more, I'm just sitting there giving advice or commenting while they do the work. There's hardly a semester when one of them doesn't say that he or she or someone else really ought to be teaching the class. Of course that's a suggestion I always take, wondering where we'll be going now. Remember Carlos, in my class at Rutgers? When he and Angela were ready with their proposal for our next project, he said "I think we oughta be doin a research paper. We gotta learn how to do references an all that stuff." So he gave us a list of topics to choose from: witchcraft, poverty, racism, crime, religion, homosexuality, and so on. Angela offered an alternative: We could each write about someone who had influenced our life, or someone whose life we had influenced. They specified a paper of at least five pages and gave us a deadline—to hell with Rouse's undemanding, easygoing ways! Most everyone chose to do the research paper, so for the next 2 weeks we met in the library. If I'd suggested doing such a project you can imagine how they would have reacted, how they would have plodded along.

One afternoon in the library I was walking around, checking to see how the work was going, and Carlos said "You can sit down, Professor Rouse—I'm in charge here." I said, "Okay, Carlos—you're right. I don't mind being put in my place," and I left them alone. Which meant that I gave them no instruction at all on how to make a reference, say, or how to write a bibliography. In Carlos' mind that was part of the research problem. And having been set free, so to speak, I spent the time doing research for my review of James Moffett's last two books.

While this work was going on, Fabiana came over to my table one day and said "Excuse me, but I know what we should be doing next." "Well, Louie just told me he does too, so maybe you can get together with him and plan something for us."

Some days later we gathered back in the classroom to present our research papers. Each was read by the writer to an audience of five or six, and the group selected a page or more for all of us to hear. I can't share any of these with you because Carlos and Angela took them—they just gave me a list of the grades they'd assigned. But I remember that one was called "I'll Put a Spell on You: Witchcraft Today", and another on homosexuality that began "We should favor love whatever form it takes." ("There was a lot of information on this," the writer told us. "I didn't know there're so many people like that.") Whatever their occasional deficiencies in expression or organization, all these papers were in correct academic form—Carlos refused to accept them until they were.

At the beginning of the next week, Fabiana took over. She said, "Louie has something for you, and so do I, and there's no choice this time. I'm asking you to write a story or an essay which expresses your own idea of true romantic love." The reaction to this was distinctly favorable. Louie said, "Then for the next paper, Fabiana an I are gonna put you together in pairs—you don't chose a partner, we'll give you one—and each pair will write a 5-minute play to act out for us. A play about some ritual aspect of life"—meaning a wedding, confirmation, prom, graduation, funeral, or whatever. He was probably influenced here by what he was learning in sociology, like your student who wrote about the Hlubi. "An we're both gonna grade you on a scale of 1 to 10." He glanced at me, I suppose because I rarely grade papers. We're getting serious here at last!

I said "Louie, why are we doing this? What are we going to get out of it?" There's always one student in the class who likes to give the professor a hard time.

"You gonna get some meaning out of it," he said. "You take one of these ritual scenes and show us some meaning in it. You have to think about this! Like maybe this couple is gettin married and the wife doesn't want to change her name and they argue about it. So what's that mean about men and women? But I'm not sayin any more, you gotta work this out for yourself. You can check your ideas with me if you want."

Later, as we were all working on our scenes, Ayesha spoke to me. "There's something else we should be doing here," she said. "You know what dot busters are?" I nodded but she went on to explain anyway. "They're people who go around beating up on Indian people." She herself had a dot between her eyebrows and was wearing a sari. "I think we should write how people feel about minorities, what they say about them. We can do some research and we can ask people about it."

"Well, I wonder what the Anglos here are going to think of that idea." Would talking about this disturb the communal spirit we'd developed?

"They're a minority in this class," she said, "so they'll have something to say."

Louie wrote a romantic short story with the title "Someday I'll Come Back", and it opens with these words: "She came through the doorway of the past into the present, and stood on the threshold of pain." It goes on to tell of a young couple who meet in high school and fall in love. The boy, whose nickname is Trick, goes away after their graduation but swears he'll come back. He never does, and eventually the girl marries and has children. One day she receives a letter with no return address, and opening it finds a message from Trick reaffirming his love. The letter ends with a poem in which he asks her to meet him "at the place where we first kissed." But then we learn that the letter was written by her husband as a test because he'd always felt he never had her complete love, and now he knows it. He leaves her.

Louie read this story to us and the others liked it very much. I said "Louie, if my ears heard correctly, then after that poem the story continues for a few lines in rhymed couplets—is that right?" "Yeah," he said. "I don't know how it happened, it just seemed like the right thing to do, it just came." "Well, that letter and the poem took her out of her ordinary prosy life and raised her spirits, so of course the story must continue at that level of feeling until we're brought back to reality by the husband. And isn't it interesting that she's been waiting in her heart for Trick, and now at the end of the story she gets a trick—from her husband. You certainly have a writer's instinct."

So here they are, Louie and the others, in a skills class for students too weak for the regular English program. Can you believe it? If no one recognizes their strength, how will they know they have it? It's left for you and me to show them how the mind, or spirit if you wish, is working in ways only half understood, so they may use it, manage it, and get control of themselves and their possibility. For most of this semester I've just been sitting there with them doing as I'm told, and commenting occasionally. And now Ayesha has started us on another project, so we're gathering information about minorities on campus.

If someone were to criticize this work they've been doing on the grounds that too much of it is insufficiently academic, this writing of short stories and plays, I would say, "Yes, these are people who really like to write!" Of course we'll teach many a semester before something like this happens, but you and I work with every group to make such an experience possible, wondering what they'll do.

But now one of your fellow lecturers tells you there's no such thing as originality or the individual self, "that every utterance is determined simply by a particular moment in the class struggle, social conditions" and so on. In other words, the utterance when it comes is not the authentic expression of an autonomous individual. So as you suggest, this implies that we might as well tell our students precisely what expression we want from them, rather than encourage them in the false belief that they can be individually spontaneous or creative in language. You have a contrary view, however, and it leads to a classroom practice that elicits such responses from students as those you've described in your letter. A practice that tends to produce a particular kind of person—one who wants to think independently rather than simply take in ideas and information from another. Surely there ought to be at least one classroom where this attitude is encouraged. But perhaps others feel that with you around they have mavericks enough.

So your fellow lecturer, as a good postmodernist, tells you that no one thinks for himself, the autonomous subject is an illusion. Well, I agree with that—in the sense that autonomy is not given to us by birth, it's the work of a lifetime: a striving to be free within the actuality to which we each belong (to draw on Kierkegaard once more). Individuality is accidental, you might say, but autonomy is an achievement.

However, postmodernist notions encourage an attitude of resignation, an acceptance of Things As They Are. In school most young people learn to go along, to present an acting self playing the part required while reserving the committed self for a life elsewhere—and the postmodern, therapeutic approach in teaching trains them to accept this division within themselves. They are to resign themselves to living in this divided way, an attitude very convenient for those in power everywhere, directing others who have learned to go along for now and have a life later.

In a therapeutic culture people are led to believe that individual autonomy is impossible, as if their birth in a particular time and place to a particular family ends their story rather than begins it. Postmodernism as expressed in our professional journals contributes to this therapeutic ethos, for it urges the same notions as various 12-step programs—that the self is a deception, individualism is unhealthy, objectivity impossible, and language is a self-contradictory prisonhouse. (Wendy Kaminer describes these programs in *I'm Dysfunctional, You're Dysfunctional.*) But you have been encouraging your students to be present in the classroom, to be fully alive and committed in the situation, with a sense of self-direction—to be a unity of the inner and outer person—and this unity is what we mean by autonomy.

Of course it's difficult to achieve, and the current popularity of postmodern notions may be seen in part as an expression of existential anxiety. Children learning the elaborated language of the middle-class family and so developing a concern for their individual identities, Bernstein remarks,

> may well develop acute identity problems concerned with authenticity [and] may come to see language as phony, a system masking the absence of belief. They may move towards the restricted codes of various peer group sub-cultures . . . (*Class, Codes and Control*, p. 186)

In other words, learning an elaborated language code we learn to distrust language and to question our own identity as authentic individuals, which makes for uncertainty about what we know of ourselves and the world. And a way to assuage this distress is to dismiss the idea of an autonomous self altogether in favor of a socially constructed reality which defines us all. What these postmodern notions come down to, then, is a nostalgic assertion of the "we" who make a world together—another expression of the unsatisfied yearning for community. The communal self given in the phatic language of peer group or local culture offers the comfort of knowing who we are and what we believe without the difficulties of developing and maintaining an autonomous identity.

There's much talk of community these days, and a great many people yearn for the existential comfort of a simpler time somewhere in a past we've heard of or seem to remember. In fact, that young woman from the Transkei you mentioned, who wrote about the fading away of African village culture, started me off on nostalgia trip of my own that took me back to the village where I grew up. Before the family moved there my father described it to us, trying to persuade us to make the move willingly. He said there was a village square with great elm trees and a bandstand, where on summer evenings the high school band gave concerts. Every weekend, people from the farms around came and sat in their cars along the square or strolled under the trees, greeting friends, going into the drugstore for a soda or into the little movie house. It was a friendly community—he knew we'd like it, and we did.

On the first of May, my brother and I each wove a small basket from strips of wallpaper, put pieces of candy in it, and that evening went out to leave the basket at a favorite girl's doorstep. This was the custom among barely pubescent boys in that village. You left your basket at the door, rang the bell and ran to hide. The girl would answer the ring and seeing the basket go searching for you. If she found you, and she always did, then she was entitled to a kiss.

It was a lovely village in a happy time for youngsters, who could not know of course they were actually living in a community more like Winesburg, Ohio, than Grover's Corners. And now there is an ugly shopping mall on the edge of town, the village square has died, even the elms are gone, lost to a blight, and everyone watches television on weekends instead people-watching in the square. Of course the youngsters growing up there today feel at home in other ways and do not miss what I knew. I suppose they too will be looking back nostalgically in later years. But the truth is that during my youth I had just one big idea: Get out of town!

It's foolish to cling to the past, and it's fear of the future that makes us do so. We should be wary of all nostalgic philosophies—like that of Heidegger, for example, who yearns for a simpler pre-Socratic time before the rise of democratic individualism. Or of those who have learned from him, like Derrida, who in his recent work sounds the nostalgic note, describing his deconstruction as done in the spirit of Marxism and confessing that he is still choked with emotion whenever he hears the *Internationale* (*Specters of Marx*). Lately I've been reading more of these plaints about the loss of communal feeling and the elevation of Self from those who dream of recovering somehow what they imagine to have been the old community spirit of the like-minded. And then of course we could deal with young people in the mass rather than having to manage them as separate and quite distinct individuals—we could give up the work of trying to make with them a community of individuals. Nostalgia is the enemy of present possibility.

There's no returning to the comfortable world of our childhood. In fact, "There is no past that one is allowed to long for," Goethe remarked—for the past is not remembered from the outside but lives and is a productive force within our innmost self. But even so, I can't help but look back sometimes like that Transkei woman, sadly.

Bye for now—JR

--- / / / ---

January 20

Dear Ed,

Surprised to be hearing from me again so soon? Well, I've just taken part in a dramatic scene and if this sounds a little breathless in the telling it's because I'm still aroused, in a don't-mess-with-me attitude. Three weeks ago I was asked to take over a class from another instructor who had left the campus suddenly for reasons not divulged to me. But after a few days in that classroom I could understand why she felt the need to seek other company. In fact, just a first look around as I came in told me this crowd could be trouble. They were quiet, but their *disposition,* their very posture, spoke loudly enough.

Two young men sat together against the left wall, one behind the other—a very tall fellow, who could be a basketball player, and behind him a large stocky boy, perhaps a football player. Between them and the rest of the class were five rows of vacant seats, the others having pulled their desks closely together on the far right side of the room. In the front row a young woman sat facing back with one leg folded under her, talking to the others. My arrival was clearly an interruption—she was telling about her travels over the weekend with her boyfriend—so I sat down with the audience and waited for my turn to speak.

It came soon. My sitting there seemed to distract her and she kept glancing at me, somewhat nervously, I thought, and then just stopped talking. An uneasy and perhaps expectant silence settled over the crowd. I continued to sit there silently among them for another moment.

Then I introduced myself casually, and getting up from my seat remarked that I too had a story for them—which I proceeded to tell, pausing from time to time. "In Africa . . . when the sun comes up, the gazelle . . . must start running to escape the hungry lion. In Africa when the sun comes up, the lion . . . must start running after the gazelle . . . or it will die of hunger. So whether you're a lion or a gazelle . . . when the sun comes up you better start running!" I looked them over. "Now what I want to know is, what do we have here—a bunch of lions or a bunch of gazelles?"

"Lions," said the football player.

"Could be. Every morning I put on my running shoes—I'm wearing them right now, see?—and I run around the park. Some mornings I feel like a gazelle and I'm just poetry in motion. Other mornings I feel like a very **hungry** lion. So what I really want to know is this: **Are you gonna run with me**?" I looked them over, then bending down to a young man I said quietly, "Are you gonna run with me?"

"Maybe."

"Wudya mean, *maybe*? Wonderin if you can keep up the pace?" and I moved on to another. "You gonna run with me?" She nodded. "Hey, this is great, I got company!" Moving on: "You gonna run with me?"

"That depends on where yer goin.'"

"Ah, you're very wise! Who knows where we'll be going?"

And when I'd asked each of them the question and gotten an answer, I said "Okay then, let's start running!" I'd told them a story, a fable, and now I asked them to each write a fable, and to help them along I supplied some key lines. "Once there was a young woman—or was it a young man?—walking alone in the woods. And she—or he, you decide—met a . . . Who or what did this person meet? Remember, in a fable anything can talk—animals, trees, whatever." And so they began running with me, going on to complete their fables, ending with "The moral of this story is . . ."

Well, not all of them were running with me. Several students came drifting into the room at various times after the start of our session. And while I sat with one young woman reading her story as the others reworked theirs, I could hear the buzz of various conversations. Getting up I looked around to see who else might like to show me a story, and noticed a young man with a magazine in hand, no work before him. I said, "You can put that away, if you will, and get on with your work."

"No I won't!" he said, quite belligerently.

"And why is that?"

"Because you didn't tell *him* to put it away," pointing to someone else. So while I was occupied the magazine had been passed on.

"I see. Well, that explains it." I left him there with his magazine.

Our classroom is quite wide and narrow, with a large empty alcove in the middle of the back wall, used at one time for storage. The next day I noticed a young women sitting in that alcove, hidden behind the other students. I said, "You can come out of there and sit with the rest of us." A day or two later I noticed *another* young woman sitting in that alcove, hidden behind the others. I said, "You can come out of there and sit with the rest of us."

As the week went on, and the next, they continued in the patterns of behavior they'd evidently developed with their previous teacher. Each day one or two were absent, two or three would wander in late. These people knew each other very well, having already spent three weeks together with their previous teacher, and they were unwilling to allow me to disturb their modus vivendi. They enjoyed sharing their fables with each other, and they were happy to give up the textbook and decide for themselves what our next project should be, for this gave them an opportunity to talk away the time. They seemed to feel that what we did there hardly mattered so long as they passed the departmental exam at the end of the term, and they evidently expected to pass. I worked with those who wanted to write with me but the critical mass was against us, so to speak. The magazine reader took to drifting about the room. It seemed to me that if I did not impose some exterior discipline, all these people would hold me in contempt for indulging them and little work would be done. But how to do that?

The two athletes continued to sit apart, against the far left wall. When both were present, a rare occurrence, they would whisper to each other, they would snicker, they would support each other in their weakness. One day when the football player was sitting there by himself, I said "Michael, you must be lonely over there, so come sit here with us ordinary people." He got up and swaggered across the room to the far right wall and sat in the back corner. But he was with the people.

The next day when the basketball player came in, late as usual and wearing his Walkman earphones, he looked around—saw the other boy and started across the room to join him. I said, "There's no room over there, Tyrone—you can sit here with us," indicating another seat.

"I'll sit anywhere I want!" he said and continued on. I think he had in mind moving someone from a seat, there were no vacant ones over there near Michael. "No, Tyrone—you'll sit right here."

"I'll sit anywhere I want, I told ya!"

"Bring your things and come with me. I think you should tell the dean how you're being treated here." I opened the door and waited for him. He looked at me for a moment, startled, then strode over and out we went.

In the corridor I moved right along in no mood to palaver. He said, "Yer only doin this cause I'm black!"

"I wondered when you'd try that one! Didn't take ya long, did it?"

Then we were outside in the quad, marching right along. Tyrone called to a young man passing some distance away: "Hey, tell the coach! He's pickin on me for no reason. Tell the coach!" Another young man passed on the other side, and Tyrone called out "Hey, tell the coach! He's pickin on me for no reason. Tell the coach!"

In the dean's office the secretary said, "But there's no one here to see him."

"Oh, he'll wait. He's looking for another class or maybe a way to stay in mine." I left him there and went back to the classroom.

As I came in, the others looked up at me and I felt a subtle change in their disposition. When I said, "Sorry about that, folks—let's get on with our work," they did. I carried my chair over to the far corner and sat down there to look at what Michael had written. Not much, but he surprised me because I could see intelligence in his words. He has a goofy look and a goofy manner, and thinks of himself as a kind of goof, perhaps. A big boy hiding in a corner of the classroom, afraid. I read one of his paragraphs to him and said, "Michael, that's intelligent—you're going to do alright here."

The time left in the session seemed to pass quickly. As the youngsters began to stir, getting up, gathering their things, the door opened and in came Tyrone followed by a short man in a long overcoat. I thought, Now who the hell is this—the coach? I got up and marched across the room to him, saying quite emphatically "And **who** are you, sir?"

"Well, I—uh, I'm—uh, well I'm, I'm Dean Jackson."

"And I'm John Rouse!" I put out my hand and gripped his quite firmly. This was not the student dean but the academic dean—a very important person, evidently come to find out why the star basketball player was having a problem here.

We waited as the students went out, Michael lingering in the hopes of hearing some of this, but then he went on and the dean closed the door. He gestured for us to sit down. The boy sat down, I sat down, the dean remained standing. I got up and stood with him. He said, "Tell me what happened here."

"Well, this young man has been absent five times, and—"

"I already told him that!"

"Yes, and now I'm telling him. Also, he—"

"Like high school!" the boy said loudly, getting up from his chair. "Jis like high school! Take ya to the principal! Can't talk man to man! Jis like a woman!" And he went on haranguing, pacing back and forth.

"You're hearing this," I murmured to the dean. "You hear it." Then, "You're hearing this. You hear it." The dean soon tired of this and motioned for the boy to leave the room. He closed the door and now we both sat down.

He said, "Tell me: Do you have assigned seating in this classroom?"

I knew where this was going. "Yes! I assigned that boy to sit *there,* and the other boy to sit over *there.*"

"Well, if you didn't have assigned seating from the first day, I think you made an error in judgment, and—"

"In this classroom we make the arrangements as we go along."

The dean got up, saying "I can't talk to you! You interrupt me, I can't talk to you!"

"Then let's talk sometime when we're both calm." I opened the door. The dean glanced at me and then went out.

That's the last I've seen of those two. I can imagine the look on this dean's face when my next yearly appointment reaches his desk for approval. Or my application for the full-time position in the writing program that's to be filled next year. So perhaps I should be calling friends and looking for work elsewhere. Tell me: Would you recommend a move to South Africa? Might I find employment at UWC?

My pot boils over—JR

- - - / / / - - -

25 January

Yo My Broer (Hello my brother),

Good news!! It finally came through, they gave it to me, a regular appointment!!! And thanks for the reference you faxed in, that helped. No more waiting every year for the next temporary appointment, I now have a full-time position with all the privileges appertaining thereto. But what a shock to find a 250 rand reduction in my monthly salary, what with increased deductions for insurance, pension, a higher tax bracket and the special election tax (democracy is not cheap). In fact, this salary does not at all meet my expenses, which as you know include a sizeable maintenance payment to my children. I'm economizing on petrol—driving the car only as far as a friend's house and then riding a bike to the university, about 12 kilometres further on. Indeed, any car repair will force me to increase the bond on this house, my one and only asset.

Sometimes I take the train to Mowbray for only a rand (although it seems like few of the other passengers in third class actually buy tickets), and then get into a minibus taxi to UWC. That costs me R3.50, which is cheaper than the bus and faster. But there are bad vibes around the taxi rank at Mowbray, and a driver was shot dead there not long ago. The two taxi organizations are in hot and sometimes violent competition with each other, and I remember Jenna, our tutor who was shot riding home in a taxi. Yesterday my driver, named Shafir, got into an argument with another driver for picking me up without waiting in rank, and I said 'Aren't you afraid of getting killed in one of these arguments?' He said, 'Well, if it's my number to go there's nothing I can do'. He had a tiny new television mounted on the dashboard, and the tape deck was howling out 'Power of Love'. As we drove along he picked up a pair of binoculars and scanned the road ahead, on the lookout for trouble.

Then today I noticed that my driver had a knobkerrie, a stick with a ball of hard rubber on the end, lying across the dashboard. 'Twenty-seven killed in Seboking', says the radio. 'Four policemen ambushed in Kwazulu. Ten bodies dug up in Boksburg. Seventeen bodies of women dug up near Attridgeville'. Are we sitting on a time bomb? With the tight controls of apartheid gone, South Africa is like one of the new democracies in Eastern Europe with the Russians gone—more crime and unemployment, and state services strained and maybe failing. There's a possibility that conditions in this country could really deteriorate, the whole economy could collapse. How can it handle the pressure of so many poverty-stricken Africans—so many expectations, dreams, angers, demands?

Just before final exams the administration threatened to exclude all students next term who have not paid their fees—some owe more than R7000—so the national body of student organizations called for a 'moratorium on all exclusions' and the trouble started. Three thousand students held a mass meeting in the Great Hall, and now every day they come toyi-toying through the campus, crowds of 20 to 400, shaking the doors of lecture rooms where lecturers brazenly continue to teach despite the boycott declared at their mass meeting.

And there was a hostage taking last Thursday when about 300 mainly African students prevented five or six members of the administration (four coloureds and one white) from leaving their offices until 3 a.m., when police were sent in. The next day there was a call for lecturers to protest against this student violence, and we agreed to meet later at the admin building. As I was walking across the campus to join the lecturers' protest, I met one my former students and he walked along with me for a bit. When I said that maybe I'd be taken hostage, he assured me that would not happen, the students didn't want hostages. He seemed embarrassed by the whole affair.

By the time I arrived the lobby was packed with angry African students. The academics had already gone upstairs to the rector's office amid the hoots and cries of the crowd, and shouts of 'Down with Eurocentric education!' I stopped to talk with a young African girl, and she was very critical of my desire to protest against the hostage taking. 'We weren't keeping any hostages', she said, 'we were simply gathered peacefully outside the admin offices, waiting to negotiate'. 'At 3 a.m.?' I asked. 'Well of course!' she said, pretending that was a perfectly ordinary thing to do. So it looks like we're in for a period of mass demonstrations and general disruption.

Then something surprising happened with the Perfect Strangers at our last meeting. We had to make good use of the little time left before the final exam, so I asked them to form groups of three or four and edit the drafts of their papers. But instead of settling down to work they were talking among themselves, laughing, and then Nomuula's standing there with a big smile saying 'I can't believe it! I can communicate in English, I can just say what I want to say to anybody!' This from a girl who'd told me on the first day that she only knew Afrikaans. Then Lucky got up and gave a little speech in my honour, some others spoke, and they gave me a large carved African mask with their names written inside it. Then they brought out a lot of food, and afterwards Faith sang a hymn for us. I wasn't ready for any of this, it was very embarrassing. And I felt guilty because there was so little time left and no work was done. Then Thobeka spilled hot water on her hand because my hot water percolator has no lid, so I just gave up any thought of going on with the work that day. It seemed they really felt something for this class of ours.

Well, this term has certainly been eventful. I was startled one evening to see Mzonke on television delivering the 6 o'clock news. He also does interviews and follow-up stories for the station, and it seems he's become their most popular news announcer. And Alistair has become a Buddhist.

So now I'm going to relax, play the guitar and sing a little, with the help of some white wine. Maybe Old Mike will come by—remember him? He showed up here last week, and lo and behold, gone were the dreadlocks, a shiny shaved pate in their stead, and he was wearing a cream-coloured jersey and good trousers. Why, the fellow looked absolutely transformed, almost resembling a graduate student at some American university. And with him was a blond, delicate and lovely lady holding a pink flower. He introduced her as Marianna, and sold me some Coke as usual. I expect that soon we'll be having coffee together at Nandos. You never know what people are capable of, what they'll do.

As I said, this has been a strange and surprising time, these last few weeks. And now I'm going to take a bit of rest.

Meanwhile, keep stirring the pot—Ed

References

Algren, Nelson. "a lot you got to holler." *The Neon Wilderness*. New York: Hill & Wang. 1960. 102-118.

Anderson, Elijah. *Streetwise: Race, Class, and Change in an Urban Community.* Chicago: University of Chicago Press. 1990.

Bader, Jenny Lyn. "Content Provided Below." *New York Times Week in Review,* Aug 1, 1999. 3.

Bakhtin, M.M. *Toward a Philosophy of the Act.* Trans. Vadim. Liapunov. Ed. Michael Holquist and Vadim. Liapunov. Austin: University of Texas Press. 1993.

Bakhtin School Papers. Ed. Anne Shukman. Oxford: RPT Publications. 1983.

Barthes, Roland. "The Death of the Author." *Image, Music, Text.* Trans. Stephen Heath. New York: Hill and Wang. 1977

Bernstein, Basil. *Class, Codes and Control.* New York: Schocken. 1974.

Berryman, John. "Of 1826." *The Dream Songs.* New York: Farrar, Straus & Girous. 1969.

Biko, Steve. "Some African Cultural Concepts." *I Write What I Like: A Selection of his Writings.* London: Bowerdean Publishing Co. 1996.

Bohm, David and David Peat. *Science, Order, and Creativity.* New York: Bantam. 1987.

Bourdieu, Pierre, Jean-Claude Passeron and Monique de Saint Martin. *Academic Discourse.* Stanford: Stanford University Press. 1994. 21.

Brannon, Lil. *Writers Writing.* Portsmouth, NH: Boynton/Cook. 1982.

Brenner, M. "Murder on the Border." *New Yorker* 69 (S 13, 1993): 52-54+.

231

Britton, James. *Language and Learning.* New York: Penguin. 1970.

Brown, Richard H. *Society as Text: Essay on Rhetoric, Reason, and Reality.* Chicago: Chiocago University Press. 1987. 164.

Brunvand, Jan Harold. *The Vanishing Hitchhiker: American Urban Legends and their Meanings.* New York: Norton. 1981.

Burroughs, William. *Nova Express.* New York: Grove Press. 1965.

Byatt, A.S. *Possession.* New York: Vintage. 1990.

Chekhov, Anton. "A Day in the Country." *The Tales of Chekhov.* Trans. Constance Garnett. New York: Ecco. 1972. 12:107-115.

_____. "At Home." *The Tales of Chekhov.* Trans. Constance Garnett. New York: Ecco. 1972. 2:259-278.

Coles, William E. *The Plural I—and After.* Portsmouth, NH: Boynton/Cook. 1988.

Derrida, Jacques. *Specters of Marx: The State of the Debt, the Work of Mourning, and the New International.* Trans. Peggy Kamuf. New York: Routledge. 1994.

Dostoevsky, Fyodor. *The Brothers Karamazov.* Trans. David Magarshack. London: Folio Society. 1964.

Elbow, Peter. *Writing Without Teachers.* New York: Oxford. 1973.

Fairclough, Norman. *Critical Language Awareness.* New York: Longman. 1992.

Foucault, Michel. "What is an Author?" [1969]. Trans. Josué V. Harari. *Textual Strategies: Perspectives in Post-Structuralist Criticism.* Ithaca, NY: Cornell University Press. 1979. 141-160.

Friedman, Lawrence W. *The Horizontal Society.* New Haven: Yale University Press. 1999.

Friere, Paulo. *The Pedagogy of the Oppressed.* Trans. Myra Ramos. New York: Continuum. 1997.

Gay, Peter. *The Enlightenment: An Interpretation.* New York: Norton. 1977.

Gee, James. *Social Linguistics and Literacies: Ideology in Discourses.* New York: Falmer. 1990.

_____. "What is Literacy?" *Rewriting Literacy: Culture and the Discourse of the Other.* Ed. Candace Mitchell and Kathleen Weiler. Westport, CT: Bergin & Garvey. 1991.

Gellner, Ernest. *Language and Solitude: Wittgenstein, Malinowski and the Hapsburg Dilemma.* New York: Cambridge University Press. 1998.

Gewertz, Paul. *Law's Stories: Narrative and Rhetoric in the Law.* New Haven: Yale University Press. 1996.

Greene, Bob. "That's Entertainment." *Esquire* (Aug. 1980). 12.

Harrington, Anne. *Reenchanted Science.* Princeton, NJ: Princeton University Press. 1996. 212.

Heath, Shirley B. "What No Bedtime Story Means: Narrative Skills at Home and School." *Language in Society.* V. 11. 49-76.

Hecht, Ben. *A Child of the Century.* New York: Simon & Schuster. 1954.

Henry, Jules. *Culture Against Man.* New York: Vintage. 1963.

Hood, Lynley. *Sylvia! The Biography of Sylvia Ashton-Warner.* New York: Viking. 1988.

Hymes, Dell. *Ethnography, Linguistics, Narrative Inequality.* London: Taylor & Francis. 1996.

Ibsen, Henrik. *Peer Gynt.* Trans. Michael Meyer. New York: Doubleday. 1963.

James, William. "Does Consciousness Exist?" *Selected Writings.* Ed. G.H. Bird. London: Everyman. 1995.

Jameson, Fredric. "Postmodernism and Consumer Society." *Postmodernism and its Discontents.* Ed. E.A. Kaplan. London: Verso. 1988. 13-29.

Kaminer, Wendy. *I'm Dysfunctional, You're Dysfuctional: The Recovery Movement and Other Self-Help Fashions.* New York: Addison-Wesley. 1992.

Katz, E. "Constructing Tutorials as a Young People's Club: An Approach to a Democratic Pedagogy." *Democracy and Education: The magazine for classroom teachers,* 12:2 (1998): 23-26.

Kerouac, Jack. *Dharma Bums.* New York: Viking. 1958.

Kierkegaard, Soren. *Concluding Unscientific Postscript.* Trans. David Swenson and Walter Lowrie. Princeton, NJ: Princeton University Press. 1968.

_____. *Either/Or.* Trans. David and Lillian Swenson. Princeton, NJ: Princeton University Press. 1959.

_____. *The Present Age.* Trans. Alexander Dru. New York: Harper. 1962.

_____. *Repetition: An Essay in Experimental Psychology.* Trans. Walter Lowrie. New York: Harper. 1941.

_____. *The Sickness Unto Death.* Trans. Walter Lowrie. Princeton, NJ: Princeton University Press. 1954.

Labov, William. "The Logic of Nonstandard English." *Report of Twelfth Annual Round Table Meeting on Linguistics and Language Studies* 1970. Ed. James. E. Alatis. Washington, DC: Georgetown University Press. 1970.

Leonard, George. *Education and Ecstasy.* Berkeley: N. Atlantic. 1987.

Liebow, Elliot. *Talley's Corner.* Boston: Little, Brown. 1967.

Malan, Rian. *My Traitor's Heart.* New York: Atlantic Monthly Press. 1990.

Malinowski, Bronislaw. "The Problem of Meaning in Primitive Languages." Supplement I, *The Meaning of Meaning,* C.K. Ogden and I.A. Richards. New York: Harcourt, Brace & Co. 1923.

Manheimer, Ronald J. *Kierkegaard as Educator.* Berkeley: University of California Press. 1977.

March, William. *Company K. A William March Omnibus.* New York: Rinehart. 1956.

Marcuse, Herbert. "Repressive Tolerance." *A Critique of Pure Tolerance.* Ed. Robert Pace Wolff et al. Boston: Beacon. 1969.

Márquez, Gabriel Garcia. *Chronicle of a Death Foretold.* Trans. Gregory Rabossa. New York: Ballantine Books. 1982.

Marx, Karl. *The German Ideology.* Trans. Eugene Kamenka. The Portable Karl Marx. Ed. Eugene Kamena. New York: Penguin. 1983. 207.

_____. *Manifesto of the Communist Party.* Trans. Eugene Kamenka. *The Portable Karl Marx.* New York: Viking Penguin. 1983. 207.

Mathabane, Mark. *Kaffir Boy.* New York: New American Library. 1986.

Mill, J.S. *On Liberty.* New York: Columbia University Press. 1989.

Mink, Louis. "Narrative as a Cognitive Instrument." *The Writing of History.* Ed. Robert Canary and Henry Kozicki. Madison: University of Wisconsin Press. 1978.

Moffett, James. *Teaching the Universe of Discourse.* New York: Houghton Mifflin. 1968.

Moss, Richard. *How Shall We Live?* Berkeley, CA: Celestial Arts. 1985.

Mphalele, Ezekiel. *Down Second Avenue.* New York: Faber & Faber. 1985.

Musil, Robert. "Helpless Europe." *Precision and Soul: Essays and Addresses.* Trans. Burton Pike and David Luft. Chicago: University of Chicago Press. 1990. 131.

Nietzche, Friedrich. *The Gay Science.* Trans. Walter Kaufmann. New York: Vintage. 1974. 167.

_____. *The Will to Power.* Trans. Walter Kaufmannn. New York: Random House. 1967. 512.

Paglia, Camille. "Do Women Ask for Rape?" *Sex, Art and American Culture.* New York: Penguin. 1992.

Pavese, Cesare. *The Burning Brand: Diaries 1930-1950.* Trans. A.E. Murch. New York: Walker & Co. 1961.

Pepetela. *Mayombe.* Portsmouth: Heinemann. 1996.

Plato. *Laws.* Trans. A.E. Taylor. *Collected Dialogues.* Ed. Edith Hamilton and Huntington Cairns. Princeton, NJ: Princeton University Press. 1963.

Podhoretz, Norman. *Making It.* New York: Random House. 1967.

Progoff, Ira. *At a Journal Workshop.* New York: Dialogue House. 1975.

Rand, Ayn. *The Fountainhead.* New York: Penguin Books. 1952.

Rieff, Philip. *The Triumph of the Therapeutic.* New York: Harper & Row. 1966.

Rorem, Ned. *Knowing When to Stop.* New York: Simon & Schuster. 1995.

Rosen, Harold. "Stories of Stories: Footnotes on Sly Gossipy Practices." *The Word for Teaching is Learning: Essays for James Britton.* Ed. Martin Lightfoot and Nancy Martin. Portsmouth: NH. Boyton/Cook. 1988.

Ross, Andrew. *Strange Weather: Culture, Science and Technology in the Age of Limits.* New York: Verso. 1991. 62.

Rouse, John. "The Politics of Composition." *College English* 41(1979): 1-12.

_____. *Provocations: The Story of Mrs. M.* Urbana, IL: NCTE. 1993.

_____. "Scenes from the Writing Workshop." *College English* 47 (1985): 217-236.

Ryan, Judith. *The Vanishing Subject.* Chicago: University of Chicago Press. 1991.

Scribner, Sylvia, & Michael Cole. *The Psychology of Literacy.* Cambridge: Harvard University Press. 1981.

Shaughnessy, Mina. *Errors and Expectations.* New York: Oxford. 1977.

Simmel, George. "The Metropolis and Mental Life." *On Individuality & Social Forms.* Chicago: University of Chicago Press. 1971.

Skinner, B.F. *Beyond Freedom and Dignity.* New York: Bantam Books. 1972. 191.

Spengler, Oswald. *The Decline of the West.* Trans. Charles F. Atkinson. New York: Knopf. 1928.

Steinbeck, John. "The Leader of the People." *The Long Valley.* New York: Penguin. 1995.

Street, Brian. *Social Literacies: Critical Approaches to Literacy in Development, Ethnography and Education.* New York: Longman. 1995.

Themba, Can. *The Will to Die.* Eds. Donald Stuart and R. Holland. London: Heinemann. 1972.

Thompson, William I., ed. *Gaia, A Way of Knowing: Political Implications of the New Biology.* Barrington: Lindisfarne. 1987.

Tlali, Miriam. *Footprints in the Quag: Stories and Dialogues from Soweto.* Cape Town: David Philip. 1989.

Tocqueville, Alexis De. *Democracy in America.* Trans. Henry Reeve. New York: Knopf. 1945.

Twain, Mark. *Tom Sawyer Abroad.* New York: Collier. 1962

Vygotsky, L.S. *Thought and Language,* Trans. Eugenia Hanfmann and Gertrude Vakar. Cambridge: MIT Press. 1962.

_____. *Mind in Society: The Development of Higher Psychological Processes.* Eds. M. Cole, V. John-Steiner, S. Scribner, and E. Souberman. Cambridge: Harvard University Press. 1978.

Williams, Raymond. *The Long Revolution.* New York: Harper & Row. 1961. 48.

Wright, Richard. *Black Boy.* New York: Harper. 1945.

Yates, Richard. "The Best of Everything." *Eleven Kinds of Loneliness.* New York: Dell. 1962. 24-38.

ADDITIONAL SOURCES

Chapter 2

p. 29: "In bad company": Bierce, Ambrose. *The Devil's Dictionary.* New York: Citadel Press. 1946.

32: "the first paragraph": Cope, Bill & Mary Kalantzis. *The Power of Literacy: A Genre Approach to Teaching Writing.* Pittsburgh: University of Pittsburgh Press. 1.

37: "Jane Tompkins": Schneider, Alison. "Jane Tompkin's Message to Academe." *The Chronicle of Higher Education.* July 10, 1999; also, letters to the editor in the issue of August 14, 1998.

"study group": Assembly on Expanded Perspectives on Learning.

"Moffett . . . outlines an instructional program": *The Universal Schoolhouse: Spiritual Awakening Through Education.* San Francisco: Jossey-Bass. 1994. Also, "Writing, Inner Speech, and Meditation." *Coming on Center: English Education in Evolution.* Montclair, NJ: Boyton/Cook Publishers. 1981. 133-181.

41: "postmodern epigones and the Marxists": Fitts, Karen and France Alan, eds. *Left Margins: Cultural Studies and Composition Pedagogy.* Albany: SUNY. 1995. 105, 221, 235, 241, 275-79, 328.

45: "identity kit": Gee, James. "What is Literacy?" Mitchell, C. & Weiler, K. eds. *Rewriting Literacy: Culture and the Discourse of the Other.* Westport, CT: Bergin & Garvey. 1991. 3-11.

Chapter 3

p.60: "some feminist academics": Patai, Daphne and Noretta Koertege. *Professing Feminism: Cautionary Tales from the Strange World of Women's Studies.* New York: Basic Books. 1994. 99, 104, 107.

61: "social ways of scientists": see also Phelps, Louise W. *Composition as a Human Science.* New York: Oxford University Press. 12.

"a recent article": Fleckenstein, Kristie S. "Images, Words, and Narrative Epistemology." *College English* 58 (1996): 914-933.

71: "visionary experiences": Noll, Richard. *The Jung Cult: Origins of a Charismatic Movement.* Princeton: Princeton UP. 1994. 209.

80: "capitalist rag": Chen, Kathy. "Chinese Families Go to the Wilds, This Time for Fun." *Wall Street Journal,* Oct. 18, 1996. A1.

Chapter 4

p.110: "The whole age": *Soren Kierkegaard's Journals and Papers, Vol. 1.* Howard and Edna Hong, eds. Bloomington: Indiana Univresity Press. 345.

Chapter 5

p.122: "Lady Francesca Wilde": Ellman, Richard. *Oscar Wilde.* New York: Vintage Books, 1987. 9, 14.

130: "Heidegger, who said": Tymoczko, Dmitri. "The Martin Chronicles." *Lingua Franca,* April 1998: 29.

139: "to paraphrase Bernstein": *Pedagogy, Symbolic Control and Identity.* London: Taylor & Francis. 1996. 158.

142: "success in many careers": *WSJ,* Dec. 29, 1998. A1.

Chapter 6

p.160: "many tribal Africans are given": Chuks-orji, Ogonna. *Names from Africa.* Chicago: Johnson Publishing Co. 1972. 81.

"Opanin Kwame Nyame": ibid. 86.

162: "Kierkegaard suggests": *Concept of Irony,* Trans: Lee Capel. Bloomington: Indiana University Press. 1965. 279.

"pedagogy of disclosure": Bleich, David. *Know and Tell: A Writing Pedagogy of Disclosure, Genre, and Membership.* Portsmouth, NH: Boynton/Cook Heinemann. 1998.

163: "Scribner and Cole's": Spellmeyer, Kurt. "Culture and Agency." *CCC* 48 (1997): 294.

165: "critical pedagogy": Fitts, Karen and France Alan, eds. *Left Margins: Cultural Studies and Composition Pedagogy.* Albany: State University of New York Press. 1995. 76, 219, 221, 235.

168: "liberties with his texts": Cole, Michael, et al., eds. "Editors' Preface." Vygotsky, L.S. *Mind in Society.* Cambridge: Harvard University Press. 1978. ix-xi.

Chapter 7

p.184: "Anxiety is the dizziness of freedom": Kierkegaard, *The Concept of Anxiety.* Trans. Reidar Thomte. Princeton, NJ: Princeton University Press, 1980. 61.

186: "confessional criticism": Veeser, H. Aram, ed. *Confessions of the Critics.* New York: Routledge. 1996.

192: "Harvard professor": Mack, John E. *Abduction: Human Encounters with Aliens.* New York: Scribner's. 1994.

"University of Virginia professor": Shroder, Tom. *Old Souls: The Scientific Evidence for Past Lives.* New York: Simon & Schuster. 1999.

"chemistry professor": Mangan, Katherine S. ""A & M's 'Alchemy Caper." *Chronicle of Higher Education,* Jan. 19, 1994. A19.

"laying on of hands": Sullivan, Ronald. "Hospitals Introducing a Therapy Resembling 'Laying On of Hands." *New York Times,* Nov. 6, 1977.

194: "Freud": Parry, Alan & Robert E. Doan. *Story Re-Visions: Narrative Therapy in the Postmodern World.* New York: Guilford Press. 1994. 7.

"Gee . . . reviewing the narrative": Gee, James. "The Narrativization of Experience in the Oral Style." *Rewriting Literacy: Culture and the Discourse of the Other.* Ed. C. Mitchell and K. Weller. New York: Bergin & Garvey. 1991.

"current issue": *College English* 59, No. 2 (February 1997).

195: "Your job is to tell a story": Spaeth, Merrie. "What You Can Learn From Brokaw & Co." *Wall Street Journal,* Jan. 6, 1996. A12.

196: "social capital": Putnam, Robert D. *Making Democracy Work: Civic Traditions in Modern Italy.* Princeton: Princeton University Press. 1994.

197: "in the CCC journal": Yagelski, Robert P. "The Ambivalence of Reflection: Critical Pedagogies, Identity, and the Writing Teacher." *CCC* 51 (1999): 33-50.

"other such articles": for example, Gallehr, Donald R. "What is the Sound of No Hand Writing? The Use of Secularized Zen Koans in the Teaching of Writing." Foehr, Regina & Susan Schiller. *The Spiritual Side of Writing.* Portsmouth, NH: Boyton/Cook Heinemann. 1997. 95-104.

Author
Index

Algren, N., 59, *231*
Anderson, E., 151, *231*
Bader, J.L., 186, *231*
Bakhtin, M.M., 116, 120, 121, *231*
Barthes, R., 175, 185, 186, *231*
Bernstein, B., ix, 4, 13, 17, 24, 43, 44, 48, 49, 50, 60, 82, 117, 134, 135, 138, 139, 140, 141, 152, 163, 174, 208, 212, 221, *231*
Berryman, J., 66, *231*
Bierce, A., 29, *235*
Biko, S., 187, 200, *231*
Bleich, D., 162, *237*
Bohm, D., 55, 60, 61, *235*
Bourdieu, P., 17, *231*
Brannon, L., 128, 133, *231*
Brenner, M., 180, *231*
Britton, J., 168, *232*
Brown, R.H., 195, *232*
Brunvand, J.H., 101, *232*
Burroughs, W., 186, *232*
Byatt, A.S., 88, *232*

Chekhov, A., 92, 119, *232*
Chen, K., 80, *236*
Chuks-orji, O., 160, *236*
Cole, M., 163, 168, 234, *237*
Coles, W.E., 146, 154, *232*
Cope, B., 32, *235*

Derrida, J., 62, 222, *232*
Doan, R.E., 194, *237*
Dostoevsky, F., 120, *232*

Elbow, P., 128, 133, *232*
Ellman, R., 122, *236*

Fairclough, N., 157, *232*
Fitts, K., 41, 165, *236*, *237*
Fleckenstein, K.S., 61, *236*
Foehr, R., 197, *237*
Foucault, M., 175, 186, *232*
France, A., 41, 165, 236, *237*
Friedman, L.W., 193, *232*
Friere, P., 163, *232*

Gallehr, D.R., 197, *237*
Gay, P., 97, *232*

Gee, J., 43, 44, 45, 46, 48, 49, 50, 139, 189, 194, *232, 237*
Gellner, E., xi, *232*
Gewertz, P., 195, *232*
Greene, B., 153, *232*

Harrington, A., 62, *232*
Heath, S., 151, *232*
Hecht, B., 186, *232*
Henry, J., 4, *232*
Hong, E., 110, *236*
Hong, H., 110, *236*
Hood, L., 193, *233*
Hymes. D., 164, *233*

Ibsen, H., 121, *233*

James, W., 185, *233*
Jameson, F., 175, *233*

Kalantzis, M., 32, *235*
Kaminer, W., 221, *233*
Katz, E., 209, *233*
Kerouac, J., 130, *233*
Kierkegaard, S., 91, 98, 105, 109, 110, 121, 125, 130, 131, 162, 183, 184, 213, 220, *233, 237*
Koertege, N., 60, *236*

Labov, W., 164, *233*
Leonard, G., 20, *233*
Liebow, E., 57, *233*

Mack, J.E.,192, *237*
Malan, R., 180, *233*
Malinowski, B., ix, *233*
Mangan, K.S.,192, *237*
Manheimer, R.J., xi, *233*
March, W., 206, *233*
Marcuse, H., 131, *233*
Márquez, G.G., 180, *233*
Marx, K., 89, 98, *234*
Mathabane, M., 131, *234*
Mill, J.S., 19, *234*
Mink, L., 195, *234*
Mitchell, C.,45, *236*

Moffett, J., 37, 133, 143, *234*
Moss, R., 53, 23453, 60, *234*
Mphalele, E., 52, 23452, 58, 71, 127, 131, 132, *234*
Musil, R., 16, *234*

Nietzche, F., 129, *234*
Noll, R.,71, *236*

Paglia, C., 202, *234*
Parry, A.,194, *237*
Passeron, J-C., 17, *231*
Patai, D.,60, *236*
Pavese, C., 93, 109, *234*
Peat, D., 55, 60, *231*
Pepetela,4, 188, *234*
Phelps, L.,61, *236*
Plato, 120, *234*
Podhoretz, N., 47, *234*
Progoff, I., 67, 70, *234*
Putnam, R.O.,196, *237*

Rand, A., 186, *234*
Rieff, P., 60, *234*
Rorem, N., 186, *234*
Rosen, H., 175, *234*
Ross, A., 61, *234*
Rouse, J., 5, 18, 74, 85, 93, *234*
Ryan, J., xi, *233*

Saint Martin, M. de,17, *231*
Schiller, S.,197, *237*
Schneider, A.,37, *235*
Scribner, S., 163, *234*
Shaughnessy, M., 18, 42, 43, 96, 140, *235*
Shroder, T.,192, *237*
Simmel, G., 81, 82, *235*
Skinner, B.F., 185, *235*
Spaeth, M.,195, *237*
Spellmeyer, K.,163, *237*
Spengler, O., 61, *235*
Steinbeck, J., 38, 58, *235*
Street, B., 135, 137, 138, 189, *235*
Sullivan, R.,192, *237*

Themba, C., 140, 156, *235*
Thompson, W., 124, 129, *235*
Tlali, M., 179, *235*
Tocqueville, A., de, 99, *235*
Twain, M., 17, 40, *235*
Tymoczko, D.,130, *236*

Veeser, H.A., 186, *237*
Vygotsky, L.S., 135, 168, *235, 237*

Weiler, K., 45, *236*
Williams, R., 17, *235*
Wright, R., 41, 96, *235*

Yagelski, R.P.,197, *237*
Yates, R., 103, *235*

Subject
Index

Academic discourse, 164, 194
Academic literacy, 32, 44, 46-47, 54, 61, 157, 163-164, 189
Afrikaans, 76
Anxiety, 105, 174, 184, 221
Autonomy, 5, 48-49, 220-221

Brain research, 13, 16

Capitalism, 73, 80, 89, 97-98, 131
Cognitive approach, 146, 154-155, 164, 167-168
Collective unconscious, 71
Communal self, 79-80
Conceptual thinking, 95-96
Confessional criticism, 186
Critical literacy, 156
Critical pedagogy, 165, 167, 188

Deconstruction, 198
Democracy, 89, 97-98, 162
Discipline, 96, 196
Discourse, academic, 42

Elaborated code, 14, 17, 24, 41, 43-44, 135-142
Emotion, 7, 15, 29, 81
Empiricist psychology, 185
Ethics, 120, 174-175, 181

Feeling,13, 16-17, 19
Form and content, 152-153
Free writing, 24

Genre study, 32, 214
Grammar, 15, 18, 32, 42

Identity, 41, 45, 121, 160, 175, 186, 190
Identity politics, 101, 193
Individualism, 97, 117, 131, 175, 187, 192
Individuality, 9, 79, 80l, 120, 165

Marxism, 41, 61, 79, 89, 98, 165, 178-179
Mysticism, 26, 28, 34, 36-38, 61-62, 122, 129-130, 185, 193

Names and naming, 29, 124, 146, 156, 159-161
Narrative, 117, 164, 175-176, 181, 194-195
Narrative therapy, 189, 193-194

Pedagogy of disclosure, 162
Personal controls, 44
Personal writing, 96, 107, 155, 174-175, 181
Popular culture, 131
Positional context, 48, 64, 132, 138, 182-183
Positional controls, 44
Postmodernism, 41, 61, 116, 122, 175, 185-186, 220, 220-221
Primary code, 139

Rationality, 13, 16-17, 19, 28, 61, 81
Restricted code, 14, 17, 24, 44, 134-142

Science, 45, 61
Secondary code, 139
Situational context, 48, 64, 132, 163, 182-184, 212
Social capital, 96-197
Social construction, 61, 175, 221
Socialism, 98
Sociolinguistics, 4, 47
Spirituality, 26, 37, 60-61

Theory, 1-42, 49
Therapy, 20, 37, 53, 60, 70, 136, 142, 193
Tolerance, 31

Urban legends, 101-102

Zen Buddhism, 197-198